DEVELOPING MENTAL FITNESS IN SPORTS

DEVELOPING MENTAL FITNESS IN SPORTS

T.K. Narasimham

CRESCENT
PUBLISHING CORPORATION

[*The responsibility for the facts stated, conclusions reached and plagiarism, if any, in this book is entirely that of the Author. And the Publisher bears no responsibility for them, whatsoever.*]

Developing Mental Fitness in Sports

First Published : 2009

ISBN 978-81-8342-118-8

Published by :

CRESCENT PUBLISHING CORPORATION
4831/24, Prahlad Street,
Ansari Road, Darya Ganj,
New Delhi - 110002
Ph. : 23272541, 23257835
Fax : 91- 011- 23257835
e-mail : campusbooks@hotmail.com

Printed at :
Roshan Offset Printers
Delhi

Preface

Mental fitness or mental wellness is the state of being robustly resistant to stress, hardy enough to challenge head-first the many challenges of life, and having the ability to enjoy the entire process and look forward to more. The brain is the "muscle" of conscious intelligence. Just like the muscles in the rest of your body, it develops and gains strength during youth, reaches a peak, and then can either be maintained over the rest of your life, or be allowed to degenerate and lose capability and agility.

The old phrase "use it or lose it" is familiar to people involved in physical fitness and sports. Muscles that aren't used lose their strength and waste away. People who don't keep fit lose not only strength, but quickness and agility in using what they have left. The remedy is to keep on working and stretching your physical and mental muscles throughout your life.

The commonly recognized ill effects of an "out-of-condition" brain are poor memory, slow thinking and difficulty in learning new things. But it's worse than that. Recent medical research indicates that people with inactive minds are more prone to contracting devastating brain diseases like Alzheimer's and Parkinson's. Staying mentally active is important in terms of preserving your quality of life, your independence, your longevity and in not becoming a burden to your family.

There is nothing inevitable about the loss of mental ability with age. The way to maintain it is analogous to the way physical strength is maintained - by exercise. This book focuses on the strategies for developing mental fitness, but it's important to be aware that research on mental aging shows that physical exercise itself, has a positive effect on combating mental aging.

To exercise one's mind is to sharpen and improve the most human thing a human being possesses. The book shows you how to do it and amply proves that the process is fun as well. It provides information about how to strengthen, flex, tone and coordinate your 'mental muscles' and eliminate mental flab. Based on pains taking research and long experience, the book bears a stamp of authority. The simple and lucid style makes the book imminently readable and informative.

T.K. Narasimham

Contents

1

Mental Fitness Training

For everything you think in your mind, your body has a reaction, regardless of whether it is real or imagined. For example, have you ever had a bad dream? Usually, you will wake up and your heart is racing, you are sweating and very agitated, even though all you were doing was sleeping.

But, in your mind there was something bad going on and your body was reacting to it. Here's another example: if you are home alone and you hear a noise and interpret it as the wind, you are fine; but if you interpret it as a prowler, your fight or flight response takes over and you become fearful, your heart begins going a mile a minute, your eyes dilate and you are scared. These are just a few examples of how strong the connection is between your mind and your body. With this premise, it becomes unmistakable how necessary it is to train both the mind and body for peak performance.

In sports, so many things are left to chance. Sports are predictably unpredictable. Why let your mental mindset be one of those things? There's no reason for your mental game to be your Achilles heel! You have the power and authority to control that. These tools and resources will help you remove psychological barriers that can get in the way of peak performance and give you some control over your own performance.

Up until about a decade ago, a Sport Psychology professional was considered a person who athletes went to see only when they had a problem, not someone who healthy and productive athletes and teams spent their time with. Luckily, this stigma is changing; the change is slow, but it is evident. Sport psychology professionals everywhere now; recreational athletes, colleges, professional teams, Olympic athletes, businesses, and corporations all seek them out. People are realising that no matter how good you are, you can always improve, and one way to improve yourself is to become well-versed in performance enhancement techniques. There is no room for complacency; the complacent ones get left behind. This philosophy holds true not only in sports but in business as well.

Athletes spend so much time physically practicing to get an edge on the competition. Yet what teams and athletes can really do to get an edge is right in front of their nose, or more accurately, right above their shoulders! You hear the same thing all the time, "Sports is 90-95% mental." Athletes and coaches at all levels say it, but how many of them do something about it? It may be common knowledge, but it is not always common practice. Maybe they don't have the time, maybe they don't have the resources, or maybe down deep they don't really believe it. Whatever the reason, the fact remains the same, they are not utilising their most powerful resource, the mind. Most athletes fatigue mentally before they fatigue physically, due to the fact that their mind is not in as good of shape as their bodies.

Competition is tight, athletes are physically fit, and the margin for victory is slim. Managers, coaches and players are realising that to get ahead they need an added resource, and that resource is a trained mind. When there are two teams that are physically equal, it is the team that works together smoothly and is mentally prepared and confident that will come out on top. Keep in mind, though: no mental training will compensate for ineffective technique. You need to be strong, technically and mentally.

Unfortunately, many times one aspect of your game is magnified at the expense of the other. You should give equal attention to both; that is the ideal approach. You are given the talent, it's your job to develop it and watch it flourish by combining physical and mental training with a great work ethic. You want you and your team to be prepared mentally and physically to the best of its' ability to increase the chance of success. If your mind is always working, why not have it work for you?

Effect of Mental Toughness

There are certain moments during competition that appear to carry great psychological significance, when the momentum starts to shift in one direction or another. These situations require athletes to remain completely focused and calm in the face of difficult circumstances. Tennis players talk of the 'big' points during a tight match, such as a fleeting chance to break serve; for an athlete, it could be the final triple-jump in the competition after seriously under-performing; for a footballer, it could be how you react to a perceived bad refereeing decision or to going behind in a match your team are expected to win. Think about times when things have not gone quite to plan and how you reacted. The journey towards peak performance is rarely a perfectly smooth road and we learn from our mistakes - or should do.

Even great athletes and teams suffer setbacks. Olympic athlete Steve Backley is a prime example. In his book *The Winning Mind,* Backley cites his psychological strengths and, at times, his weaknesses as major determinants of whether he performed near to or below his own strict targets in competition. He talks of the transition from young up-and-coming javelin thrower to major international competitor when, after experiencing success so often as a junior, he found himself under-prepared for the mental hurdles and barriers created by higher-level competition. Backley says psychological strategies were the key to helping him to deal with this competitive stress.

Most top athletes and coaches believe that psychological factors play as crucial a role as physical attributes and learned skills in the make-up of champions. When physical skills are evenly matched-as they tend to be in competitive sport—the competitor with greater control over his or her mind will usually emerge as the victor. Mental strength is not going to compensate for lack of skill, but in close contests it can make the difference between winning and losing.

A key question for sport and exercise psychologists is whether champions have simply inherited the dominant psychological traits necessary for success or whether mental toughness can be acquired through training and experience. Recent research has attempted to explore the concept of mental toughness in sport more thoroughly, and it appears that, while some people are naturally more tough-minded than others, people can be 'toughened-up' with the correct approach to training.

Mental toughness is probably easiest to define in terms of how it affects behaviour and performance. A mentally tough athlete is likely to:

— achieve relatively consistent performances regardless of situational factors;

— retain a confident, positive, optimistic outlook, even when things are not going well, and not 'choke' under pressure;
— deal with distractions without letting them interfere with optimal focus;
— tolerate pain and discomfort;
— remain persistent when the 'going gets tough';
— have the resilience to bounce back from disappointments.

Personality

These characteristics are obviously related to success in most life situations. But it seems that some of us may be tougher than others because of personality traits and learned ways of coping. Personality research has always stirred up controversy- usually because researchers have not been able to agree on the correct approach to studying it. Some have taken what is known as the 'trait' approach, which views personality as stable and enduring, based on individual characteristics. However, others see personality as shaped by environmental influences, while 'interactionists' view individual traits and the environment as codeterminants of behaviour.

In recent times, this latter position has tended to predominate, based on the view that personality structure involves both a stable core of attitudes, values and beliefs about self, that remains relatively unchanged after early childhood, and more changeable, dynamic behaviours that are influenced by our environment.

Research on the relationship between stress and illness has revealed that some people have characteristics that act as buffers against stressors, making them less likely to succumb to ill health in difficult times. The leading researcher Suzanne Kobasa showed in one study that a personality characteristic known as 'hardiness' was a key factor in whether or not highly-stressed executives succumbed to illness. The hardy executives, who avoided illness, tended to perceive stressors as 'challenges' rather than threats, so maintaining a sense of control over events.

Kobasa suggested that hardiness incorporates three key elements:

— *Control* -the perceived ability of the individual to exert influence rather than experience helplessness;

— *Commitment*-ie a refusal to give up easily;

— *Challenge* - involving a person's ability to grow and develop rather than remain static, and to view change rather than stability as the norm.

Until recently, few studies had attempted to transfer the concept of hardiness to sport and exercise settings, but it seems very similar to the idea of mental toughness outlined earlier. One study on the relationship between hardiness and performance in basketball showed that seven out of eight season-long performance indicators were significantly correlated with a total hardiness score. This finding needs to be interpreted with caution, however, since correlations do not necessarily reflect causation.

A key development has been the development of a questionnaire to assess mental toughness that can be used to assess its influence in experimental studies. The Hull researchers carried out two studies to show how mental toughness was related to performance and cognitive appraisal. In the first study, 23 volunteers performed 30-minute static cycling trials at three different intensities of 30, 50 and 70% of their maximum oxygen uptake, rating the physical demands of the trials at five-minute intervals.

Participants were classified as having either high or low mental toughness based on their responses to the above-mentioned questionnaire and, as predicted, those with higher levels of mental toughness reported significantly lower perceived exertion at 70% of maximum. No significant differences were noted at lower levels of exertion which, as the researchers acknowledged, is consistent with the cliché that 'when the going gets tough, the tough get going'. The observed differences at higher levels of exertion could reflect a tendency of the more tough-minded to somehow act on the incoming stimuli before it reaches the level of perception, to reduce the perception of strain. Mentally tough exercisers might perceive themselves as having greater control during such conditions, or interpret the higher intensity as a challenge rather than a threat.

The second study, on 79 participants, considered the influence of mental toughness on resilience in adverse situations. Participants were given either positive or negative feedback after completing a variety of motor tasks, and then asked to perform a planning task which was used as the objective performance measure. The key question for the researchers was how participants would respond to feedback that could alter their confidence. As predicted, mentally tough participants performed better on the planning task, delivering relatively consistent performances whether their feedback had been negative or positive. However, those with lower levels of mental toughness performed significantly worse after negative feedback, confirming the greater resilience of those with high levels of mental toughness.

'4Cs' Model of Mental Toughness

Confidence (as well as control, commitment and challenge) is a key element of mental toughness. This has given rise to the '4Cs' model of mental toughness.

Research on mental toughness in sport and exercise has focused largely on individual differences, in which mental toughness is viewed as a relatively stable characteristic. Weiss and colleagues observed a toughening phenomenon after exposing animals to cold-water swimming, electric shock treatment or injections over a 14-day period. Specifically, the usual decrement in performance following aversive stimulation was not observed after the 14-day period. The intermittent exposure to aversive stimuli had apparently led to the animals becoming more tolerant of — and resilient to — such stimuli.

Although this finding does not necessarily transfer to human subjects, there are distinct parallels with various techniques commonly used as interventions in sport and exercise environments. For example, a technique known as 'stress inoculation training' gradually exposes the individual to more threatening situations while self-control is acquired as a means to combat learned helplessness. The stress response is gradually diminished as exposure renders the situation less threatening and the individual experiences a growing sense of control.

Of particular importance here is the idea that exposure to stress in controlled situations is much more powerful than stress reduction or removal, which will not help an individual cope with future exposure to the same stressor. One researcher has proposed four major influences on toughening, as follows:

— *Early life experiences*. Both human and animal studies have shown links between exposure to stressors in early life and reduced fear or emotionality when exposed to threats in adulthood;

— *Passive toughening*. Intermittent exposure seems to protect against depletion of 'stress hormones' and is linked with their quicker returns to baseline levels. In other words, people become less sensitive and more tolerant of stress;

— *Active toughening*. Physical fitness gained through aerobic conditioning is thought to be an important means of self-toughening. This could be related to the application of control;

— *Ageing*. This has the opposite effects to the other three, tending to make people more sensitive to and less tolerant of stress.

Clearly, active and passive toughening are the most relevant manipulations for athletes and can be applied in a number of practical ways. Stress inoculation training is an obvious application, but this is probably best approached with the aid of a sport psychologist. Since a sport psychologist, will give some examples of how mental over-load may be applied to training sessions in order to achieve some degree of toughening.

Rod Laver, the Australian tennis legend, has described how he used practice sessions to simulate 'tough' match conditions. Laver felt that fatigue placed great strain on the concentration which was crucial to success in long matches. To simulate these conditions, Laver forced himself to concentrate and work even harder during the latter stages of training sessions, when he was tired, so that he became used to the mental strain of such conditions. He has cited this as one of the key factors in his long-lasting success.

Simulation training is a great way to prepare mentally for the challenges of competition, and this can include mental as well as physical stressors. For example, a tennis player could increase the mental pressures in a practice match by starting each service game 0-15 down, and thus getting used to 'rebounding' after losing the first point. Alternatively a player with an over-reliance on his first serve could be restricted to one serve only and be forced to become extremely focused and accurate with what is, in effect, a second serve.

To enhance the stress still further, players could practise by playing tiebreakers, or play practice matches in front of an audience. The coach might use bad line calls or spectator noise as a way of exposing players intermittently to distractions and giving them practice at dealing with them.

Tennis is a game with plenty of breaks between play that allow time for dwelling on past events or self-doubting. Using imagery and positive self-talk during dead time in order to remain calm and in control can be an effective strategy. Mentally tough competitors are likely to use strategies that reinforce their self-belief at times of crisis. And these strategies can be rehearsed in practice situations. With a little invention, simulation training can be used for most athletes, and the opportunity to deal with mental stressors in controlled situations can be an invaluable way to toughen up in preparation for the very real challenges of competition.

Mental Imagery

A few years ago, a close-up shot of former world motor racing champion Damon Hill in his Formula One car as his head swayed from side to side. There was nothing new about TV producers wanting to get closer to the action, but the odd thing about this shot was that Hill was sitting in a stationary car, waiting to exit the garage in an attempt to qualify for the race. In fact there was a simple explanation for Hill's behaviour: like many other top sports people, he was using the time leading up to a performance to mentally rehearse and (in his case no doubt) imagine steering the correct racing line through each corner.

On top of the time spent honing skills and developing physical readiness, studies of top performers have shown that the élite from a variety of different sports complete many laps of the track, lengths of the pool or throws of the javelin in their minds before major competitions.

Once learned, imagery can be applied in many different ways to aid sports performers, and is one of the most regularly used tools of the sport psychologist. However, recent research evidence suggests that to achieve maximum benefits athletes and coaches should select the content of their images very carefully.

Scientists have now turned their attention from the question of whether imagery works—given the strong evidence that it does—to the question of how it works. On this issue opinion remains divided and a healthy debate continues. Some experts believe that small neuromuscular 'firings' that have been demonstrated in some research studies provide sufficient feedback from imagined stimuli to allow for changes in performance.

Mental Blueprint

The evidence suggests that imagery may work more indirectly—facilitating changes in someone's psychological state by building confidence, promoting motivation and reducing performance anxiety. At present, the exact mechanisms by which imagery works remain unclear, although recent work using brain imaging techniques has advanced our knowledge by confirming that the right hemisphere of the brain is the primary imagery centre.

If you watch children playing, you can rapidly appreciate how creative and imaginative they are. As children play with dolls and toys they create their own inner worlds, thereby engaging the right hemispheres of their brains. Unfortunately, much systematic education focuses on logical and analytical processes, which use the left hemisphere and tend to be more highly valued by adults.

The trouble is that without constant practice the brain's imagery centre reacts in much the same way as your muscles do if you stop training—ie it atrophies. Again using a body analogy, when you return to using this part of your brain after a long lay-off, it's like doing that first exercise session all over again. However, as with physical exercise, the more you train, the faster you adapt and the easier it gets.

Although imagery can be applied in very dynamic situations, it is best to learn how to do it in quiet, relaxed, non-competitive settings. You need to start by relaxing—closing your eyes and focusing on deep rhythmical breaths. You cannot afford to be half-hearted, so commit yourself to the process and try to decide beforehand what you are going to imagine. Some people might even decide to record a series of instructions onto a cassette tape to help direct their images.

Development Plan

Sport psychologist Rainer Martens suggested that, in developing a systematic approach to using imagery, people should first work on increasing overall sensory awareness. A fundamental point that must be made at this juncture is that visualisation and imagery are not one and the same; imagery should involve far more than visualisation, including the feelings of movements, sounds, emotions and, in some cases, even smells.

A cricket batsman, for example, might attempt to become more aware of sensory process by recalling the important visual environmental features, as well as the sound of the bowler running-in and the noise the ball made through the air. He may recall the feel of swinging the bat and making contact with the ball. The subsequent sounds of bat on ball and the call of his partner to run may also be considered. The sense of control as the ball reached the boundary, a feeling of determination and the smell of freshly mown grass may help to stimulate all the senses. So Martens proposes a first stage dedicated to appreciating things that the individual may have come to take for granted.

The next step is to develop vividness. It is true that some people are able to recall or create very clear and vivid images, while others may struggle to get an image at all. With practice, though, most people are able to sharpen their images so that recognisable sensory experiences are evident. This is the stage to be creative and experiment by using scenes and experiences that are very familiar to you. These exercises do not need to be sport-specific at first, as the general idea is to promote overall clarity. You might like to try exercise 1, above, to help develop vividness.

The final stage of your development plan involves control. If you are mentally rehearsing what you are going to do, it is important to have control over your images. That is because imagery can be destructive as well as helpful. If, for example, a golfer is imagining the path of the ball on the green but continually sees herself missing the putt, this is hardly likely to help. The great thing about imagery is that, even if the golfer has missed putts in reality, imagery provides an opportunity to correct errors.

This stage is more sport specific and should incorporate your desired outcome. You should feel the movement and see a positive result, such as the golf ball following the correct path and entering the hole. If you do start imagining negative outcomes, try to recall a previous success—or even watch another person successfully complete the skill and try to replicate this in your mind, with yourself in the role of successful performer.

Although the most obvious application of imagery is in the learning and performing of sport skills, there are many other ways to use the technique. For example, imagery can also be used to practise strategies, manipulate levels of arousal, manage stress, build confidence, deal with pain and periods of injury and develop an appropriate focus.

Recently researchers have suggested that, for maximum effect, athletes should match the content or type of imagery with the desired outcome. Towards this end, you should think carefully about the components of your imagined experiences and ask yourself what you want to gain. Do you seek to facilitate learning and performance of skills and strategies, or are you attempting to build confidence or even psych yourself up?

The five main categories of imagery have been identified as follows:

— *Motivational-specific (MS)*—This involves seeing yourself winning an event, receiving a trophy or medal and being congratulated by other athletes. MS imagery may boost motivation and effort during training and facilitate goal-setting, but is unlikely on its own to lead directly to performance benefits;

— *Motivational general-mastery (MG-M)*—This is based on seeing yourself coping in difficult circumstances and mastering challenging situations. It might include maintaining a positive focus while behind, and then coming back to win. MG-M imagery appears to be important in developing expectations of success and self-confidence;

- *Motivational general-arousal (MG-A)*—This is imagery that reflects feelings of relaxation, stress, anxiety or arousal in relation to sports competitions. There is good evidence to suggest that MG-A imagery can influence heart rate—one index of arousal—and can be employed as a 'psych-up' strategy;
- *Cognitive specific (CS)*—This involves seeing yourself perform specific skills, such as a tennis serve, golf putt or triple-toe-loop in figure skating. If learning and performance are the desired outcomes, evidence suggests that CS imagery will be the most effective choice;
- *Cognitive general (CG)*—This involves images of strategy and game plans related to a competitive event. Examples could include employing a serve-and-volley strategy in tennis or a quick-break play in basketball. Case studies support the use of this type of imagery, although controlled experimental evidence is still needed.

Clearly there is potential for these types of imagery to overlap if, for example, you imagine specific sports skills, such as a golf putt (CS), with the accompanying positive outcome and tournament-clinching result (MS). However, research suggests that if you choose the wrong type of imagery, you may not achieve any benefits. For example, one study showed that CS imagery significantly improved sit-up performance, while MG-M imagery was ineffective. Conversely, other studies have shown MG-M imagery to be more effective than CS imagery for boosting self-confidence. The trick is to decide what it is you want to achieve, then make the imagery content match your goals.

FITT Principle

In designing imagery training programmes, FITT principle, which has often been associated with physical training.

F is for Frequency. Aim to incorporate imagery into every day of your training schedule. For busy people, just before you sleep could be a good time, and it helps if you are in a relaxed and tranquil state;

I is for Intensity. Try to create an all-sensory experience that is as vivid and clear as possible. Initially, practising in a quiet environment can help to minimise distractions and facilitate clear images;

T is for Time. Imagery should make big demands on your attention, so short (5-10 minutes) frequent quality sessions are preferable to long ones;

T is for Type. Remember to decide on your desired outcome and select the type of imagery to match it.

Effect of Mental Fitness

Mental toughness is what makes Michael Jordan and Pete Sampras so special. These athletes know their real battle is not so much on the court, but inside their heads. You absolutely must manage your mental side if you want to be the best. If you are one of those athletes who spends all your training time on technique and fitness while paying no attention to your mental side, you are doing yourself a serious disservice. We know from countless studies that mental skills are acquirable and you can, with practice, learn to perform mentally. You can improve your confidence, concentration, motivation and anxiety levels if you chose to.

Principles

Feelings affect your performance. Whether you are aware of them or not, how you feel affects how you perform. Feelings are based on what you imagine or interpret from an event and not from the event itself. Two players appearing in the Wimbledon final for the first time will imagine different things about the match. One might imagine she will be unable to play well in such a big final. This player is likely to feel nervous and uncertain and her performance will be poor. The other might imagine it as the experience of a lifetime for her to go out and enjoy - she might feel liberated and relaxed and her play is likely to reflect these emotions. The same event evokes two different responses which result in two very different performances. The message here is very simple - learn how to change your interpretations and you learn how to manage your emotions. When you can manage your emotions you can perform at your best.

The mind and the body are inextricable linked - how you feel physically affects how you feel emotionally. This means that we can improve our mental performance using physical interventions (relaxation exercises) and vice versa. You operate within a system - your performance is just a symptom or outcome of how your system operates. The parts of your system are all interrelated. A cricket player's confidence may be affected by his technique, which may be affected by his fitness, which may be affected by his lifestyle which may be affected by his time management. It is always more potent to look to remedy the underlying causes of a problem than the symptom itself.

If Alan Shearer is not scoring goals, the problem might lie not with him but with the midfield who are not creating chances for him (a moot point in this case). In situations where your performance was greatly influenced by your relationship with another person. As humanistic psychologists, we believe that under the right circumstances you will want to reach your potential. Our focus is not just on your performance but also on your welfare. Often the two are linked. You can divide mental skills training into two approaches: individual work and group work. A standard programme for both may last for a minimum of six weeks with sessions of 60-90 minutes.

Influence of Mental Fatigue

Theories about mental fatugue abound, but one popular hypothesis is that most of the lethargy is caused by a chemical called tryptophan. Tryptophan is an amino acid which normally rides through your bloodstream attached to a very important blood plasma protein, albumin. However, when blood fat levels rise, as they do during prolonged exerclse, the fats 'kick' tryptophan loose from its albumin moorings. This 'free' tryptophan then enters the brain in large quantities, where - converted to another chemical called serotonin - it may induce fatigue and produce a drop-off in performance (serotonin is noted for its calming and even sleep-producing effects on brain cells).

This biochemical scenario has a protective effect: before you exercise so long that you tear your muscles to shreds, your brain fills up with tryptophan and you go to sleep - or at least you lose the willpower to force your muscles to keep going. However, if you're an athlete, you would like to keep exercising at a high level until you reach the finish line or the end of the match, so how can you prevent your brain cells from taking a tryptophan bath? Exercise physiologists have had two answers: you could try to limit the natural rise in blood fats, the ascendancy of which frees tryptophan to do its wicked work on the brain, or you could pop some branchedchain amino acid (BCAA) tablets as you carry out your extended exercise.

Since everyone, even the skinniest Kenyan runner, has fat cells which insist on releasing fat into the blood during exercise, the latter strategy has gained a certain appeal. BCM-popping is an intriguing idea because BCMs 'compete' with tryptophan to enter the brain. As blood-BCAA levels increase, less tryptophan enters the neuron palace. If you're an athlete with high blood-BCM levels, you should be able to stay fatigue-free for a longer period of time as you exercise.

However, as BCAA-expert J. Mark Davis of the University of South Carolina points out, there are some problems with the BCAA-ingestion strategy. If you take a moderate dose of BCMs as you exercise, blood levels of BCAAs probably don't increase enough to thwart tryptophan. Large servings of BCAAs might work, but the problem is that hefty helpings reduce the absorption of water in the gut, potentially producing dehydration. High BCAA intakes might also increase your blood concentrations of ammonia, a toxic chemical which has been linked with fatigue. Not surprisingly, researchers in a number of studies have had a very hard time linking BCMs with improved exercise performances.

Fortunately, a tried and-true strategy - taking in carbohydrate during exercise - may have a profound effect on mental fatigue. Scientists have known for years that ingested carbohydrate keeps muscles perking along at a high level during triathlons, extended bike rides, marathons and multi-game squash or tennis matches, but they're just beginning to realise that carbohydrate may also have a profound effect on brain cells. It happens this way: carbohydrate feedings during exercise reduce the amount of fat circulating in the blood. As a result, less tryptophan is freed from its tenuous marriage with blood albumin, and so a lower amount of tryptophan enters the brain. Your nerve cells can't chill out on serotonin.

According to Davis, the realisation that carbohydrate delays central (mental) fatigue leads automatically to the following practical recommendations:

— Don't fast before workouts or competitions. Fasting raises blood-fat levels, an effect which lets tryptophan do its dirty brainwork.

— Avoid fatty foods during the 12-hour period before training sessions or competitions (fatladen foods increase your blood-fat concentraitions and launch a cascade of tryptophan towards your brain).

— In order to reduce blood-fat levels, eat a carbohydrate meal two to four hours before workouts or competitions.

— Take in three to four swallows or more of a sports drink every 10 minutes or so during extended exercise to delay the onset of mental fatigue - and improve your performance.

Mental Strength

A friend was in a cancer ward and his treatment involved going without food and water for eight weeks. He survived on a drip and lost three stone in weight. Around him other patients frequently died. It was a depressing period. Nearly 40 years ago the great Australian runner Ron Clarke broke world records for two miles, three miles and six miles, and 3000 and 5000m, as well as the distance run in one hour. The 10,000m world record, however, had eluded him many times, and on one of his training runs by the sea, he was pondering why this was so when, in the distance, he heard much squealing and splashing coming from a rocky alcove.

The word 'recreation' literally means recreating our mind and body. Because we can, we should. If we enjoy sport we will enjoy it more if we get better at it. Improving involves the allocation of time. Our lives revolve around the three eights - eight hours work, eight hours sleep, eight hours free time. Some of the free time is required for taking meals and for travelling to and from work. At the very least we can find one hour a day to practise our sport. When we choose that hour is our prerogative.

The world's first sub-four-minute miler, Roger Bannister, was a medical student at St Mary's Hospital, Paddington. He chose to use his lunch hour for a 10-minute jog to Paddington track. There he ran 10 x 440yds in about 60secs with two minutes rest, then he ran back to work. The whole procedure took exactly 48 minutes, leaving him time for lunch. If you want to train for sport you can always fit it in somehow.

We are at our physical peak in sport for about five years, although we may compete in one way or another for 25 years. This means that you should regard every training session - like every day - as a precious piece of your time. Regard it as an investment which will pay dividends in the future.

Reduce Stress

Mental stress can hurt your performances in a variety of different ways. It can raise heart rate and oxygen consumption, harming your exercise efficiency and causing particular workout and race speeds to feel tougher than they actually should. It can increase muscle tension, reducing stride lengths (if you are a runner) and making your legs and arms considerably less 'springy' and powerful. On a cognitive level, stress prevents you from 'mentally managing' your tough workouts and races; instead of relaxing and focusing on the task at hand, you are preoccupied with stressful thoughts and emotions, so the quality of your performance decreases.

If you feel stressed-out before and during your competitions or hard training sessions, what can you do to control the stress, and thus increase your chances of performing at your highest-possible level? Sport psychologists have proposed a number of different stress-managing techniques over the years, but one of the most successful has been something called 'stress-inoculation training'. Developed in the late 1970s and early 1980s by

Donald Meichenbaum, a psychologist at the University of Waterloo in Canada, stress-inoculation training takes its name from the fact that it exposes individuals to stress in manageable but gradually increasing amounts, thereby enhancing 'immunity' to stress for the persons practising the technique.

The key, however, to stress inoculation is not simply that stress levels are increased in a governable way during training; athletes also learn skills for coping with psychological stress and enhancing performance, including the development of productive thoughts and self-statements and the utilisation of centring strategies. There are usually three stages in the overall stress-inoculation process:

1) A conceptualisation phase, in which an athlete becomes more aware of how positive and negative thoughts, self-talk, and imagery influence performance,
2) a rehearsal period, during which an athlete learns to use centring, positive self-statements, and other coping skills, and
3) an application phase, in which the athlete actually practises his/her skills, first in low-stress situations and then in settings in which stress levels are gradually increased.

Stress-inoculation training was originally developed for the public-at-large, but psychologists quickly realised that it could be applied to sports settings. They knew that many athletes unwittingly respond to stress with maladaptive thoughts and images which greatly hinder performance. Once such athletes understand how their unsuitable 'headwork' is keeping them from reaching their potentials, they begin to eagerly construct new self-statements and images which can have a profoundly positive impact on their performances.

Scientific studies concerning the effects of stress-inoculation training on exercise capacity have generally been positive: In one study, two sessions of stress-inoculation training per week for 5.5 weeks improved the running economy of eight male collegiate cross-country runners. Stress-inoculation training has also been linked with improved performance during abseiling (descending mountain faces) and lower stress levels during squash competitions, and it has been particularly effective at boosting the performances of gymnasts.

Not too surprisingly, a number of sport psychologists have examined the effects of stress-inoculation training on basketball players, particularly with regard to free-throw shooting, which is often a high-stress activity within the game. One study found that stress inoculation improved both free-throw and field-goal shooting, and a second investigation (carried out with just three players, however) determined that free-throw shooting accuracy increased from 50 to 88 per cent and self-statements changed from 86-per cent negative to 71-per cent positive after just 10 hours of stress-inoculation training. In practical terms, here's how stress inoculation works:

Conceptualisation phase

If you are interested in managing your stress more effectively, you begin by keeping track of the things you say to yourself about your training and performances. You may want to write these things down, unless you are able to keep a fairly clear 'mental log' of your self-statements in your head. It's important to bear in mind that no statement you make about yourself and your running is 'too small' to record, and you should also make note of the emotional content of your self-statements.

Here's a specific example of a common self-statement which endurance athletes make, along with an explanation of why they make it and what it does to their performances. Many athletes do quite well with their workouts but have problems delivering good race performances (i.e., they 'choke' on race days). After their races and at various times during their daily routines when they think about their racing, it's typical for such athletes to utter self-statements along the lines of 'I just have to face the fact that I am not a good racer.'

Here, poor race performance is the stressor. The bad races are making the athlete feel bad about himself; he feels that he is not measuring up to the expectations of himself, his loved ones, and peers. And since he lives in a culture in which winning is highly valued, he feels that his bad races brand him a 'loser'.

The statement 'I just have to face up to the fact that I am not a good racer' is the anti-stressor, the temporary relief from the anxiety associated with racing so miserably. It is anti-stressful, because it implies that nothing can be done about the horrible race performances. If nothing can be done, then there is no longer any need to worry!

And the anti-stressor statement works, to a small degree, if modest and temporary reductions in anxiety are the ultimate goal. However, the statement is not functional at all if the ultimate goal is to learn to handle stress more effectively and perform up to one's capacity. The statement 'I just have to face up to the fact that I am not a good racer' encapsulates a sense of hopelessness and futility, which will make it impossible to ever race well. In fact, such a statement is an inoculation for failure, rather than a true stress-reliever. It ensures poor performances - and it is the type of statement which makes it certain that stressors will never be met head on.

Here's another fairly common situation: a female marathon runner who performs very well in 5Ks, 10Ks, and half-marathons consistently experiences problems after the 20-mile mark in her marathons. In the last six miles of the race, her pace falls off so much that her finishing times are considerably slower than expected or predicted. As she looks ahead to an important marathon and begins to feel anxious about how well she will run after reaching the 20-mile point, she develops the following self-statement: 'I just have to accept the fact that my speed is going to drop off after 20 miles or so.' As race day approaches, she makes a similar statement to herself every time she worries about the final portion of the impending race.

The stressor in this case is the last 6.2 miles of the marathon, or more specifically the runner's inability to perform well during this portion of the race. The transiently stress-relieving but basically negative statement 'I just have to accept the fact that I am going to slow down after 20 miles' takes away some of the burden of stress, because if nothing can be done about the velocity downturn, then it is not necessary to worry about it.

However, the emotional content of such a self-statement expresses a strong sense of futility and hopelessness. As such, it can not help the marathoner perform well in the marathon itself (secretly, she hopes to do well even though her self-statement admits defeat), nor can it help her train effectively and completely for her big race.

Competition and Emotional Control

Competition can bring out the best or the worst in athletes, and the psychological demands are especially high when individuals or teams are striving to achieve the same goals. When physical skills are evenly matched, it is often the competitor with the stronger mental approach, who can control his or her mind before and during events, who wins. However, many athletes wrongly assume that mental aspects of performance are innate and unchangeable when, in reality, systematic mental training can have a similar impact on performance as physical workouts. Getting into the correct mind-set prior to competition is one of the most crucial aspects of top performance.

In fact, a study of Olympic athletes by Orlick and Partington showed that the combination of mental and physical readiness was a key factor that distinguished more successful athletes from their less successful counterparts in the Olympic Games. Perhaps even more impressive is the finding that, of the three states of readiness assessed (mental, physical and technical), only mental factors were statistically linked with final Olympic rankings.

If you have ever observed performers during the lead-up to competition, you can't have failed to notice that behaviour starts to change. As the anticipation builds, athletes and coaches cope with the demands of the situation in various ways, some becoming withdrawn and quiet and some more aggressive than usual, while others disappear frequently to the toilet. Emotional reactions to stressful situations can drain an athlete's resources and impact negatively on performance if poorly-managed. That is why it is important to have in place a strategy to deal with pre-performance stress.

Emotions can be defined as brief positive or negative feelings occurring in response to meaningful or important situations, which can influence mood states. Basic emotions such as fear, anger, joy and surprise are commonly experienced in sport, although complex mixes of emotions are often evident. Positive emotions can help sustain motivation and enable us to approach events with enthusiasm and energy. Negative emotions, by contrast, are linked to avoidance behaviours and withdrawal.

Emotions in the sporting arena can be triggered by many things personal to an individual, including memories, conversations with other people, seeing the competition venue, weighing up the opposition etc. Researchers have studied emotions in order to determine why they occur and what impact they have on behaviour. At first it was thought that emotions were simply the result of physiological changes, since physiological symptoms, such as increased heart rate, were commonly observed in such reactions. To test this theory, scientists injected volunteers with the so-called 'stress' hormone epinephrine (adrenaline) to see if emotions could be generated in the laboratory.

A small minority of participants reported feeling genuine emotions (usually sadness) while most reported physiological changes (to be expected after administration of adrenaline) and 'as if' emotions—feelings closely associated with being happy, sad or angry, but not the 'real thing'. Subsequent research demonstrated that emotions could be induced by directing participants' thoughts to emotional triggers, such as deceased relatives (sadness) or past achievements (pride). In summary, research in these areas has shown that both physiological arousal and the cognitive interpretation of that arousal are important in determining the emotional response.

During the lead-up to an important competition, the body starts to prepare for the demands to come by releasing hormones such as epinephrine into the bloodstream, setting in motion the physiological changes associated with increased arousal (sometimes referred to as the 'fight or flight' response). In addition, changes occur in the attentional system, as athletes become more focussed and alert, with increasingly active minds. This overall increase in arousal can be your best friend or your worst enemy: and the key to achieving an appropriate mind-set is to analyse the changes in a rational manner and channel your emotions in a positive direction.

This positive interpretation of the arousal response usually leads to more positive emotions and optimistic outlooks. Conversely, some athletes interpret physiological changes like an increased heart rate as anxiety, worry and apprehension, with a negative impact on emotions that is not conducive to good performance. The most important thing to remember is that your interpretation of physiological changes directs your emotional response. However, the relationship between thoughts and emotions works in both directions: although emotions are the result of cognitive interpretations, they can also impact on your thoughts, giving rise to a vicious circle of negative thoughts and emotions.

The good news for athletes who experience unhelpful emotions before competition is that you can gain more control by altering your focus of attention. The next time you feel these unwanted changes occurring try going through the following psychological routine:

— Tell yourself 'this is my body preparing me to perform well', and repeat the affirmation as necessary;

— Try to recall an image of yourself either winning or performing well, and connect this with the feelings you experienced at the time.

You will need to practise this routine on a regular basis in order to establish it as a habitual response that will help you feel more composed and energised before competitions. If negative images jump into your mind during this time, try to visualise the most successful athlete in your sport and the way he or she runs, competes, enjoys performing—in short every positive thing about them; Then visualise yourself with similar positive attributes. Even experienced athletes get nervous and irritable before competing, and a little tension (as long as it is controlled) is often necessary to inspire maximal performance.

The techniques outlined above will not remove all the tension, but they should help you to channel your emotions more positively, which is what top athletes have to learn to do. The difference between winners and losers often boils down to coping skills, in that some athletes have learned to cope with competitive situations better than others. It is important to challenge the belief of some athletes that emotions and mood states are simply reactions to external events; in fact, the athlete has considerable capacity for control in this area.

A recent study by Stevens and Lane identified a number of strategies employed by athletes to regulate their moods. Although unique strategies were employed for specific mood dimensions, results indicated that 'changing location' and 'listening to music' were among the most commonly used strategies. Various research studies have demonstrated the ability of music to impact on emotions and mood by either calming or stimulating the individual as required—although careful consideration is needed in the selection of appropriate music. Listening to music or engaging in a mentally active process, such as a crossword, can help to stop the mind wandering in the hours leading up to competition, although immediately beforehand athletes need to be completely focused on the task in hand.

Such a coping response puts the athlete in control by creating a familiar psychological comfort zone regardless of whatever is going on in the external environment. One of the biggest triggers for anxiety is uncertainty, which is, of course, inherent in all sporting events. The key principle for the athlete is to control the things you can control but not to waste energy on things you can't control. Many top athletes have found, to their cost, that giving attention to how opponents might perform or how technically good others were in the warm-up has a negative impact on their focus. The one thing you can control is your own preparation, so that should have your full focus. By developing consistent routines and ways of coping with distractions, uncertainty can be reduced and you are less likely to be negatively affected by external factors.

Because athletes have varying requirements, it is impossible to standardise the pre-competition preparation. However, you may wish to adopt some of the ideas below in creating your own pre-performance strategy to achieve the desired emotional state. These ideas are all designed to be put into practice in the hour before competition, although the principles can be adapted for other times.

Physical Preparation

The warm-up period can be an important psychological aid as well as preparing the body for the rigors of competition and helping to prevent injury. By developing a relatively stable warm-up routine, including mobility work, stretching and increasing deep muscle temperature, uncertainty can be reduced and the athlete's attention directed to appropriate cues, such as quality technique and body awareness. The development of routines in sport has consistently been shown to be important in directing attentional focus to important cues, so aiding performance.

Although during last summer's major athletic events it was impossible to observe what was going on inside the minds of the sprinters, you could clearly observe the regularity of the warm-up routines and the intense concentration written on athletes' faces prior to taking their marks. These routines are not haphazard, but have been systematically designed to promote optimal functioning in the final few minutes before performance.

Golfers have routines that allow them to prepare in the same way for each shot, as do some rugby place kickers, and tennis players before serving. The key to any routine is that it provides the athlete with control and directs attention to the important cues. Coaches and athletes should work together in deciding the key attentional cues and the sequence in which these should occur. Such routines are the opposite of superstitious rituals that take control away from the performer, as with superstitions outcome is essentially believed to be controlled by sources other than the self.

Mental Preparation

The mental aspects prior to performance should involve focussing on what you are going to do during the event. This can include specific strategies, and the establishment of optimal attentional focus. Some athletes will like to use imagery to recall positive past experiences and generate a sense of confidence. Imagery is a very flexible method to employ prior to competition but it needs to be used correctly for maximum effect. Imagery is not just a form of visualisation, but moreover an all sensory experience that should involve the kinaesthetic sense, emotions and auditory experiences to increase the impact.

Many people use imagery to simply see themselves winning but it can be employed to imagine good technique, coping with difficult situations, recreating emotional feelings and rehearsing the up-coming event in the mind. Imagery is a powerful technique since the brain interprets the imagined scenarios very literally, so directly enhancing such psychological variables as confidence. Always keep imagery sessions short (no more than a few minutes) and simple just before competition. Tailoring the imagery to the desired outcome is essential, so if you want to improve your mood, imagine a realistic scenario that makes you feel good. For more advice on incorporating imagery into your preparation, you may like to read a very practical book entitled *In Pursuit of Excellence*.

Mental preparation can include the repeated use of positive self-statements (affirmations) such as 'I have trained hard, and am in great shape'. These affirmations act by occupying our attention in such a way as to change our belief system over time, so that we begin to attend to feelings or happenings than are consistent with these new beliefs.

2

Psychological Interventions in Sports Training

Psychological interventions can help athletes to recover more quickly from injuries, experience more positive mood states during recovery and maintain confidence. For example, one study examined the effects of imagery and relaxation on knee strength, levels of anxiety and perceptions of pain during anterior-cruciate-ligament rehabilitation. Thirty injured athletes were equally divided into three experimental groups and exposed to either no intervention; a placebo intervention, involving attention, encouragement and support; or an imagery plus relaxation intervention. Results revealed that participants subjected to the imagery and relaxation intervention reported significantly less re-injury anxiety and lower perceptions of pain. Additionally, greater knee strength was reported, which seems to support both physical and psychological benefits of this intervention strategy.

Serious athletes channel large amounts of energy into their physical training and when this is not possible because of injury, channelling these energies into something positive is essential. Otherwise, long lay-offs can become the breeding grounds for depression, anxiety and self-doubt. Mental training can provide a positive outlet that the athlete can equate with progress and moving towards his or her goals. It is often not a perfect substitute for physical training far from it in many cases but it can help to promote a sense of exerting some control over the situation and act as a new challenge. In essence, the time spent during periods of injury can be destructive if the athlete allows his/her mind to wander; alternatively, it can be seen as an opportunity to develop skills that might ultimately lead to even better performances. Which would you choose?

Matching Individual Needs

The key element of any psychological skills training programme is matching the intervention to the client's specific needs. Since imagery can be used in many different ways, and the content of imagery training can vary considerably, selecting the correct type of imagery was essential in this case. One particularly useful imagery model based on an interpretation of many past studies suggests that in order to facilitate self-confidence, the content of the imagery sessions should involve the athlete seeing him or herself mastering difficult situations and overcoming obstacles. Imagining a positive outcome is very important as this is what boosts self-confidence in much the same way as achieving real goals. This type of imagery is particularly pertinent in the case of injured athletes who need to see themselves succeeding and eventually returning to competitive action.

A Three-stage Approach to Intervention

Stage one involved a detailed discussion concerning the injury, what it meant to the client, how the client was feeling and coping and any particular concerns that were troublesome. These specific concerns were noted and used later during imagery sessions as the client imagined mastering these scenarios. At this stage the extent of the injury was discussed as the athlete affirmed the physiotherapist's conclusions and physical recovery recommendations. The injury was not severe but a three-week layoff from training was likely, so the client and psychologist negotiated the aims of the upcoming psychological training sessions. A unified approach was agreed. Second, the intervention itself initially involved the client recalling positive performance indicators from recent matches and reliving these via vivid repetitive images. This was essentially for confidence maintenance and to promote a positive mind-set where successes were recalled to working memory and acted to restrict access to pessimistic, negative memories such as sustaining the injury.

The specific images used included recalling goals scored, outpacing defenders, good link-up play with team-mates and quick reactions in tight situations. In each example the psychologist guided the client through these images and attempted to focus on the clarity of visual image, the sounds involved such as when striking the football, the feel of the movements and the excitement and exhilaration involved with successful outcomes. The client reported feeling energised, optimistic and eager to return to playing as soon as possible, following this initial session.

Eventually, stage three of the intervention commenced as the client was preparing to return to physical training and then competition. A number of concerns that were highlighted during the initial meeting were used as a means of psychological strengthening. Specifically, the client reported that speed was his biggest asset and he worried about not being able to accelerate away from defenders over uneven ground due to the after-effects of his injury. He also mentioned making sharp, angled turns and 50-50 challenges as situations within a game that might be troublesome.

In response to this, the client was guided to create up-coming scenarios against known opponents that involved these concerns. These included both training and match scenarios. He saw himself out-pacing defenders and finishing clinically, making quick-angled turns pushing-off with the previously injured knee and making solid contact and winning 50-50 tackles against tough defenders. A scenario was also used where the player imagined waiting to be introduced as a substitute and dealing with the feelings associated with this. The client was encouraged to create vivid, realistic images that included kinaesthetic feelings of the movements and mood states during practice. Much as in real situations, the client reported feeling a little tense when imagining these potentially threatening challenges, but after a short time, this tension dissipated as successful images were produced. This form of simulation training allowed confidence to be gradually enhanced by mastery imagery.

Outcomes

The client made a successful return to competition following a three-game absence. Although he reported a degree of tension while waiting to be introduced as a substitute in his return to action, this quickly decreased as he made some early positive contributions to the game which closely matched his previous imagery experiences. Over the period of injury, interviews and questionnaire responses revealed that confidence was successfully maintained at a level corresponding to that immediately prior to injury.

Over the entire intervention period of six months, a significantly positive change in mental attitude and psychological characteristics was noted. Most importantly, the imbalance initially reported between anxiety and self-confidence was removed and normal levels of each variable achieved. Although the client still had areas for improvement, significant progress had been made and despite missing four games over the season due to injury, he reached his goal-scoring targets set pre-season. The use of mastery-type imagery appears to have positively influenced self-confidence, and supports the mental imagery model and research previously mentioned.

In regard to the period of injury, the psychological training appeared to help maintain self-confidence, provide a positive training focus that aided motivation and facilitated the adjustment of goals. It appears that channelling one's energies into training that can ultimately lead to higher levels of performance is a most constructive way of approaching injury lay-offs. This can be an especially good time to introduce the athlete to psychological skills training since many athletes neglect these skills in favour of traditional physical practice during regular training periods.

The intervention highlighted in this study was specifically tailored to the individual's needs and many other various techniques and strategies can be employed to aid the recovery process. Psychological training should always be viewed in conjunction with the work of physiotherapists and other relevant professionals, and should be used to develop realistic confidence (not over-confidence). For longer periods of rehabilitation, imagery could involve the athlete imagining regaining full range of motion at a joint, or completing a set of rehabilitation exercises that have yet to be accomplished in reality.

Overtraining Syndrome

How important is non-training stress in the development of the overtraining syndrome? At some point during their career, a number of endurance athletes report experiencing a suppressed athletic performance, often in conjunction with one or more other physiological and/or psychological symptoms. Among others, these symptoms may include chronic fatigue, disturbed mood states, increased susceptibility to upper respiratory tract infections, changes in resting heart rate and disturbances in sleep patterns. Athletes experiencing such symptoms may be suffering from, or are at increased risk of developing, the overtraining syndrome.

At times, the symptoms associated with the overtraining syndrome can be severe and full recovery may take a number of weeks or months. For some athletes, the outlook may be even bleaker. Athletes involved in our recent investigations reported suffering from symptoms of the overtraining syndrome for as long as two years. In such cases, athletes have been unable to continue participating in their sport.

Despite being recognised as a serious problem for endurance athletes, understanding of the overtraining syndrome is limited. A number of difficulties exist with regard to the recognition and diagnosis of the overtraining syndrome, and uncertainty exists in relation to its cause. The aim of this article is to consider the causes of the overtraining syndrome, in particular, the role that non-training stress may play in the development of the syndrome. In doing so, an overview of the possible causes of the overtraining syndrome will be provided, together with the presentation of two case studies of athletes diagnosed with the overtraining syndrome. Practical information will then be provided to aid athletes and coaches in its prevention.

Too much training, too little recovery?

Historically, training stress has been reported to be the major cause of the overtraining syndrome. Overtraining, a process that involves performing an excessive training load, coupled with inadequate recovery, is frequently suggested to be the major cause. This is often thought to result from a poorly planned training programme. Foster and Lehmann report that no cases of the overtraining syndrome have been diagnosed in athletes undergoing a period of 'easy' training.

Evidence to suggest that training stress may play a role in the development of the overtraining syndrome is provided by the findings of studies that have been carried out in an attempt to investigate the process of overtraining and also from anecdotal reports. Essentially, these studies have focused on manipulating athletes' training loads. Some have increased the intensity of the training load, whereas others have increased the training volume. Generally, the findings from these studies suggest that athletes may be at an increased risk of developing the overtraining syndrome following a training overload of three weeks or more. Despite these findings, a number of problems exist. These studies have essentially been single disciplined in nature, predominantly from the physiology discipline. Furthermore, findings from such studies have demonstrated that individual differences exist in response to the training load. What constitutes overtraining for one athlete may constitute optimal training for another. Possible explanations for such differences have not been explored.

'There is some evidence to suggest that the overtraining syndrome may be a response to an accumulation of both training and non-training stress'. Recently, it has been suggested that non-training stress in the form of environmental and lifestyle stressors, such as examination and relationship stress, may contribute to the development of the overtraining syndrome. It is proposed that the overtraining syndrome may be a response to an accumulation of both training and non-training stress. Although limited at present, some evidence does exist to support this suggestion. Evidence is provided from those studies that demonstrate the existence of individual differences in response to the training load. Some of these studies have reported that a small number of such athletes were experiencing additional non-training stress at the time of the study. As well as supporting the claim that non-training stress, together with the stress of training, may lead to the development of the overtraining syndrome, these findings may go some way to explaining the individual differences that have been unexplored in other studies.

Due to the dominance of single disciplined work in investigating the overtraining syndrome, little further evidence exists to support the notion that non-training stress may be a precursor to the syndrome. However, an abundance of literature exists that provides evidence to suggest that life stress and daily hassles may increase the incidence of illness and athletic injury, and although limited, research also exists that suggests social and lifestyle factors may be involved in the development of the chronic fatigue syndrome.

Symptoms of the chronic fatigue syndrome are similar to many of those reported by athletes diagnosed with the overtraining syndrome. Although further work needs to be carried out, evidence of this relationship between life stress and health outcome, together with the existence of individual differences in training load tolerance, may go some way to suggesting that non-training stress does contribute to the development of the overtraining syndrome.

Because of the uncertainty that exists in relation to the recognition, diagnosis and cause of the overtraining syndrome, our recent investigation took a more individual and holistic approach to investigate the syndrome. Findings from the investigation highlight the role that non-training stress may play in the development of the overtraining syndrome. Following diagnosis by a sports medic, five endurance athletes presenting with symptoms of the overtraining syndrome were given two psychological questionnaires: The Coping Response Inventory and The Athlete Daily Hassle Scale. On completion of the inventories, each athlete was interviewed in depth about their experiences of the syndrome. Based on the information gathered, a case study of the overtraining syndrome experience was written for each athlete.

Sports Injury Prevention

Anyone playing sport is to a greater or lesser extent at risk of injury, the intensity, frequency and type of play being only some of the factors that may influence physical damage. Thus, although the ideal may be to prevent injury, the practical goal should be to minimise it.

Perhaps the most basic way to reduce injury is to play according to the rules, though if the media are to be believed this presents the greatest growth area in the league table of sporting trauma. The laws of all sports were designed to ensure a level playing field but the increasing use of blatant fouls and cheating as the prizes grow larger can only contribute to the growing toll of injury. Pressure on umpires and referees comes from all directions. They are branded incompetent when the slow-motion TV camera picks up a missed infringement, overzealous if they apply rules to the letter, and berated by players where decisions go against them. And all for the love of sport and travel expenses!

That money is a factor in the attitude of sportsmen cannot be denied. With some professionals retiring by the age of 30 to draw pensions it is vital for them that these are topped up in their playing years. So if bending the rules or fouling helps that fund...well, that's the name of the game - isn't it?

Newton and the Strike Angle

Injury may come from various directions. In contact sports, external trauma from an opponent, accidental or premeditated, causes a very high percentage. However, it is not only the intensity of the contact that produces damage but also the angle of strike, the part of the body affected and the forces enacted according to Newton's laws that determine the extent of the injury. To help minimise this, the industry of protective body wear has developed, leading in its most extreme case to that grotesque caricature of sport, the American Footballer. The wonder is that he can manage to run at all, kitted out like Mr Blobby!

Nevertheless, sensible protection will spare players many injuries. A man who plays games involving small hard spherical objects and fails to look after his own is risking more than leisure pursuits. The footballer who will not wear shin pads could be deemed negligent in a sport where so much lower-limb contact occurs within the rules. The list of sensible protective clothing and equipment is endless, the necessity and suitability of much of it producing a fine line, in any active sports, between flexibility and relative immobility.

Successful teams and players usually have good coaches. To gain the highest professional qualifications most coaches will have undergone both generalised and sports-specific training under the auspices of such bodies as the National Coaching Foundation. As their courses include anatomy, physiology, psychology, nutrition, performance and injury prevention within their modules, there should be no excuse for coaches who are unaware of the effect their training programmes may have upon their charges.

Not only will intelligent coaching help to develop efficient and powerful players, but sensible adaptation of the regime can also allow an injured player to maintain a degree of fitness while the injury heals. Further than this, liaison with sports scientists, whose use of the slow-motion camera has revolutionised our perception of biomechanical movement, can often pinpoint the cause of an injury or even predict the one that occurs as a result of poor technique.

Coaches also have pressures upon them to produce their strongest teams and may play their least-injured players rather than their fittest, Armageddon occurring when the two are synonymous. Playing with an injury invites problems on two fronts: first, the original injury may be reactivated, and second, the stresses induced by favouring it may place intolerable strain on other structures which then break down.

So if injury is to be prevented, the player must start with no injury. This somewhat chicken-and-egg situation can be minimised if adequate precautions are taken. The necessity for warm-up has often been stressed, the similar need for a warm-down and the will to perform it rather less emphasised. The warm-up itself must be scientific - a five-minute jog followed by a couple of efforts merely scratches the surface. During competition the joints involved are liable to be used not only through their normal range of flexibility but also, often at the behest of an opponent, into angles of extension not previously contemplated. So before a warm-up, which often only increases the heart rate to competition levels and prepares muscles for aerobic exercise, there should be a programme of movement for each joint to take it to its extremes and to lengthen muscles and tendons so that the shock of competition does not immediately tear them.

Flexibility should therefore be built into every training programme, but a survey of the tight hamstrings of nearly every distance runner shows the futility of suggesting such exercises. An inability to comprehend that much of the lower-back pain from which they suffer is related to stiff and unstretched hamstrings is accompanied by the unspoken fear that time spend in stretching equals time and mileage lost in training, and all runners know that low mileage means poor results, don't they? However, lengthened hamstrings could allow an increase in stride length and performances to match, but how to persuade the blinkered mileage freak?

Sit back and ask yourself why

The trained athlete has one other source of injury - overuse. Repeated movement and actions, especially within the one plane, can induce injury that insufficient recovery will accentuate. Unfortunately, fitness is a knife-edge - under-training equals under-performance while over-training equals over-use injury.

There is no single way to prevent this, though varied training in terms of effort, intensity, terrain, environmental conditions and distance may all minimise the risk. The runner with a set 50-miles-per-week routine will probably suffer more from injury over a four-week period than the one who runs 35, 60, 45 and 60 miles in successive weeks, allowing time for recovery after harder and longer efforts.

Objective coaching can educate, not only with regard to lower limbs, but also in the case of the racket player with tennis elbow, the swimmer with shoulder impingement pain, and so on through the endless list of over-use damage. If a single piece of advice existed for prevention of injury, many medical and paramedical staff would be out of work. However, if present trends continue the need for medical care of injured players will increase rather than decrease. That, however, does not prevent each individual from sitting back dispassionately from his sport and, with the help of a coach, knowledgeable friend or even training companion, trying to analyse why any previous injury has occurred and outlining the measures necessary to prevent the most common cause of human beings ceasing to participate in one of life' s greatest pleasures.

Overtraining Syndrome

All five athletes that had been diagnosed with the overtraining syndrome experienced some form of non-training stress prior to their symptoms presenting. Each athlete described this non-training stress to have caused them varying amounts of stress at the time. Interestingly, none of the athletes reported a significant increase in their training load in the six-month period leading up to their symptoms presenting. Although further investigations are required, findings such as this suggest that the overtraining syndrome may be a response to an accumulation of both training and non-training stress, where an athlete's ability to adapt to his/her normal training regimen has been compromised. Such findings have a number of implications for practice which should be considered when working with competing athletes. The purpose of this article, therefore, is to follow on from that written previously and to provide some practical guidance on how best to minimise cases of the overtraining syndrome.

Obvious Steps

Before considering how we might practically take into account the factor of non-training stress when trying to minimise the ill effects of the overtraining syndrome, there are a number of obvious steps that should be considered when working with competing athletes. Without doubt, one of the most important factors in the prevention of the overtraining syndrome is for coaches to ensure that the training programme is well structured.

Training programmes should provide athletes with an appropriate balance between training stress and recovery. Unfortunately, however, the recovery process is frequently overlooked as the 'more is better' myth often takes priority.

The recovery process is one of the most important aspects of a training programme as it is when adaptation is reported to take place. If sufficient attention is not given to the recovery and adaptation process, then the body will have little time to adapt to the training stress imposed upon it and the ill effects of overtraining may be difficult for an athlete to avoid. A further consideration that should be taken into account when devising a training programme is to recognise that individual differences exist with regard to training-load tolerance.

Athletes are able to tolerate different levels of training and may also require different lengths of recovery. Therefore, a training programme that has led to an optimal performance for one athlete may lead to the demise of another. It is, therefore, essential to ensure that training programmes are individualised as far as possible. Unfortunately, despite numerous studies being carried out in an attempt to identify reliable physiological markers that indicate when an athlete is unable to tolerate the training load, a single consistent marker has not yet been identified. As a result of such inconsistencies, it is recognised that being able to confidently devise a training programme that optimises an athlete's performance, while at the same time avoiding the devastating effects of the overtraining syndrome, is an ongoing problem for many coaches.

Non-training Stressors

In addition to ensuring that athletes have both individualised and well structured training programmes, non-training stressors should also be considered when working with competing athletes. Traditionally, training programmes have taken a narrow view of the athlete, simply considering him/her in terms of their training and competitive schedules. Little consideration has been given to the non-sport environment in which an athlete must operate on a daily basis. The importance of considering this aspect of an athlete's existence is paramount if we consider the role that non-training stress may play in the development of the overtraining syndrome. Rather than leaving it unrecognised, coaches must consider modifying their athletes' training loads during times in which they are experiencing non-training stress. For example, to name but a few, examinations, the birth of a child and relationship difficulties.

If training loads are modified, athletes may then be able to accommodate the accumulation of stress that they are experiencing, ensuring that their ability to adapt is not compromised. It must be stressed that modifications to the training load must take place even if such training loads have optimised performance in the past. The athlete may not have been experiencing such non-sport stress when the training load in question led to optimal performances.

The Role of Sport Psychologists

In order to ensure that the non-sport environment in which an athlete exists is considered and understood when planning his/her training programme, it is suggested that experts such as a sport psychologist become more involved in developing and monitoring training programmes with coaches. This may ensure that unique training programmes are designed for athletes following a thorough consideration of them and their day-to-day existence. Furthermore, coaches and athletes alike may be more likely to consider modifying training programmes if the monitoring process indicates that an athlete is experiencing non-training stress at any point during his/her athletic career.

As well as aiding in the monitoring process, the sport psychologist may be able to help athletes gauge the degree of non-sport stress that they may be experiencing and provide them with appropriate intervention strategies so as to limit the stress from accumulating unnecessarily. There are a number of intervention strategies that a sport psychologist might consider, and as with any training programme the strategies employed will be those that are most suitable for the athlete in question. However, it has been suggested that the most effective prevention efforts might be those that enable an athlete to appropriately manage his or her stress levels. For example, for some athletes it may be appropriate to educate them on appropriate coping strategies and stress reduction techniques when dealing with the multiple contexts that they operate within.

A final piece of advice for any coach who is trying to optimise athletic performance and thus minimise the development of the overtraining syndrome is to ensure that athletes listen to their bodies. An athlete's body is the most useful tool for detecting maladaptations to the training load. Suppressed athletic performances and/or complaints of other symptoms indicative of the overtraining syndrome that do not usually occur in response to training may indicate that the athlete is not tolerating the training load. At such times, modifications should be made to the training programme in response to such symptoms in an attempt to facilitate adaptation.

Unexplained Underperformance Syndrome (UUPS)

The 'unexplained underperformance syndrome' (UUPS) is defined as a history of objective loss of performance, without a medical cause and despite two weeks of rest. This definition was arrived at by a group of experts in

Oxford in 1999. They chose to call the syndrome UUPS as opposed to 'over training' to avoid restricting the cause to training per se.

UUPS is almost exclusively a condition of endurance athletes, commonly occurring after a period of heavy training and competition. There is often a his-tory of frequent minor infections. Anecdotally it is thought that between 2% and 10% of elite endurance athletes suffer significant episodes of UUPS during their sporting careers. Often the condition occurs insidiously and remains undiagnosed for many weeks. The athlete typically will have sought advice from many quarters and have tried short periods of rest without success. Ideally the diagnosis of UUPS should be one that both athlete and coach agree upon.

Fatigue is the key presenting symptom. This fatigue persists despite rest and leads to underperformance. The athlete may lose motivation and often complains of sore muscles and poor sleep. Sometimes they may experience a loss of libido and appetite. They also often become depressed, and when this is clinically significant, it requires pharmacological treatment. It is often difficult for the athlete to determine whether the depression is the cause or the effect of the UUPS, but in my experience, if you do not treat the depression, you are likely to delay the resolution of the syndrome.

The onset of UUPS may coincide with upper respiratory tract infections, particularly viral. It is common, in taking the patient's history, to find that they have trained intensively through a viral upper respiratory tract infection, leading to symptoms of fatigue. Less common symptoms of UUPS include:

— stiff, sore muscles

— nocturnal hot sweats

— minor changes in bowel habit

— an elevated heart rate at a given intensity of training
— an elevated resting heart rate.
— an inability to alter pace at the end of a race.

Sometimes the athlete has difficulty in raising his/her heart rate in exercise and a profound loss of motivation. It is important to stress that none of these symptoms are diagnostic or consistent across all UUPS subjects. Chronic fatigue syndrome is distinct from UUPS in that it is a more severe condition in which sufferers usually cannot even contemplate doing sport, and they recover less quickly.

Despite much ongoing excellent research work, there are as yet no unequivocal diagnostic serological (blood analysis), physiological or psychological markers for UUPS. Observations have included raised stress hormones and reticulocyte (immature red blood cell) counts, increased cortisol to testosterone ratios, raised neutrophil to lymphocyte ratios and lower branch chain amino acids. Some researchers have shown a relative loss of sympathetic neural tone in athletes with UUPS; this is the part of the nervous system which, among other things, increases heart rate. A loss of heart rate variability (HRV) occurs during morning postural testing and this reflects the loss of sympathetic neural tone. This may be useful in monitoring rehabilitation intensity during recovery from UUPS because the loss of HRV can be quantified and recovery thereby monitored.

Mood scores, whilst a helpful psychological tool in confirming the diagnosis, are neither sensitive nor specific. Serological markers may in future help provide a more accurate clinical diagnosis.

UUPS must not be confused with other medical causes of under performance. There is an extremely long list of differential diagnoses for fatigue in athletes, many of which can be excluded by taking a good history and examination of the athlete.

The key to managing UUPS lies in a multi-disciplinary approach by a team of sports specialists, including physician, nutritionist, psychologist and physiologist. An experienced nutritionist should analyse a nutritional diary and the athlete's carbohydrate ingestion before, during and after exercise. It is important to be able to rule out an eating disorder: the SCOFF questionnaire may be useful.

Many athletes with UUPS have coincident social, financial, domestic and career stresses, which a psychologist will need to explore. Physiologists with experience in heart rate variability monitoring can lead athlete and coach through the pulse-dependent rehabilitation that follows, and an early meeting between them is good practice.

The successful resolution of UUPS depends on clear communications between the multidisciplinary team and the athlete, their coach and family. It is really important to give the athlete a clear understanding of what is happening, and to make time to answer their questions throughout treatment and rehab. In my experience, recovery to full training often takes 10 to 15 weeks, during which time there should be regular team meetings, and meetings with the athlete and coach.

Psychological support throughout the whole process is very important to address the concerns of the athlete, family and coach. It is difficult for the athlete to accept that there is no 'quick fix' for UUPS and experienced consultation skills are required to address questions on the aetiology of UUPS where our know-ledge is, at best, incomplete. The multidisciplinary team must reflect regularly on the athlete's clinical status, changing management swiftly when appropriate.

Table 1 Score symptoms

Date	*Fatigue*	*Muscle aches*	*Motivation*	*Upper respiratory tract symptoms*	*Other*	*Total*
Range	0-10	0-10	0-10	0-5	0-10	
1.02.03	5	5	6	5	8	29
2.02.03	5	6	5	4	6	26
3.02.03	5	6	4	4	5	24
14.02.03	2	1	1	0	1	5

There is no published evidence that one programme of management of UUPS is better than another. What follows is a pragmatic approach that has been adopted in the south-west region of the EIS, and which is regularly revised. Our strategy is based on symptom scoring and pulse-dependent rehabilitation (PDR). The athlete is asked early to score his/her symptoms in certain key areas (Table 1). Significant symptoms are scored 1 - 10, less significant symptoms are given less weighting and are scored 1 - 5. Daily totals are collated (high is 'bad', low is 'good') and used to determine the progression of the PDR programme. We leave one column for 'other' symptoms that may be specific to the individual athlete's history.

The PDR programme is agreed with the athlete and coach, and starts with a few weeks of complete rest, during which time the nutritionist and psychologist work with the athlete. The rate of progress thereafter is governed by improvements in the heart rate during exercise. The physician incrementally increases the volume and intensity of exercise based on heart rate response (table 2).

Table 2 Pulse-dependent rehab programme for a triathlete

Week	*Plan*
1	Rest
2	Rest
3	HR <120; 20 mins turbo training; 2 days off
4	HR <130; 20-25 mins TT; 2 days off
5	HR< 140; 30 mins TT; alternate days run 20 mins; 1 day off
6	HR < 150; 30 mins TT; run 20-30mins, swim 2k; 1 day off
7	HR 150-160 add short sprints (<10 secs)

In institutes of sport and high performance centres the prevention of UUPS should be high on the agenda. The prevention of UUPS is beyond the scope of this article but the main issue is education of athletes and coaches. Overall attention to the 'basics' of sports exercise physiology; periodised training, carbohydrate and fluid replenishment and a holistic approach to athlete-centred training intensity are fundamental to maintaining the good health of the athlete.

Prehabilitation

When an injured athlete has got to the point of needing joint surgery, it's all too easy to 'write them off', leaving them to fend for themselves until after the operation, when the sports therapist can pick up the important task of organising their rehab. But this is to miss a significant opportunity to work with the injured client on prehab - preparation leading up to surgery. By designing a prehab programme, a good support professional can prepare their patient mentally and physically for surgery, so that the chances of a successful outcome are maximised.

Mental Preparation

After an injury to an athlete's limb, the injured athlete

and their surgeon have agreed that surgery is required. Typical examples are: unstable shoulder resulting from repeated soft-tissue damage to the joint; torn meniscus from a rotatory injury to the knee; or ruptured ligaments of the ankle after an awkward tackle on the rugby pitch.

Patients are often nervous about surgery and will probably have failed or forgotten to ask the surgeon the right questions. Prehab allows the procedure to be explained and the patient to discuss their rehabilitation programme in detail, so that they fully understand what is expected of them. The process of allaying the patient's fears and answering their questions will allow them to go to surgery with a positive mental attitude.

This mental preparation enables the patient to be both confident and realistic about setting and achieving postoperative goals. Without it, they are much more likely to become frustrated and demotivated when recovery seems to be taking a long time, because they never had a realistic understanding of the time-frame in the first place.

After ACL reconstructive surgery of the knee, patients are not usually allowed to run until 12 weeks post-op, or to resume serious training for four to five months. Yet they may have picked up very different timescales from a combination of hearsay and media reports of very unusual cases, which could have set up vastly different expectations about the speed of their recovery.

Moreover, many orthopaedic surgeons have their own specific protocols for post-op programmes, so the prehab period is a valuable opportunity for the patient to learn about this, and even to practise the exercises.

Physical Preparation

The basic principles of physical preparation apply to all

joint surgery. However, the nature of prehab for acute injuries (those needing surgery within the first few weeks, such as an ACL rupture) will be somewhat different from that needed for chronic injuries (those needing cold surgery such as an osteoarthritic knee awaiting joint replacement). The main focus below is on the former group.

Acute Injuries

After a traumatic injury a joint will experience several possible inflammatory reactions to varying degrees. Pain and swelling occur at the site of injury, followed by reflex inhibition of the surrounding musculature, which in turn leads to joint stiffness and muscle weakness. Rehab must therefore commence from the time of injury, not from the time of surgery, in order particularly to help minimise the muscular weakening.

A skier twists their knee awkwardly when their skis fail to come off. The diagnosis of an ACL rupture is made. Because the success of surgery is significantly enhanced if the joint is calm prior to the operation, the surgeon has given the patient three to four weeks to prepare the knee so that it is non- inflamed and has good strength, full flexion and hyperextension.

If a surgeon operates on a swollen, stiff and weak knee, intra-articular fibrosis is more likely to occur postoperatively, causing joint stiffness and possibly affecting the long-term outcome of the surgery. This would have implications for private medical insurers, who are keen to minimise the number of post-op physio treatments.

Reduce pain and swelling rapidly

All inflamed joints will benefit from RICE: rest, ice, compression and elevation. RICE initially causes vasoconstriction in the area to reduce the blood flow and stop the bleeding of the injured tissue. Cooling by ice also reduces the perception of pain. Ice can be applied as an ice pack, wrapped in a towel for compression, for 10-15 minutes every 2 hours. The patient must rest with the limb elevated, so that gravity helps the swelling to reduce. For a leg injury the foot is supported higher than the hip; an injured arm is elevated on pillows so that the hand is higher than the shoulder.

If our skier's ruptured ACL happens to be combined with a medial collateral ligament injury then their knee joint will need to be supported in a brace to help protect against further injury. The skier will also be partially weight bearing on crutches to reduce pressure through the joint.

Ice and compression can be given in the form of a cryo-cuff, a pouch filled with iced water which compresses the joint. The advantage of this method of cooling is that the cuff can stay on the skin for longer (eg 30 minutes) and applications can be easily repeated throughout the day.

Restore range of movement

As the pain and swelling start to reduce, gentle mobilising and stretching exercises will encourage a return to as near normal range of movement as is possible. It is important for the client's trainer to be involved at this point, as they can supervise and encourage the client to maximise their potential for improvement prior to surgery.

Upper limb injuries respond well to active/assisted exercises, eg gripping fingers together and using the stronger arm to take the weaker arm into further flexion, or using a rope and pulley system to similar effect. For lower limb injuries, hydrotherapy or gentle exercises in water are very effective. The buoyancy of the water can be used to assist or resist movement.

For the athlete with the ruptured ACL, gentle flexion/extension exercises are used for knee joint mobility. It is important to restore full hyperextension prior to surgery, because swelling in the knee joint can only be fully compressed by a maximal isometric contraction of the quadriceps muscle when it is in the locked or hyperextended position.

If an athlete has a bucket-handle tear of the meniscus that is blocking the knee joint by 20-30 degrees from full extension, early arthroscopy is necessary. The quadriceps muscle will weaken rapidly if extension is not restored within a few days.

Full hyperextension can be achieved by using passive hamstring stretches such as knee hangs with only the heel supported on a pillow, or prone knee hangs (the patient lies on their stomach and allows only the thigh to be supported while the lower leg hangs over the end of the bed).

To improve knee flexion, the patient can sit on a desk with legs dangling and knees bent at 90 degrees. They then use the good leg to push the injured one gently back into further flexion. Alternatively, the patient can sit with their legs straight in front, bend the injured leg at the knee and use their hands to grip the ankle, easing the leg into greater flexion.

Gain muscular control of the injured limb

The pain and swelling arising from acute inflammation produce reflex inhibition (reflex weakening) of the muscles surrounding the injured area. Neuromuscular control needs to be restored prior to surgery in order to facilitate muscle recovery post-operatively. The stronger the muscles are, the faster they will recover afterwards.

Prehab strengthening exercises for all limb injuries would include isometric contractions, progressing to isotonic exercises against light resistance. The athlete may even be able to do light resistance training using gym machines, but they must understand that prehab exercises have to be closely monitored and that the joint must not be aggravated. If they end up provoking further pain and swelling, it may even delay surgery.

For knee prehab, isometric cocontractions of the quadriceps, hamstring and calf muscles will help reduce atrophy and can be performed sitting, lying and standing. Once the patient can maintain full hyperextension with a maximal isometric quadriceps contraction, begin straight leg raises.

Patients must gain active muscular control of hyperextension so that the knee does not 'flick' into that position during weight bearing. Where an ACL rupture has left an unstable knee, closed kinetic chain exercises are best, as muscular co-contraction occurs around the joint and reduces the anterior shear force on the tibia. Closed chain exercises also improve proprioception around the joint. These include static cycling, cross trainer, half squats, lunges and leg press.

Encourage proprioceptive awareness and normal movement patterns

Any sporting action, whether it's kicking a ball or throwing a javelin, depends on the co-ordination and fine-tuning of the neuromuscular control of all the soft tissues contracting around the joint. Joint injuries involving soft tissues that contain proprioceptors will have reduced awareness of joint movement. For athletes the importance of restoring neuromuscular function, including balance reactions and proprioception, cannot be over-emphasised.

A gymnast who has to balance her body weight through her arm on the beam must be able to feel where the joint is. Proprioceptive exercises need to be started prior to surgery to stimulate the neuromuscular mechanisms and make them more responsive after surgery.

Examples of upper limb proprioceptive exercises are press-ups over a Swiss ball, or pushing a soft ball on to the wall with one arm, then rolling it in different directions.

Anyone with a painful and swollen knee will normally limp. And as the symptoms improve, they often continue to limp because the motor cortex of the brain has accepted the changed motor pattern as normal. The correct gait pattern can be re-learnt prior to surgery to reprogramme alignment, weight transmission and proprioceptive input. This helps to facilitate a normal postop gait pattern.

For ACL-deficient knees, gentle balance exercises can be introduced, such as balancing on one leg with eyes open and then closed. A brace may have to be worn during exercise if the knee is very unstable. Balance boards and balancing on trampettes are also options. Most proprioceptive training comes postoperatively, once the knee has been stabilised with the new tendon graft.

Chronic Joint Injuries

If an athlete has suffered with a chronic joint injury over a long period and the joint has become increasingly stiff and painful, the body will almost certainly have developed compensatory movement patterns to try to offload the affected joint. Prehab is the place to try and reduce these movements and work on correct movement and recruitment patterns.

Weak, unstable shoulders will often compensate by over-using the trapezius muscle so that the position of the scapula becomes elevated and protracted. The humero-scapular area is not stabilised and this may lead to impingement problems of the rotator cuff or to neck and shoulder pain. A typical example of lower limb compensation would be a former footballer in his fifties who had a total medial meniscectomy in his twenties and has developed medial compartment osteoarthritis. The decision has been made to perform a hemi-arthroplasty on the medial side of the knee joint.

The footballer, not surprisingly, limps. This causes the hamstring and calf muscles to tighten and places extra pressure on the patello-femoral joint, causing it to become painful. A degree of chronic swelling will be present which can contribute to weakened musculature on the affected side. Limping can also place pressure on the lumbar spine or sacro-iliac joints and cause low back or hip pain.

This patient would need to start a prehab programme at least one month prior to surgery so that the limb can be mobilised and strengthened. His prehab programme would include:

— Deep soft-tissue massage and stretching of the hamstring and calf muscles (release of posterior tightness will allow increased extension, helping to prevent flexion contractures post-operatively);
— Mobility exercises (eg flexion/extension) and gentle stretching into the end of range of movement;
— Manual mobilising techniques and possibly McConnell taping to loosen the patella and improve alignment in the trochlear groove of the femur;
— Quadriceps, hamstring, calf and hip abductor strengthening exercises within a pain-free range of movement (isometric and isotonic concentric and eccentric muscular contractions);
— Gait re-education and proprioceptive balance work (the motor pattern of a limp feels normal to the

patient and he will have to re-learn the correct pattern of walking).

By the time the moment of surgery has arrived the patient will be feeling more confident about the strength and function of the knee and will be motivated to work harder at the post-op programme to achieve best possible results.

Pain Perception

Most patients come to see sports therapy practitioners because they are in pain; others because they have had pain and want to know what they can do to prevent a recurrence. And so, not surprisingly, as practitioners we tend to focus on the mechanisms that have caused the pain: whether, for instance, certain structures are hypermobile or hypomobile, and how the body is compensating for this. What we are less good at is taking into account the possible effects of any previous experience of injury, in particular the potential damage done by the stress/emotional strain that accompanies injury and/or the degree of neuroplasticity (change to the nervous system) that results from pain. In fact, the level of pain experienced is a poor guide to the degree of tissue damage: pain perception can operate alarmingly independently of the severity of mechanical injury.

This is because pain relates to context. The pain an athlete feels will be closely linked to their perception of its cause. So if an athlete with low back pain is told by his health professional that he has a massive bulging lumbar disc, he will probably feel more unpleasant pain than if he had been told that bulging discs are reasonably common and not always painful.

We all learn how to respond to pain early on in our lives. Have you ever seen an infant hurt themselves and then look at their parents before starting to cry? If the parents indicate that the child should be experiencing pain, the child will receive this stimulus and learn from it.

In general, pain is a useful and healthy signal. Thus the runner who has increased their mileage too quickly may start to develop Achilles pain. This allows them to realise that they have incorrectly increased their workload and need to modify it.

But the message of pain is not always so obvious. Take the athlete who is nearing competition and has not unwisely changed their workload, but who suddenly develops soreness in an old injury site. What processes are occurring here? You cannot underestimate the effect of emotional stress on the musculoskeletal system. There are other things going on.

Pain and the Brain

Without delving too deeply into neurophysiology, there are three components to the pain experience (the pain cycle):

— *Reception of pain stimuli:* this occurs in the peripheral nerves and is detected by nociceptors or pain receptors;

— *Transmission of pain signals:* from the peripheral nerve to the spinal cord and up to the brain for interpretation;

— *Perception of these pain signals:* this is the balance between the information from the periphery and the resulting interpretation from the brain. This is where we decide how we feel about the pain and what we are going to do about it. The brain allows input from various areas relating to emotion, memory of previous pain, sympathetic nervous system responses, immune system responses and so on. So if we believe there is a threat to our health then we will feel pain.

Stresses and trauma, including past injury, can prompt changes in the nervous system that will alter its behaviour. In the peripheral nervous system (which provides information to the spinal cord about the muscles/joints etc) these changes include:

— More receptors activated;

— Receptors more easily excited;

— Receptors firing off spontaneously;

— Normally quiet receptors becoming 'inapprcpriately' receptive, making it more likely that stress/emotion will cause pain.

The central nervous system may undergo central sensitisation. This is where the spinal cord has greater excitability to all degrees of input from the peripheral nervous system. Normal stimuli can be interpreted as pain, and moderately painful stimuli can be interpreted as extremely painful.

The higher centres of the central nervous system in the brain are also susceptible to change. This is where the centres responsible for emotion, memory, the autonomic nervous system and motor responses are situated. There is always an emotional component to our experience of pain: how an athlete will interpret this depends on previous injuries, when they occurred and the extent of the time away from competition. If an athlete is returning to an arena where they previously sustained an injury, the combined influence of memory and emotion may well cause them to feel the old injury site start to ache or feel tight - even though there is nothing wrong with the body part.

Decode and Damp Down

The therapist therefore has the tricky task of forming an opinion about the patient's pain in relation to the objective level of tissue damage. In making this assessment, here are some points to consider:

— *Time since injury.* If sufficient time has elapsed since the injury for inflammation, scarring and remodelling of the tissues to have occurred, yet the patient is still in pain, then broader questions have to be addressed.

— *Signs of increased sensitivity* to normal sensation such as touch.For instance, the lumbar spine patient who feels pain just on light palpation of the lumbar tissues is experiencing 'allodynia', a sign of changes in central nervous system processing;

— *Negative test results.* If reliable objective mechanical tests are negative (for instance, upper limb tension tests are normal while the patient reports neural symptoms), ask questions;

— *Adverse response to small changes in temperature.* An example would be when cold-weather training causes an old injury to start aching even though nothing is wrong with the tissues. Ask questions;

— *Raised level of emotional stress.* As an important competition looms, for instance, the athlete's sensitivity to an injury site can increase;

— *Number of helpers.* The size of the entourage accompanying the patient into the physio's consulting room can be inversely proportional to the seriousness of the injury - and with some patients, the additional company seems to magnify their pain;

— *Response to treatment.* This can be influenced by previous treatment the patient has had or their understanding of treatment. A recent patient of mine who had ruptured his posterior cruciate ligament was doing really well with his rehab until he met a friend who'd had the same injury and told my patient that he, too, would need surgical repair. It was not until my client received positive reinforcement from the surgeon that his pain subsided and rehab was successful.

The course of pain over time

By attending to broader contextual issues and with good management, the therapist can reduce this magnified pain response. Indeed, the patient comes to the therapist with expectations, and the level of confidence that they have in the 'expert' will in itself make a tremendous difference to their response to treatment. Even the certificates and plaques that professionals display on the walls of our clinics are part of that process of establishing our clients' confidence in us. Here are some more measures you might deploy to help reduce pain:

— Positive reinforcement about the injured tissue; for example, that it is mechanically sound and objective tests are normal;

— Explain the pain cycle: as Moseley et have demonstrated with low back pain sufferers, by explaining the way pain works, you can help diminish the patient's pain levels and reduce their anxiety about what they are feeling;

— Use movement therapy not just for mechanical effect but also to reduce pain levels by damping down the nervous system's centralised sensitivity. Passive movement of injured tissue can help speed the brain's winding down of pain responses;

— Advise the client about self-care; eg, to stretch an old injury site just before a competition, not simply to warm up but also to act as reassurance that no harm will come to that limb because it is feeling good, working well and is properly prepared;

— Be ready to revise the pace of your graduated rehab programme. Your main aim will be to allow healing tissue to strengthen and regain extensibility at a safe and efficient rate of progress, but the client's previous injury experience and preconceptions about pain may interfere. Their brain may be instructing the body to slow the process down if it perceives that the speed of rehab may in fact exacerbate the damage;

— Reduce the threat of further injury: probably the most important factor here is environment. The rehab environment should feel safe and not related to the scene of the injury. But as healing progresses you will gradually need to introduce stress/pressure to simulate the sporting environment.

Finally, devise preventive or proactive work that can help the athlete minimise their associations with pain:

— Mental rehearsal of movements that have previously injured body parts - using good technique. Thus, a high jumper who has hurt her back because she is extending too much through the lumbar spine can visualise performing her jump using the stabilising muscles to protect her back;

— Change exercise position: perform the rehab process in different positions that stimulate different thought processes, eg vary quad/gluteal exercises against a wall and on a leg press machine to try and break any negative thought processes attached to a specific movement or exercise pattern;

— Add differing degrees of balance challenges/ different surfaces: again, the idea here is to re-educate the brain about an acceptable normal range of movement patterns and bio-feedback;

— Design situations of emotional stress into the rehab, eg the injured rugby player who has sustained a medial ligament injury will need to progress to stepping off that leg when pressured from a would-be tackler. The challenge here is certainly physical, but also hugely psychological;

— Add distractions, simulating the playing environment with noise etc;

— Use visual inputs to reinforce the value of the rehab: the positive effect of specific exercises can be enhanced by showing the client the beneficial changes to their body. For instance, use of real-time ultrasound in retraining the transversus abdominis muscle can convince the patient of its attachment into the deep parts of the lumbar spine. Imagery is very important as a reinforcement tool.

3

Sports Motivation Training

Motivation has been defined as 'the direction and intensity of ones efforts'. Direction refers to the decision to commit and to turn up to training on a regular basis. The intensity dimension is about how much people are prepared to give in each training session. In sport, these dimensions are often related, with committed individuals attending training on a regular basis and working hard during their sessions.

Some coaches believe that motivation is a fixed personality trait or characteristic — that you either are or aren't a motivated athlete. In fact, though, motivation is not quite that cut and dried since the motivational climate created by the coach will impact on the motivation of the athletes under his or her guidance.

Reinforcement and Punishment

Reinforcements and punishments can be either positive or negative. However, to avoid confusion, you must think of positive and negative in this case in terms of either adding something or taking something away, not in terms of good or bad.

Whereas classical conditioning works by forming an association between two stimuli (eg a 'clicker' and a treat in dog training), operant conditioning forms an association between a behaviour and a consequence. There are four possible consequences to any behaviour, as follows:

— Something good can start or be presented;
— Something good can end or be taken away;
— Something bad can start or be presented;
— Something bad can end or be taken away.

Anything that increases a behaviour — makes it occur more frequently, makes it stronger or makes it more likely to occur — is termed a reinforcer. Normally a person will perceive 'starting something good' (positive reinforcement) or 'ending something bad' (negative reinforcement) as worth pursuing and will repeat the behaviours that seem to cause these consequences.

Anything that decreases a behaviour — makes it occur less frequently, makes it weaker, or makes it less likely to occur — is termed a punisher. Normally a person will perceive 'ending something good' (negative punishment) or 'starting something bad' (positive punishment) as worth avoiding and will not repeat the behaviours that seem to cause these consequences.

Note that these definitions are based on their actual effect on the behaviour in question — ie they must reduce or strengthen the behaviour to be defined as punishment or reinforcement. Pleasures meant as rewards that do not strengthen a behaviour are indulgences, not reinforcers; would-be punishments that do not weaken a behaviour are classified as abuse.

Sport psychology research evidence overwhelmingly supports the use of a predominantly (80-90%) positive approach, with punishment kept to a minimum. Behavioural modification techniques based on positive reinforcements have been successfully used to increase output during training sessions, improve performance, and reduce errors. It's at this point in lectures that some students tell that they prefer a more authoritarian coach, even one who shouts. That way they know what is expected of them — and that there will be negative consequences if they fail to live up to those expectations.

However, it is important to point out that a positive approach doesn't mean being 'laid-back', having few rules and even fewer expectations of your athletes: far from it. A positive approach is as demanding as a negative one, except that rewards tend to predominate over punishments as the route to better performance.

A predominantly positive approach to coaching will sometimes involve punishment. If, for example, one of your athletes has been late for training a number of times you might need to criticise them in order to ensure better timekeeping in future. Letting someone know you are unhappy is perfectly justified — as long as you limit your criticism to the particular behaviour that has made you unhappy rather than indulging in more general character assassination.

Taking a positive approach to coaching is not about praising athletes continuously, regardless of success or failure, but about giving praise when it is merited. That means recognising and rewarding not just successful overall outcomes — ie winning — but also performance improvements, improved approximations (like a more technically correct forehand in tennis) and effort. One study showed that children who were praised for their efforts following failure were more persistent, enjoyed the task more and performed better than children praised for having high ability.

The scheduling of positive reinforcement is also an important factor. Continuous praise is actually a bad thing — unless you are working with novices—as it devalues the reward, which is seen as too- easily obtained. In this kind of climate, players essentially switch off. You also need to be aware of how your behaviour may be perceived by others. If, for example, you adopt a predominantly positive approach, using positive reinforcements, but for some reason remain fairly quiet during a session, your behaviour may be interpreted as a withdrawal of the normal praise and hence a punishment.

Sandwich Approach

At times coaches need to be critical, but this can lead to defensive behaviour on the part of the athlete, as criticism can be perceived as a threat to self-esteem. One way to avoid this is to 'sandwich' your corrective feedback between two positive statements. Let's take an example of a football coach being critical of a striker who has missed a relatively simple chance to score. Rather than berate the player, the coach might consider something along the lines of the following feedback sandwich:

'That was a great run you made to create space...

— '...but it was a poor finish. You were leaning back on contact and that's why the ball lifted over the bar. Next time try to keep your head over the ball.

— 'Keep going because you are stretching their defence.' When presented in this way, the feedback becomes more constructive by balancing praise and criticism while also providing instruction.

Why should a negative approach to coaching, using more punishment and criticism than positive reinforcement, be discouraged when there is evidence to show that punishment can help to eliminate some unwanted behaviours? There are three serious drawbacks to incorporating punishment into your coaching style:

— The predominant use of punishment normally works by creating a fear of failure, and this can often lead to performance decrements as athletes focus on the consequences of losing or making mistakes rather than on what needs to be done to be successful. Fear of failure can promote indecision, with consequent tentative responses and a tendency to choke in high-pressure situations. In hockey, for example, a winger needs to take risks by running at the full backs and committing his opponents; this will not always be successful but it only has to work once for a match-winning goal to occur. However, if the player fears a backlash from his coach if he loses the ball, he might become tentative and avoid responsibility by passing to a team mate. 'Playing it safe' is often a counterproductive tactic which has been linked to poorer performances. Fear of failure has also been linked to less enjoyable experiences in sport and increased dropout rates.

— If you are working with athletes who are attention seekers, making an example of them by punishing them in front of others can actually reinforce the behaviour you want to eliminate. Poor behaviour, such as constantly turning up late for practice, is sometimes designed to provoke a response. The best way to deal with such behaviour is on a one-to-one basis in a private setting; otherwise it is likely to recur as it gives the attention seeker exactly what he craves.

— The predominant use of punishment as an approach to coaching doesn't promote good relations between coach and athlete. It can lead to the build-up of hostility, resentment and discouragement, resulting in loss of motivation.

There are some players for whom a negative approach to coaching might be effective, but you really need to know your athlete before employing such tactics. Creating the most productive motivational climate depends on many interrelated factors, including the characteristics of the group and individuals, their preferred style of coaching, the qualities of the coach (knowledge, expertise etc), situational factors (eg the dangers involved in a given activity) and, of course, the coaching style favoured by the coach.

In experience, the best coaches are flexible and able to adapt to the requirements of different situations. This will nearly always involve criticism or punishment as well as praise, but will rely primarily on a positive approach in order to motivate players to perform at their best.

Getting your athletes to change an old habit or adopt a new behaviour is often crucial to whether they will achieve their goals or respond correctly to a treatment. Success depends not only on what happens when the athlete is with you but also on what happens when he or she are on their own, looking after themselves.

The following examples should illustrate the point. You coach an athlete who trains very well, achieving all your planned sessions. However, his eating habits are poor and even though you have told him what to eat many times, he doesn't seem to want to change his diet. Or, if you're a therapist, you treat an injured client who needs to do some rehabilitation exercises, such as stretches, at home on his own as well as when he visits you for treatment. Although you've instructed him what to do, he doesn't carry out the exercises regularly to get the benefits required. So what's the solution? Improve your motivational skills.

In 1983, two researchers called Prochaska and DiClementi introduced the Transtheoretical Model of Behaviour Change (TTM). The TTM very simply describes how people go about changing their health or lifestyle behaviours by defining five 'stages of change'. The TTM suggests that, for people to make positive change, they must go through a process of increasing their readiness to change. In other words, before a new behaviour or action can occur, the individual must have the right attitudes and beliefs to embrace it. Each of the five 'stages of change' depicts a distinct level of attitude and action for behaviour change. For example, the following are the five stages applied to changing eating habits:

— Precontemplation: not changing diet and not intending to start to change.

— Contemplation: not changing diet, but intending to change.

— Preparation: making some changes, but not fully, though intending to change fully.

— Action: achieved all diet changes regularly for less than six months.

— Maintenance: maintained all diet changes for longer than six months.

What the TTM tells us is that the type of strategies needed to get people to change their diets, for example, will depend on their current stage of change. If you give an athlete or client a diet sheet to follow, they will only adopt the new diet if they are at the preparation or action stages. At these stages they would be ready to respond to this 'action-oriented approach'. If, however, the athlete or client is only at the precon-templation or contemplation stages, they will be unlikely to respond to the new diet. So with individuals at these stages of change, the strategy is to motivate and persuade them that changing their diet is important, beneficial and achievable. In short, increasing their readiness to change by taking them on to the preparation stage.

At these lower stages, the strategies used are not 'action-oriented', such as the diet sheet, but more motivational and attitudinal. To progress from the lower stages, an individual must believe that the new behaviour is important and worthy, and that the 'pros' for adopting it outweigh the 'cons' of changing. This is called 'decision balance' and the strategies used in the lower stages must aim to shift the decision balance in favour of the 'pros'. For instance, the pros for changing diet such as feeling better and losing weight must counter the cons of not being able to eat pizzas and chips every night.

A person must also believe in him/herself to be ready to make a behaviour change. This is known as 'self-efficacy' and is the individual's belief in him/herself to perform a task successfully. Often, individuals at the lower stages have low self-efficacy regarding their behaviour. For instance. they don't feel confident about changing their diets. To progress through the stages, strategies to build self-efficacy must be used to help trigger the change.

Research with the TTM suggests it can be used across a range of health and lifestyle behaviours and that the strategies it supports are effective in helping individuals to make positive changes. For example, Marcus et al found that people in a group became more active when they received motivational materials relevant for their stage of change. Prochaska et al studied why it was than in a worksite weight-loss programme there was an 80 per cent dropout rate. They found that the weight-loss programme had been action-oriented, involving exercise classes and diet plans, and yet most of the participants were still precontemplators and contemplators.

So the reason why the athlete won't change his diet, or the patient won't follow stretching instructions, or the fitness client doesn't train by himself is that they are being given 'action-oriented' instructions that don't match their readiness to make that change. The beauty of the TTM is that, unlike other social psychology models, it not only describes the theory behind how behavioural change occurs but also gives us the practical strategies to use at each stage of change.

The athlete that won't respond to the diet instructions needs first to have explained to him the benefits of changing his eating habits. Pointing out to him that his performance will improve, that he will recover quicker from training and have more energy for training if he eats correctly. will help shift the 'decision balance' in favour of the 'pros' for changing diet. Discussions about how to make healthy but tasty meals, what to buy from the supermarket instead of unhealthy snacks, and about how other athletes eat well will help build 'self-efficacy' about changing to healthier foods. These discussions may need to take place over a period of time and the messages should be reinforced with handouts or articles about the benefits of proper nutrition. How long it takes to progress to the higher stages will depend on the athlete's initial readiness to change and his/her ability to take on board the new messages. In general, though, the strategy for getting the athlete to change involves education, persuasion and practical advice.

Building up self-efficacy is obviously important for the patient who doesn't do the rehab exercises at home or the client who doesn't train alone. It may simply be that the exercises in the rehab programme, say, are new or difficult and the patient may have low self-efficacy about performing them alone. In this case, it is worth spending extra time teaching all the exercises involved in the programme, providing clear instructions and demonstrating the techniques so that the patient can remember the exercises and how to perform them. Writing out the programme clearly and providing pictures should be useful in helping build the patient's self-efficacy towards performing the exercises alone.

The same goes for the athlete who is unable to do solo workouts. In this case, simply providing a fitness plan to follow isn't enough to help the individual achieve his training sessions. The athlete with low self-efficacy about training alone will find it hard to surmount the normal obstacles that make exercising harder, such as bad weather or finding the time. Such an individual must be helped to plan when he can train alone so that it fits easily into his lifestyle—for example, before work or at lunchtime. At the same time, make sure that the workouts you plan are practicably achievable.

If you compile complex workouts that take over an hours to perform, the athlete may be put off attempting the session. He will feel more confident about performing simple, short workouts on his own. You also need to teach the solo workouts in full. Your clients are unlikely to perform something alone that they have not first performed with you at least once. For example, you may decide that the athlete should do a 40-minute run on his own and a short run plus some resistance exercises when he is with you so you can supervise the technique. This is a reasonable decision, but you may find that unless you spend at least one training session doing the long run with the athlete he will not have the confidence to perform it alone.

These examples help illustrate the TTM and the process of changing behaviours. The key message is that the strategy for change you use and the individual's state of change must be matched. Those at the lower stages need motivational, thinking strategies that boost their self-efficacy and promote the 'pros' of change. Those at higher stages will respond to action-oriented instructions and programmes.

Motivation Intrinsic

Physical activity is necessary to produce fitness improvement and benefits to health. Motivational studies have long focused on factors that initiate, influence, and modify behaviour. Early theories dealt essentially with the deterministic aspects of those factors; focusing on instinctual drives, physiological drives, or environmental influences. Although these theories had (and still have) considerable value, their apparent view of people as passive beings that are pushed and pulled around by their physiology or environment has given rise to concern and criticism.

A major development of White's monograph is represented by the addition of a formal statement of cognitive evaluation theory. Cognitive evaluation theory states that intrinsic motivation is driven by an innate need for competence and self-determination in dealing with one's surroundings. The intrinsic rewards for the behaviours motivated by this need are satisfying feelings of competence and autonomy, positive emotions such as enjoyment and excitement, and possibly the sensation of flow (complete absorption in the activity). These feelings, in turn, serve to maintain or increase a person's intrinsic motivation for the particular behaviour.

In a nutshell (according to the theory), an individual's desire to pursue a particular activity depends upon whether his or her feelings of competence, autonomy, and positive affect persist over time. Conversely, if an individual begins to perceive him or herself as incompetent at the activity and/or under external control to do it, then his or her intrinsic motivation is undermined. The outcome is then either a state of extrinsic motivation (the activity might continue dependent on the continuance of external rewards and/or coercion), or a state of amotivation (further activity unlikely because the perceptions of incompetence lead to a sense of futility).

A wealth of studies in general psychology have supported the validity of cognitive evaluation theory. Many studies have clearly shown that when individuals receive information that undermines their sense of competence and/or perception of self-determined choice, their intrinsic motivation declines.

Losers' Intrinsic Motivation

In the present study, researchers also examined possible ways of counteracting what they expected would be strongly negative effects on intrinsic motivation of losing the competitively contingent reward. They began by nothing that, with competitively contingent rewards, losers get the negative performance feedback implicit in losing and they also fail to get the desired rewards. Thus, they considered two possible approaches to counteracting the negative effects of losing the competitively contingent reward: (1) providing positive feedback on the quality of performance, and (2) providing a performance-contingent reward to make up for the competitively contingent reward they failed to win. Consider these in turn.

Positive Feedback for Losers

Positive performance feedback has generally been found to enhance intrinsic motivation. Further, the initial study of the effects of competition on intrinsic motivation indicated that when people received implicit positive feedback, namely seeing that they solved puzzles faster than another participant, they were significantly more intrinsically motivated than people who won a competition. Together these findings suggest that positive performance feedback can be a powerfully positive motivator.

Researchers hypothesised that, if losers of a competitively contingent reward received positive competence feedback about their actual performance at the activity, they would be significantly more intrinsically motivated than comparable losers who did not receive the positive feedback. In other words, the positive feedback should help to counteract the negative feedback implicit in losing a competitively contingent reward. In the present experiment, one of the groups of participants who were told they could win a competitively contingent reward but in fact lost it were also told at the beginning of the experiment that if they solved three out of the four puzzles, they would be doing very well because they would have performed better than 70% of previous participants. These participants, all of whom did in fact solve at least three puzzles, thus got positive feedback about their performance, and they expected them to show significantly higher intrinsic motivation than those who lost the competitively contingent reward but got no positive performance feedback.

Monetary Rewards for Losers

As noted, losing a competitively contingent reward means not only that participants get implicit negative feedback but also that they fail to attain their goal of receiving the reward. As such, it is possible that, even though they lose the competitively contingent reward, receiving a reward for doing well that is comparable in magnitude to the reward they losing the counteract the negative effect of losing the competitively contingent reward.

Tangible rewards, collapsed across type of contingency, have been found meta-analytically to undermine both behavioural and self-report measures of intrinsic motivation. However, the meta-analysis showed that performance-contingent rewards undermined the behavioural measure of intrinsic motivation, but not self-reports of enjoyment. Researchers interpretation of this seemingly disparate result is based in the idea that people enjoy receiving a performance contingent reward because it represents competence affirmation. Specifically, although tangible performance-contingent rewards tend to-be experienced as controlling and thus to decrease self-initiation of the activity, the message of competence conveyed by the performance-contingent rewards promotes enjoyment.

As such, a performance-contingent reward should be nearly as effective as positive feedback in terms of promoting enjoyment because in both conditions people will feel more competent. However, if people are controlled by a performance-contingent reward, they should not self-initiate the activity in the absence of an operative reward contingency, because research has shown that perceived competence does not enhance intrinsically motivated behaviour if people do not feel autonomous. Accordingly, they hypothesised that performance-contingent rewards given to the losers of a competitively contingent reward would lead to less intrinsic motivation behaviourally assessed than would positive feedback given to losers of the competitively contingent reward, but that the levels of enjoyment for the two groups would not differ.

Recently, although the evidence for this is relatively scant, Harackiewicz and Sansone argued that a condition in, which participants get performance contingent rewards for matching evaluative norms should yield higher levels of intrinsic motivation than a condition in which people are told their performance will be evaluated and are then given positive feedback for matching evaluative norms. In the current study, losers in the positive-feedback condition and the performance-contingent rewards conditions were given evaluative norms before they began the puzzle solving. Thus, counter to the predictions that performance contingent rewards would undermine free-choice behaviour but that the two groups would not differ on enjoyment, if Harackiewicz and Sansone were correct, then the performance-contingent rewards condition should have a higher level of both free-choice behaviour and self-reported enjoyment than would the positive feedback condition.

Measuring Intrinsic Motivation and Ego-Involved Persistence

Past experiments have used two different measures of intrinsic motivation. The behavioural measure assesses behaviour during a so-called free-choice period subsequent to the performance period, and the self-report measure assesses participants' reports of interest/ enjoyment for the activity, which is also done following the performance period. Consider the behavioural measure because it relates not only to intrinsic motivation but also to ego involvement that can be easily stimulated in competitive situations.

The free-choice behavioural measure involved leaving participants alone with the target activity and interesting alternative activities for a period of time when the participants assumed that no one would know what they were doing and they would not be asked to work more with the target activity. If participants spent time with the target activity, they were assumed to be intrinsically motivated. The number of seconds spent with the target activity was the measure of intrinsic motivation.

This free-choice behavioural measure has been widely used, and it worked extremely well to assess intrinsic motivation following an experimental manipulation in which an external contingency was presented and subsequently removed. However, it ran into problems when research began to investigate the effects of ego involvement on intrinsic motivation. Specifically, when the experimenter did a manipulation that resulted in people's egos or feelings of self-worth becoming contingent on their performance at an activity, there was no easy way for the experimenter to remove the contingency.

Two approaches have been used for dealing with this problem. First, Ryan et al. suggested that if free-choice behaviour is really intrinsically motivated, the person should be experiencing interest/enjoyment while doing it; in other words, the free-choice behaviour and self-reports of interest should be positively correlated. On the other hand, if the free-choice behaviour is ego involved, free-choice behaviour and self-reported interest should not be correlated. Ryan et al. further suggested that when ego-involved people do badly at a task, they will be driven to persist during the free-choice period in order to regain a sense of self-worth, whereas if they do well, they will not need to persist because their good performance will have confirmed their worth.

The researchers did an experiment in which, in some conditions, any free-choice behaviour was expected to be intrinsically motivated and in others free-choice behaviour was expected to be ego-involved persistence. Results indicated that in the conditions where intrinsic motivation was expected, free-choice behaviour was significantly positively correlated with expressed interest; whereas, in the conditions where ego-involved persistence was expected, free-choice behaviour was not correlated with expressed interest. As such, Ryan et al. were able to separate the two types of free-choice behaviour. However, the disadvantage to this approach is that the free-choice period behaviour was defined as either intrinsic motivation or ego-involved persistence at the level of the experimental condition rather than within individuals.'

The second approach to distinguishing intrinsic motivation from ego-involved persistence during a free-choice period was suggested by Reeve and Deci. They partitioned the free-choice measure into two categories: (a) working with new puzzle configurations, and (b) working with the previously encountered configurations. The reasoning was that, if people are intrinsically motivated for an activity, they would seek novelty and challenge because of interest, so working with new puzzles was considered an indicator of intrinsically motivated persistence. In contrast, if participant are working to regain their feelings of worth-for example, after having failed while ego involved-they would return to the puzzles on which they had done poorly in order to try to feel better about themselves. Thus, working with old (previously-encountered) puzzles was considered an indicator of ego-involved persistence.

As already mentioned, competition tends to promote ego involvement, and failing at a task in which one is ego involved can promote ego-involved persistence. It was thus necessary to have measures of both intrinsic motivation and ego-involved persistence in the current study.

Method

Participants

A total of 25 male and 55 female University of Rochester undergraduates volunteered for the experiment and received extra course credit for doing so. Most of the participants were Caucasian in the age range of 18-23 years old.

Experimental task

The experimental task was a spatial-relations puzzle called Happy Cubes. Past studies with college students working on the Happy Cubes puzzle indicate that participants find it to be a highly interesting activity and persist at it during the free-choice period. Participants were provided with drawings of three-dimensional configurations that they were to reproduce with the mechanical puzzle.

Procedure

Participants arrived at a waiting area where they were welcomed by an experimenter and taken to the experimental room. The experimenter then went to an adjoining room from where he observed participants through a one-way mirror and communicated with them over an intercom.

The experimenter explained that the purpose of the study was to examine motivation for working oh a spatial-relations puzzle task. Participants were randomly placed in one of the five experimental conditions. Those in the four competitive conditions were told that their same-sex opponent had already arrived and was settled in the adjoining room.

The experimenter used a sex-appropriate name to refer to that "other participant." In reality, there was no person in the next room, but the purpose of this pretext was to help create a competitive atmosphere. All five conditions were (a) the Happy Cubes puzzle, (b) two drawings of three-dimensional configurations that the participants would attempt to duplicate with the puzzle during a practice period, and (c) a selection of popular magazines that served as an alternative activity during a later free-choice period. The experimenter explained that there would be a series of six puzzles to solve.

Before starting the practice puzzles, participants received experimental instructions appropriate to their experimental condition. In the no-competition/nofeedback/no-reward control group (Condition 1) the experimenter simply asked the participants to work on the puzzles, "doing your individual best." In each of the four competitively contingent reward conditions, the experimenter told participants the following: "The purpose of this competition is to try to outperform the other person by solving your puzzles faster than he or she." Thus, participants were led to believe that they would to be competing against the same-sex participant who had been said to be in the adjacent room. "To win the game you will need to solve the puzzles more quickly than your opponent. You will have four puzzles to solve and you will have four minutes to solve each puzzle.

It does not matter whether you figure out how the puzzle works, the important thing is to win the competition. So, focus your attention on being the winner." In all four competitively contingent reward conditions (Conditions 2-5), participants were told that "you can make $3 by winning the competitive game; in other words, you will get $3 if you solve more of the puzzles more quickly than your opponent."

People in Conditions 4 and 5 were given the following additional instructions: "if you manage to 'solve three out of the four puzzles correctly, regardless of whether you are slower or faster than your opponent, you will have done better than 70% of the participants in their previous studies. So, the purpose of this competition is twofold: first, to try to beat the other person by solving your puzzles faster than he (or she) does, and second, to try to surpass the 70th percentile performance standard by correctly solving at least three of the four puzzles within the allotted time."

People in Condition 5 were then given an additional instruction, namely that "if you meet the 70th percentile performance standard by correctly solving at least three out of the four puzzles, you will receive a $3 reward. So, there are two ways to earn a reward of $3; one way is through beating the other person and the other is by performing well, namely by solving three out of four puzzles correctly. If you solve three puzzles and win the game you will earn $6." The researchers was to find four puzzles that would be as challenging as possible but would allow all participants to solve at least three of the four.

The amount of money given for the performance contingent reward was $3 just as the amount given for the competitively contingent reward was $3. This was done so the losers of the competitively contingent reward in Condition 5 would receive the same amount of money from the performance-contingent reward that the winners of the competitively contingent reward received in Condition 2, and also so the losers in Condition 5 would lose the same amount as the losers in Conditions 3 and 4 who ended up without any monetary reward.

The losers in Condition 5 would have imagined that the winners had made three dollars more than they themselves received. Similarly, the losers in Conditions 3 and 4 would have imagined that the winners had made $3 more than they did from winning the competition. As such, for each comparison, the amount of money believed to have been won and/or lost was controlled across relevant comparisons.

Before starting the performance puzzles and after receiving the instructions, participants in all conditions were given two practice puzzles. After the first, participants in the four competitively contingent reward conditions (Conditions 2-5) were informed that their opponent had failed to solve the puzzle in the allotted time, so the participant would have won on that puzzle. After the second practice puzzle, participants were told that their opponent had solved the second puzzle faster than they did. Puzzles had been preselected so that the participants would not be able to solve the second practice puzzle within the allotted time, but could solve the first practice puzzle. This matching of practice outcomes in the competition conditions was intended to convey the impression that the two people were roughly of equal ability and was also intended to create the perception of a challenging game. After the two practice trials the, experimenter told participants the practice period was over.

The experimenter then entered the room to remove the practice configurations and leave six more configurations. The period of working on the performance puzzles then began. In each of the competitively contingent reward conditions, the experimenter provided comparison feedback after each trial by telling the participants over the intercom which of them had won on that puzzle. The feedback that was provided had been predetermined according to condition.

The win versus lose outcome was manipulated by the experimenter as follows. The score of the competitive set of four performance puzzles was always 3-1. Participants in the win condition (Conditions 2) were told they won the first, third, and fourth trial and the opponent had won the second trial.

Participants in the lose conditions (Conditions 3-5) were told they lost the first, third, and fourth trial, but they had won the second trial. This way, the score after two trials was equal (1-1) in all competitively contingent reward conditions to further the feelings of competition and challenge. If participants won a puzzle, they had to wait an additional minute or so, in order to give the impression that their opponent was still working on the puzzle.

After the four performance puzzles were completed, participants in all competitive conditions were given the results of the competition, and those in Conditions 4 and 5 got additional feedback. Specifically, participants in Condition 2 were informed that they had won the competition and would receive their $3 for winning at the end of the experiment.

Participants in Conditions 3, 4, and 5 were informed that they had lost the competition and would not receive the competitively contingent reward. In Conditions 4 and 5, participants were told that, "although you lost the competition, you still managed to solve at least three out of the four puzzles correctly. I can tell you that you did very well because you reached the performance standard of doing better than 70% of the participants in previous experiments." For participants in Condition 5, the experimenter also said, "So, at the end of the experiment you will receive the $3 reward I promised you." Because the four performance puzzles had been pretested all participants were able to solve at least three of the puzzles within the allotted time, so all competitive losers in Condition 4 received the positive feedback and all competitive losers in Condition S receive the performance-contingent reward.

After the four performance trials, the experimenter entered the experimental room and told participants that the puzzle-solving phase of the experiment was over and that he needed to go to another room to get a final questionnaire for them. Because the appropriate questionnaire was to be prepared by the computer based on their performance, it would take him just a few minutes to get the two correct questionnaires and drop off the one for the opponent. The participants were left alone for a 6 mn free-choice period, during which they could do whatever they wanted to do in the experimental room until the experimenter returned.

During this period an observer recorded the amount of time the participants spent on the new and the old puzzle configurations. The observers had been trained to be able to look through the one-way window and identify whether particular puzzles were the performance-period puzzles (i.e., old puzzles) or the free-choice-period puzzles (i.e., new puzzles).

After the free-choice period, the experimenter re-entered the room, administered the postexperimental questionnaire, debriefed the participants, and gage the reward to those who had been told they would receive it.

Behavioural measure

The behavioural measure of intrinsic motivation was taken during the 6-min free-choice period subsequent to the feedback that was provided at the end of the performance period. Specifically, the amount of time participants spent working with new puzzles during this free-choice period was recorded by the observer who was blind to the hypotheses and experimental conditions. The amount of free choice time spent on previously-encountered (i.e., old) configurations was also recorded as the measure of ego-involved persistence.

Questionnaire measures

Participants completed a questionnaire after the free-choice period. This postexperimental questionnaire included 13 items (scored on 7-point scales), 7 items measuring "enjoyment of the activity" which was used as the self-report measure of intrinsic motivation; and 6 items measuring "perceived competence" which was used as a manipulation check to ensure that winners felt more competent than losers and that losers who got positive feedback felt more competent than losers who did not. Also, because past studies have shown that perceived competence mediated the effects on intrinsic motivation of winning versus losing a competition and of positive feedback, its inclusion allowed us to test whether it would mediate any condition effects in this study.

Influence of Time on Motivation

Abraham Maslow, the American psychologist whose seminal work on human motivation resulted in his Hierarchy of Needs, made two profoundly important statements in relation to achievement: "Man is an ever-wanting animal" and "All behaviour is goal oriented." These are my jumping off point for this article; they can be combined in the single question, what do we want to achieve? That is, and more explicitly in relation to the athletes whom you coach, what is it that at a deep emotional level drives them and, by implication, needs satisfying?

Carrot or Stick

An athlete's psychological relationship to time will influence their motivation; equally, it will inform their response to your coaching style and further, it should direct whether you emphasise the "carrot" or the "stick" when coaching them to convert athletic potential into actual achievement.

People can be divided broadly into "In Time" or "Through Time" types. What differentiates them is the direction of their Time Line. A Time Line is an imaginary or virtual line linking a person's past, present and future. People will "see" their Time Line running in one of two alternative directions, relative to the position of their body; it is where their Time Line runs that defines whether a person is "In Time" or "Through Time".

With "In Time" people their Time Line dissects their body: they are, as it were, "In Time". "In Time" people not infrequently see their past and sometimes a part or the whole of their present in front of them. It is not uncommon for "In Time" people to also 'see' their future behind them: their past, which can be in front of them, can be so influential it continues to inform, colour and shape what an "In Time" person 'sees' when they look ahead to tomorrow.

Clearly, there is a high likelihood that an "In Time" person will apply the usual distinguishing definitions of 'past', 'present' and 'future' less strictly; that is, 'past' is not always 'behind', 'gone' and 'future' is not always 'ahead', 'yet to happen'. Such a person's psychology can mean these three periods can be found in front of, or inside or behind their body. An "In Time" person must therefore metaphorically turn their head, to look behind themselves, to 'see' some part of their Time Line. On the other hand, a "Through Time" person will 'see' the whole of their Time Line in front of them, and whether it is organised horizontally in front of them, vertically in front of them or, for some individuals, in a V-configuration on a horizontal or vertical plane in front of them, past, present and future are always in view without any need to metaphorically turn their head to 'see' a part of their Time Line.

A person's Time Line configuration will have an effect on their perception of time; indeed, a Time Line's course, plus the proximity of past, present and future to each other on it, plus the psychological nearness in space of these periods on the Line to the person's body will have a predictable effect on time-related behaviours and practices. The major distinction, however, is that for an "In Time" person a part of their Time Line will be behind them and for a "Through Time" person the whole of their Time Line will be in front of them.

In Time people

A person's Time Line influences their behaviours and practices, how might we generically describe "In Time" and "Through Time" people? "In Time" people typically:

— Fully associate themselves in a memory; that is, they can see themselves in the memory through their own 'real time' eyes and again hear the sounds, taste the tastes and feel the feelings vividly that were experienced originally

— Are less aware of duration (passing time) than "Through Time" people

— Get caught up in the 'now' and are not troubled by lateness or overruns; indeed, the 'now' for "In Time" people can run on and on and this allows them to stay intensely focused for long periods

— Prefer open-endedness and to keep their options open. This can make them seem undependable to others

— Have difficulty prioritising tasks, because to do so limits their options and gives their activities a finite structure and definite end, rather than an open end

— Stray from the 'track', due, mostly, to the 'track' shifting (i.e. priorities changing, thus switching a present priority to a past or future priority) but leaving the "In Time" person still in their 'now' and focused on the old, superseded priority

— Have strong memory recall, and rely on past experience to inform them; they are thus not infrequently liable to be motivated by 'Away From' goals

— Tend to live a less orderly, more spontaneous and flexible existence

— Tend to dislike rigorous planning, preferring to take things as they come and adapting to life and work as they go. They tend to avoid closure and deadlines

— Identify with sensations such as 'perceiving', 'feeling', 'thinking', 'touching' and 'tasting'. In a word, "In Time" people are Kinaesthetic.

Through Time people

On the other hand, "Through Time" people typically:

— 'See' time as continuous and uninterrupted: time for them is linear.

— Are acutely aware of duration, and judge their relationships and involvement in activities according to how much time was spent and whether they got value from their investment of time. Time and value are often synonymous to "Through Time" people.

— Stick rigidly to appointment times, and instinctively judge fairly accurately such factors as travelling time (to get to a meeting, for example), elapsed time and even the time of day, without looking at a clock.

— Use time as a life reference point. A

— Tend to be dissociated from their memories; that is, they see themselves in the memory as a 'third person' rather than looking through their own eyes. Consequently, they can be less able than an "In Time" person to feel the feelings, taste the tastes, etc experienced originally.

— Experience difficulty in recalling and accessing a specific memory, since they tend to collapse several experiences into a single experience.

— Set and keep to deadlines.

— Foresee, plan, schedule and complete activities on time. However, some "Through Time" people can have difficulty focusing on the 'now' because their future is there, always there, on full view. Thus, "Through Time" people can dislike working in an untidy environment or in a role where priorities change rapidly: to them, this is chaos, which to people who need the security of sequence, planning and order can be quite unsettling.

— Differentiate work and play.

— Need finite and closed-end projects.

— Identify with sensations such as 'judging', 'value-for-money' (or 'value-for-time') and 'visioning'.

Clearly, "In Time" and "Through Time" people have different perceptions of time and consequently tend to behave differently, not least due to the influence of their deep lying emotional drivers - those that spur them on to achieving their goals. So now let me turn to the subject of goal achievement.

Goals

Every person moves either towards their future or away from their past; which movement is predominant will depend on their Time Line and the influential power of their past, present and future. It is the predominant direction that is important: whether most of the time in most situations the person is motivated by approach, attraction and reward, i.e. a "carrot"; or avoidance, repulsion and punishment i.e. a "stick". In other words, a "Towards" person will move towards what they like and want to achieve in the future, whereas an "Away From" person will move away from what they don't like or from some troubling past. The outcome could well be the same, that is a notable achievement, but what drives a "Towards" person will be the magnet of a clearly seen future, and what drives an "Away From" person will be the repulsion of their clearly seen past. Consider two world-class boxers, Muhammad Ali and Mike Tyson.

Expressed very simply, we might say that all of Tyson's behaviours speak of someone whose past is always with him, whose past is a constant influence and from which he ceaselessly tries to move away from; whereas Ali's behaviours spoke, and still speak, of someone whose future is the attractor and to which he constantly moves towards. Of course, at some level or other everyone will experience a drive to move towards or away from something; but generally "Through Time" people are driven by moving towards future goals and "In Time" people are driven by moving away from their past.

"Towards" people

A "Towards" person will be motivated by their desires; so to motivate them, they need a reward or a goal. In terms of achievement, a "Towards Goals" person will be motivated by a strong desire to improve personal efficiency even more - to get more value from an activity or life in general. Any system or technique that will help them do this will be welcomed. On the other hand, motivating a "Towards Goals" person with a 'stick' will only serve to make them antagonistic.

"Away From" people

As "Away From" people move away from what they don't like, they can best be motivated by their fears. Trying to motivate such a person with a 'carrot' will rarely work well: they will care little for it. In terms of achievement, then, the 'carrot' of greater personal efficiency, or of winning per se, might not in fact be as powerful a carrot as assumed because they are not motivated by "Towards" goals. They could well be motivated, however, by something significantly negative that they want to move away from, for example a memory or a negative life experience.

Some people can convince themselves they are a "Towards" goals person, but their direction is merely apparent for their inner representation, their deep and truer psychological or emotional stimulus, is "Away From". Hence they repeatedly sabotage their own efforts to achieve a sustainable "Towards" goals direction or outcome by acting according to the "Away From" motive. In a sense, they behave like the Moon circling the Earth: the Moon is always attempting to shoot off into outer space but is held back, in a fixed orbit, by the Earth's more powerful force.

The Moon can thus be said to be in a stuck state. People in a stuck state will never resolve their dilemma until they are able to free themselves from whatever is preventing them seeing their future unencumbered by the influence of their past. Again somewhat simplistically, we might suggest that all Tyson's achievements have been motivated by his drive to get away from his past, but because his past is probably always there in front of him he will see his future through the influential lens of his past, and until he is helped to change the configuration of his Time Line his behaviours will continue to be coloured by what he is trying to get away from. In Maslow's language Tyson's goal-oriented behaviour is designed to dwell upon his past, not to achieve a future, but as his past continues to anchor him in a stuck state he replays his self-sabotaging behaviours.

Is "Achievement Goal Theory" reality or just a myth

Individuals have a 'personal theory' about what achievement means to them for that specific situation or task. The characteristics of the situation and task interact to impact the state of the goal the individual adopts. Achievement behaviour is "the behaviour in which the goal is to develop or demonstrate to self and others high ability or avoid demonstrating low ability". Ability is constructed in two ways. Firstly, ability can be judged high or low with reference to the individual's own past performance or knowledge. In this context, gains in mastery indicate competence. Secondly, to demonstrate high capacity, one must achieve more with equal effort or use less effort than others do for an equal performance.

Achievement goals

The two types of achievement goals could be activated, depending on which conceptions of ability were held salient at that point in time. When gains in mastery indicate competence, individuals are said to be task involved. On the other hand, when achievement of more with less effort than that of others indicates competence, they are said to be ego involved. There is a plethora of literature on the goal perspective theory (GPT).

There is also a vast amount of literature, which offers a critical view on the Achievement Goal Theory. Many authors take the view that the notion is a myth. Other literature stated that the Achievement Goal Theory did not correlate with the goal-setting literature. It stated that goals motivate and direct behaviour as an ego orientation and cannot be detrimental to performance because high-class athletes would naturally set outcome goals. Current literature also shared the consensus that successful performers have multiple perceptions of their competence and would integrate the use of performance, outcome and process goals to good effect. This therefore indicates that individuals can have both high ego and a task orientation at the same time. As a result, the theorists highlighted conceptual and measurement (psychometric) inconsistencies of the goal perspective theory.

Conceptual

— Confusion over orthogonality

— Association between goal & the differentiation of effort & ability
— Meaning of task involvement in sport

Measurement

— Validity of TEOSQ
— Inability of TEOSQ to discriminate among people who are truly high, moderate or low in each orientation

The Task and Ego Orientation Questionnaire (TEOSQ)

The Task and Ego Orientation in Sport Questionnaire (TEOSQ) is a psychometric measurement, which attempts to assess the preferred goal perspective of an individual. The original TEOSQ is a 13-item questionnaire whereby the subjects indicate their degrees of agreement with each of the items on a 5-point Likert-type scale. The original TEOSQ, developed by Duda and Nicholls was modified by adding six additional questions in order to reflect the new 3rd self-referenced construct of the goal perspective theory, suggested by Harwood, Hardy and Swain [5]. The modified version of the TEOSQ was used as part of an initial baseline assessment in order to select those participants required to partake further in the study.

The findings of research carried out on individuals' motivational climate concluded that an ego-involving context is an environment in which athletes perceive that poor performance and mistakes will be punished. It also concluded that high ability team members will receive the most attention and recognition. It finally concluded in an ego-involving context that competition between team members is encouraged by the coach. In terms of a task involving context is an environment in which athletes are reinforced by the coach when they experience improvement, work hard and help each other learn.

Nicholls concluded from the research carried out that athletes should be encouraged to set performance rather than outcome goals. Nicholls also suggested that high levels of ego orientation were associated with cheating. Finally, Nicholls concluded that people who want to compete i.e. have a strong ego orientation are "bad guys" and people who want to "play nicely" and not participate in competition are "good guys".

Harwood et al proposed an alternative conceptual approach, which incorporated three goal perspectives. These are outlined as follows;

— Pure task involvement = concern is with learning and putting in effort with no direct or observable competence outcome
— Self referenced ego involvement = concern is with the adequacy of personal ability associated with the level of current skills, i.e. the achievement goal is centred on demonstrating the adequacy of current personal skills, irrespective of the skills of others
— Norm-referenced ego involvement = concern is with the current definition of ego involvement, wherein achievement is conceived of as demonstrated ability that compares favourably with the ability of others.

The tripartite aspect of the critique demonstrates the potential link between the three goal dimensions and elements of the goal setting literature.

Conceptual		*Technique*
Task orientation - Process	→	Process goals
Task orientation - Product	→	Performance goals
Ego orientation	→	Outcome goals

The proposals put forward in this article are; firstly, achievement goals and goal involvement states can be manipulated by the manipulation of goal setting.

Secondly, goal-setting techniques can be implemented so that they influence individuals to take on certain thought processes. Finally, goal setting can be used by coaches and individuals alike, in order to set up a kind of 'personal development plan', which is designed to allow the individual to move in and out of states as the situation requires. As a result of the new developments in the goal perspective literature, the additional third domain has been integrated into this study in the form of a new, modified TEOSQ, which incorporates the new construct.

Research Methodology

The methodology of the work for this article was as follows: the interpretist approach was used, with the use of individual case narratives, in order to obtain in-depth information from each athlete as individuals. The post-positivist paradigm was also incorporated in which;

- 14 subjects from local swimming clubs were requested to complete the modified TEOSQ
- Results were analysed and screened and 3 subjects selected for further study
- These 3 subjects were then interviewed throughout the study (over a five month period)

The interviews lasted between 20 and 45 minutes and were recorded throughout their entirety. They were all conducted by the same researcher, thus providing a constant across the interviews. The interviews are outlined as follows:

- Interview 1 = baseline assessment of the subjects, i.e. allowed the researcher to get a complete picture of each subject and therefore build a rapport with them
- Interviews 2 & 3 = competition interviews, i.e. the subjects were interviewed about specific interviews they had recently participated in

— Interview 4 = confirmatory interview, i.e. the subjects were asked to reflect on their experiences and to confirm or reject the information received over the previous interviews

The work predominately focused on two aspects of the conceptual critique, these arguments are; firstly, the tripartite approach to the achievement goal theory; and secondly, the integration between goal involvement states and goal setting cognitions.

The results provided the following significant support for the tripartite approach to the achievement goal theory;

- The response of the subjects to the completion of the questionnaire
- The results from Sarah's interview, as she defined success in terms of effort, yet appeared not to have achieved success, as no improvement was experienced
- Clear distinctions were made between the three involvement states
- In training contexts, self-referent ego involvement and pure task involvement are more likely to predominate
- Competitive sport promotes ego involvement, and, although pure task involvement may be present, what researchers previously labelled as task involvement in a competitive setting is what Harwood et al refer to as self-referenced ego involvement
- It is the individual's cognitions about achievement and his/her reasoning behind what is required to maximise a sense of achievement that occupy his/her thought processes

The results provided significant support for the integration between goal involvement and goal setting cognitions;

— The language of the athletes in the interviews made a connection between the goal involvement literature and the goal-setting literature

— The states of involvement adopted are subconscious states and are not discreet goals set by the subjects but instead are psychological states that reflect their beliefs about achievement for that task at that time

— Particular goal-setting strategies can be applied in order to influence the tone of an individual's achievement context and so encourage an athlete to adopt specific goal achievement states.

Golf - It's All in the Swing and the Mind

The psychology in the world of sport is a rapidly growing field of interest and involvement. Described by Williams and Straub, as "the youngest of the sport sciences", sport psychology has, until recent years, been over looked by both players and coaches alike. This Coaching Portfolio relates the theme of psychological coaching to the sport of golf. The mental concentration and cognitive ability required in golf, makes this an excellent sport to involve psychological training methods.

Golf is classified as an individual, target sport requiring predominantly fine motor skills. Although the golf swing is a self-paced executive programme, the game itself is an open one, vulnerable to environment impacts. The average club level golfer is usually described in the 8 to 12 handicap bracket. This may include less experienced, but improving performers who are looking to reduce their handicap and develop further as players, or more experienced participants who have peaked at this standard of play.

Club level golfers will be well into the associative stage of learning, where there is good knowledge of the activity and models of the swing. Performers will also have the ability to detect and correct errors in performance, however technique may be variable and potentially inconsistent. Some club level golfers will be heading towards the autonomous phase of learning, whereby movement has become automatic and attention can given to environmental aspects and strategic play.

Planning

A club level golf season would begin in April and continue through until October. This period of play would gradually increase in intensity, peaking around July and August, before reducing into September and October. Over the season, players will regularly practise physical elements of the game (e.g. swing fundamentals). During the closed season, very little physical practise will occur, and during both periods, very little or no psychological practise/coaching will take place.

In order for a coach to design and implement a coaching programme, he/she must consider when each type of training would be best suited in relation to the athlete's calendar of events. The majority of club level golfers will do very little training during the off-season and begin work shortly before the season starts. Psychological training is most effectively used during the pre-season months (January - March). This period is an excellent opportunity to educate the performers in mental development and also can be introduced gradually as not to put the athletes under unnecessary stress due to their lack of experience is this area of training.

Methods learnt pre-season will be fully understood and feel more natural by the start of the season and will strengthen the participants' performance during the season. The coach will study the schedule and reinforce techniques prior to key times in the season to aspire towards peak performance for important competitions. Psychological training can also be of particular use during rest periods between events or more so during spells of injury and recovery, when physical training may not be possible.

Setting Objectives

A crucial area for a coach to begin a programme with is that of setting goals. Setting goals in the industrial and organisational world has proved to be a tool to motivate and enhance performance. To a certain extent, sporting success and setting performance related targets have been apparent, however, Burton, D. explains of the 'Jekyll and Hyde' problems that can occur when goals are not set appropriately. It is paramount to a teams' success that the coach and players create and record realistic, specific and challenging, long and short-term goals. The coach should take the performer through the stages of setting goals, usually beginning with an evaluation of the athlete. 'Performer Profiling' is one way a coach can brake down areas of a sport and let the athlete rank themselves on their own ability in each.

Viewing the results can help players set more specific goals and hopefully increase motivation. Once goals have been set, they should be discussed between coach and performer and decide what steps or measures need to be taken in order to reach the targets. For the golf season, its will be necessary to set a long-term goal, which should contain aims to meet by the end of the season. Short-term goals are equally important, stating specific targets for a shorter period of perhaps a week or a month and hence will be evaluated regularly and changed according to the intensity or schedule of forthcoming events.

Goal Setting

By setting goals, you will be able to focus on areas you wish to improve, while continuing to perform in strong areas of your game. Goal setting helps to motivate during practise.

— Where do you want to be?

— Which parts of your game need most attention?

— What specific measures will you take to succeed?

Goal setting is a simple, yet often misused motivational technique which can provide some structure for your training and competition program. Goals give a focus, and there are two well known acronyms to guide goal setting.

SMART or SMARTER

— S - goals must be Specific

— M - training targets should be Measurable

— A - goals should be Adjustable

— R - goals must be Realistic

— T - training targets should be Time based

— E - goals should be challenging and Exciting

— R - goals should be Recorded

Make specific targets for:

— Fairways hit

— Greens hit in regulation

— Putts per round

— Up and downs (chipping rate)

— Sand saves

Goals should be both long and short term and written down to refer back to. Discuss them with your coach so you can both work towards these shared goals. Recording your emotions before and after competition can also help future results.

Sports Psychology

Relaxation and Imagery are techniques that have proved effective in improving golfers' performance. Relaxation coaching aims to teach players how to completely remove tension, both muscularly and mentally, before a shot is performed. To begin with it will take a while for a club level performer to relax each muscle group, but with practise, this time can be reduced and eventually can be used in a competitive situation in the form of a pre-shot routine, which the coach will help the pupil to create. To increase the chance of a successful shot being performed, the coach will stress how important the behaviour prior to the shot is and that it should be the same every time a shot is played. Within this routine, a coach will include the use of imagery and will work on a one-to-one basis with the performer in a number of short, intense sessions. Imagery training, taught following relaxation periods, will involve the golfer using all necessary senses to create a mental picture of both the flight of the ball and the swing mechanics, using muscle memory. The athlete must remain focused without speaking, listening to the coaches calm descriptive tone. The players may visualise in the form of watching themselves complete the successful shot from outside their body (external), or by actually experiencing the shot through their own eyes (internal).

If such psychological training methods are incorporated around physical swing practises as part of a full training programme, club level athletes should benefit enormously. A varied and structured coaching programme should raise self-motivation for training and consequently increase confidence and competitive success.

Steps to Success

1. Decide on club selection and type of shot to be played (spin/wind/flight path)
2. Take a practise swing, feel the muscles in position. Rehearse movement
3. Stand behind ball. Focus on breathing. Relax muscles and entire body
4. Look at the ball and the target. Visualise a line between both, this is the flight path the ball will take
5. Visualise the perfect swing, smooth tempo and balanced finish
6. Take stance over ball, get comfortable, check target last time
7. Use a 'mantra' (a word or phrase to trigger the movement to begin, recalling all feelings from muscle memory.) e.g. "turn and release" .
8. Swing and believe.

Motivation to Move

There are a number of ways in which people can be motivated. In addition, it is important to understand what motivation is in the context of sport and participation. Brasile, Kleiber, and Harnisch state that motivation is "a process through which persons take available resources - time, talent, and energy - and distribute them in a way they choose." This process is called the personal investment theory, and it incorporates a two-stage causal process.

The first stage involves the effects of external factors and their influence on how an individual perceives a particular situation. In the second stage, the individual undertakes a personal investment in the situation. The personal investment involves an inner drive, an impulse, or an intention an individual possesses as a reaction to external influences. The key question is, What motivates athletes to dedicate themselves to sport?

Everyone has different motives for participating in sports: enjoyment, physical fitness, social relationships, or goal attainment. As noted, there are two types of motivation that enable people to accomplish a particular goal or task. First, extrinsic motivation in sports participation comes from outside influences or people. People are extrinsically motivated to gain compensation, social approval, or rewards.

Second, intrinsic motivation is an inherent characteristic that feeds off one's inner drive to accomplish a goal or objective. According to Seifriz, Duda, and Chi, "focusing on a task for its own sake, having a sense of self-determination, and perceiving oneself as able to meet the demands of a task are all assumed to be fundamental to intrinsic motivation." This concept to motivational effects on high-school basketball players. Results indicated that players were primarily motivated to participate in basketball to improve and potentially master their skills, not to compare their skills against those of other players.

The motivational climate evolved around a mastery-focused environment. Players were task-oriented because they were primarily concerned with personal improvement, trying their best, and experiencing maximum enjoyment while playing basketball.

Sir Ludwig Guttmann, founder and director of the National Spinal Injuries Center, developed a philosophy of sports participation among people with disabilities. His philosophy and subsequent years of investigation have supported recreation as an excellent tool to rehabilitate and develop self-confidence, personal skills, physical ability, and determination to pursue other challenges in life.

Basketball has been a part of United States sports culture since the late 1800s. For paraplegic, post-polio, amputee, or mobility-impaired athletes, since its development as a rehabilitative method following World War II, it is the country's most popular wheelchair sport. There are men's and women's divisions, an intercollegiate division, and a youth division within the National Wheelchair Basketball Association. The youth division was developed to provide support for adolescents who were learning the sport.

Getting the Wheels Rolling

With an increase in participation in wheelchair sports, it has become clear that adolescents with disabilities are motivated to remain healthy, competent, and socially active. Research has supported the view that social support alleviates the effects of stress and reduces injuries.

When comparing wheelchair sport participants and nonparticipants, those engaging in physical activities or sports have a positive well-being and higher vigor with lower tension, depression, anger, and confusion. These benefits are influenced by many factors. White and Duda suggest that success in wheelchair sports stemmed from a number of factors, including perseverance, overall health, and quality of equipment.

To better understand how athletes are motivated, a goal perspective theory is used as a contemporary social cognitive approach, suggesting that task and ego involvement are associated with how people define success and judge their competence. The personal investment theory encompasses three major categories: task, ego, and social incentives. These incentives are the primary factors used when researching motivation.

The first category is task incentives. Task incentives occur when a participant chooses to engage in an activity for enjoyment and personal reward. The participant is in total task absorption and pursues activities where each task's demands only slightly exceed the individual's capacity. He or she is intrinsically motivated to participate for the purposes of improved competence, enjoyment, personal improvement, and mastery of a task. Research by Brasile and Brasile et al. revealed that individuals participated in sports for intrinsic and task-oriented reasons, which means they were internally driven to accomplish performance goals rather than to win or compare themselves with others.

Ego incentives are derived when comparing one's abilities, actions, or competence to the performance of another individual or group. The results of the comparison assist in the development of social realities. In competitive situations, it becomes important to be more competent. However, ego involvement can result in a negative response in achievement because of a lack of confidence in one's ability. When an athlete's abilities do not compare favorably with those of another, adverse effects may occur. Adolescents with low perceived competence have a tendency to foster maladaptive behaviors such as cheating, giving up, or risking health for success. Often, the effects of comparison can alter one's thinking about one's self, abilities, competence, or health.

Social integration incentives are another important factor. Many enjoy sports for the companionship, social interaction, recognition, respect, and feeling of belonging. These factors reinforce participation in sports and are often encouraged by friends, family, and health professionals. Martin and Mushett explain that social support alleviates the effects of stress and reduces injuries.

Fitness and health and social affective incentives are two other types of motivation that Brasile and Hedrick and Brasile et al. suggest as important factors in sports participation. People participate in sports to remain fit and healthy. They are motivated by their understanding of the harmful effects of a sedentary lifestyle and the positive effects of physical, emotional, and spiritual well-being.

Another scope of motivation, social affective incentive focuses on the reintegration or socialisation of an individual into society. Involvement in physical exercise gives an individual with or without a disability the means for escaping an aversive atmosphere in which he or she has been confined. As related to sports, it is important to understand the personal feelings, dispositions, attitudes, or emotions an athlete experiences through cooperative social involvement.

A study by Brasile and Hedrick compared the participation incentives of adult and youth wheelchair basketball players. Task, ego, social integration, fitness and health, and social affective responses were analysed. The top four responses of both youth and adult participants were team interaction, improving ability, testing against standards, and excitement. Adult and youth participants were similar in their perception of motivation participation. Intrinsic task-oriented activities were equally important for adults and youth, but ego and social integration were observed to be more important to youth. Youth responses included, "It gives me the opportunity to be with friends," It pleases others who are close to me, "It gives me a chance to use good equipment," and "It offers me the opportunity to be independent."

Benefits of Participation

Some 10,000 spinal cord injuries occur in the United

States each year; 20 percent of these involve people under the age of 21. It is important for adolescents with disabilities to participate in sports or adventure programs. Many benefits - improved physical fitness, social interaction, family cohesion, and risk taking - are derived from participation in physical activities, all of which help improve self-esteem, quality of life, independence, and competence. Axelson states that physical activity improves emotional and spiritual attributes, which include greater self-confidence and increased feelings of "inner peace."

White and Duda, 59 athletes with physical disabilities completed a 13-item task and ego orientation in a sport questionnaire that was specific to wheelchair basketball. The results revealed two distinct goal-belief dimensions. First, success was the result of task orientation associated with practice, exerted effort, and external factors. Second, it was determined that ego-orientation leads to the belief that ability, chance, or taking an illegal advantage may result in accomplishment in sport. Therefore, it is important to note the advantages of supporting task-oriented approaches to sports.

Coaches, parents, peers, teachers, and players need to understand that task-oriented activities are beneficial because athletes are not focused on winning or comparing themselves to other athletes' abilities or skills. Even though it is important to incorporate task-oriented activities, it should be noted that taking an illegal advantage through drug doping or cheating needs to be eliminated from wheelchair athletics.

Participation in sports can lead to the development of athletic identity and sport orientation. Martin, Adams-Mushett, and Smith researched the development of adolescent swimmers with disabilities. The Athletic Identity measurement scale and the sport orientation questionnaire were applied to 27 female and 30 male youth swimmers with disabilities. The average age was 16.2 years. The adolescent swimmers reported a secure self and athletic identity, strong competitiveness and goal orientation, and a moderate to strong social identity. The results also indicated that some swimmers strongly identified sports as an indicator of social status or acceptance among peers, family, and people without disabilities.

Campbell and Jones studied the psychological well-being of wheelchair sport participants and nonparticipants. The participants demonstrated a positive well-being and higher vigor with lower levels of tension, depression, anger, and confusion. Also, greater levels of mastery and positive perceptions of heath and fitness were exhibited by sports participants. Nonparticipants often perceive their environment or situation as frustrating and stressful.

Brasile et al. researched the five participation motivation incentives among athletes with and without disabilities. At the time, there was little empirical evidence devoted to the value of understanding what motivates athletes with and without disabilities to participate in sports. Results indicated that there were more similarities than differences among those with and without disabilities in terms of incentives for participation in sport. It was discovered that task incentives and fitness were important to all athletes seriously involved in sports. Participants also reported ego incentives as important. Social integration and social affective incentives had less impact on participation motivation. Social integration incentives were more important for athletes with disabilities.

Hatfield investigated motivational incentives among collegiate athletes with and without disabilities. The participants completed a respondent information form and a participation reasons scale. Participants in this study included division I and II athletes from seven universities. Of the 128 respondents, 37 were males without disabilities, 49 were females without disabilities, 37 were male wheelchair athletes, and five were female wheelchair athletes. The results showed that athletes with and without disabilities appeared to participate in collegiate sports for similar reasons. The only difference was found in the fitness incentives, which were higher for athletes with disabilities. Ego, task, social integration, and social affective incentives were similar.

The motivation of male adolescent basketball players with and without disabilities to participate in sports was researched. Using an instrument developed by Brasile, and used by Hatfield, Bartle found that the only significant difference between the two groups was that the adolescents with disabilities placed more emphasis on the motivational force of social integration factors. Contrary to Hatfield's collegiate athletes, these adolescent wheelchair athletes rated fitness motivation lower than did basketball players without disabilities. However, mean scores for the factors of task- and ego-oriented incentives were the highest.

Advertisement

When it comes to socialisation, adolescents with and without disabilities have similar views on social support and acceptance. Martin, Adams-Mushett, and Smith discovered that adolescent swimmers strongly identified their role in athletics as being the most important social role they filled. It is believed that youth, in general, need peer-group acceptance. This is often established when comparing one's abilities, competence, or status with another's.

These ego-oriented motives are especially significant among boys, who often determine status among peers by comparing themselves to others. When faced with competition, athletes with and without disabilities internalise their egos when having a negative experience. This could cause an individual to take an illegal advantage, develop a poor work ethic or negative behaviors, or discontinue sports.

It is apparent that task-oriented sport achievements are the main focus among athletes with and without disabilities. Martin et al. stated that the level of competition and importance of goals determines whether adolescents are concerned with personal achievement or nonachievement goals (social interaction, having fun, learning skills). However, adolescents with disabilities also specifically attribute success to external factors such as equipment and the influence of the coach's expectations. It is legitimate that equipment is an important factor because the quality of equipment adds to the quickness and maneuverability of the individual who uses a sports wheelchair.

During adolescence ... the need for group identification and social interaction is at its peak. It is an important developmental time for independence, but an injury brings about regression to dependence. Therefore, it is essential to promote positive social integration and physical activity to alleviate any added pressures for social acceptance, and to avoid a passive lifestyle. Awareness of these issues is especially important for coaches, programmers, and parents of adolescents with disabilities.

Implications of Participation Motivation

Coaches, programmers, and parents should be aware that their athletes might be highly invested in sports. These researchers further explain that "expressing low performance expectations or patronising attitudes toward performance potential can be psychologically and athletically harmful." But stressing ego-driven motives to the participating athletes could cause an adolescent to attempt to succeed (or avoid perceived failure) by taking an illegal advantage, having a poor work ethic, developing negative behaviors, or discontinuing sports. Dichotomising participants into either winners or losers can have harmful effects on future participation, since ego-driven athletes are constantly comparing their competence and skills with other athletes. When the comparison is not equal, problems can occur.

Past research has proven that intrinsic task-related activities drive participation in sports for people with disabilities. This reflects a dominant motivational factor, which is internally driven and emphasizes personal accomplishment relevant to performance goals.

Therefore, coaches, programmers, and parents should emphasize instructional and participatory activities to enhance participation and continued involvement through challenging but attainable goals. This allows all participants, regardless of abilities and skills, the opportunity to develop self-concept, feelings of accomplishment, and acceptance of disability by participating in activities.

4

Psychological Skills Training

Psychological Skills Training (PST) is an individually designed combination of methods selected to attain psychological skill needs. There is no single idyllic PST package, each program must be individualised based on the psychological state of the individual and, the sport. To assemble a successful PST program it is important to distinguish between PST skills and PST methods. PST skills are the psychological qualities or attributes that need to be developed (i.e. confidence, concentration), the PST method is the tool that will be used to help improve the PST skill. Much of the early research utilising prescriptive PST programs used single PST methods and examined their effect on performance. Thelwell and Greenlees argue that when implementing a PST program, it is improbable that a single method will be employed by a sports psychologist. Thelwell and Greenlees highlight that it is more effective to employ a combination of mental skills that relate to the specific sport.

Gymnastics

Men's artistic gymnastics is competition on which the athlete must perform on a total of six pieces of apparatus; these include vault, high bar, parallel bars, rings, pommel horse and floor. During major competitions such as the commonwealth games the athlete must perform three pieces on two consecutive days. The athletes are given a score out of 10 for their performance on each piece. Athlete score more marks for more difficult sequences and less for easier routines. For each apparatus the athlete is scored based on: difficulty of routine, composure, timing, combination of movements and execution of movements.

To compete at the Commonwealth games 2006 the athlete must have attained scores higher than the lowest qualifying scores form the commonwealth games apparatus finals in 2002 (See Table 1). These scores must be achieved during recognised gymnastics competitions such as: Northern European Championships, Scottish Championships, Welsh Open and British Championships.

Table 1. Lowest qualifying scores from the commonwealth games 2002

Apparatus	*Grade*	*Apparatus*	*Grade*
Floor	8.80	Vault	9.125
Pommel Horse	8.90	P Bar	8.70
Rings	8.80	High Bar	8.65

Thewell and Greenlees note that the effectiveness of PST packages is positive within sports of all natures. Fournier, Cakmels, Duran-Bush and Saimela reported a 10% improvement in the bars, beam, and floor when compared to the control group. The PST program used by Fournier et al., consisted of a five step intervention using relaxation, self talk, goal setting, focusing and visualisation. Fournier at al., also reported that imagery and relaxation were the most effective methods utilised.

The purpose of the study it to develop a PST program for an elite male gymnast. The PST program will be implemented to optimise performance for the forthcoming Commonwealth games in Australia with specific consideration to emotions and self-confidence.

Self confidence

Self confidence may be the most critical self-perception in sport psychology. Self confidence is defined as a global and stable characteristic which, in reality bares little use within the sports domain. The athlete must be confident they can perform well when placed in their competitive environment, i.e. Tiger Woods would be confident of making the final putt on the 18th green at Augusta in the Golf Masters, however, may not feel too confident taking the final penalty kick in the World Cup final. Self-efficacy is a situation form of self-confidence or the belief that one is confident and can perform within a specific situation. Gill suggests that the most consistent difference between elite and less successful performance is that elite athlete possess greater levels of self efficacy.

Self confidence/self-efficacy

Theories Bandura stipulates that self-efficacy is directly related to athletic performance. Increases in self-efficacy are mirrored by improvements in performance. Subsequently decreases in performance limit both performance and training. Prior experiences effect efficacy expectations, the probability performing to a high standard is much greater if you believe in your abilities, therefore efficacy has tremendous explanatory power when comparing fluctuations in performance.

Self efficacy is very important in a sport like gymnastics, the performer must believe they can perform well at the required time. Efficacy can fluctuated between apparatus, therefore within gymnastics it is important to increase self-efficacy for each piece of apparatus. Initially low levels of self-efficacy may transfer form piece to piece and negatively influence the whole performance. Therefore, initially high levels of efficacy will improve performance and should be maintained throughout the duration of the competition. As with many psychological components rarely does a single component work in isolation. Decreases in self-efficacy could alter important performance variables such as arousal, stress and anxiety which may have a snowballing effect on performance.

Emotions

Emotion in sport is much more than a reactive expression to victory or defeat. Sports scientists have argued that pre-competitive and competitive emotional states can influence the athletes ability to perform. Emotion is not a single construct, it can be sub-divided into emotional components. Researchers have demonstrated that a wide range of emotions are associated by changes in performance. Many athletes report that heightening levels of arousal facilitates their performance. It is reported to increase anaerobic power. However, emotions can have a negative effect on some motor skills through increasing muscular tension which ultimately effect co-ordination, both detrimental to a sport like gymnastics.

Arousal

Arousal is referred to as a unitary construct that embraces both the psychological and physiological energetic systems. Some define arousal as an energising function that is responsible for harnessing the body's resources for intense and vigorous activity. Arousal is perceived to vary along a continuum which runs from 'deep sleep' to extreme excitement. Arousal can be measured using self-report questionnaires such as the Thayer Activation-Deactivation Check-list. Arousal can also be measured using simple physiological tests; heart-rate, blood pressure, respiration rate and biochemical indicants such as; epinephrine or adrenaline.

Anxiety

Martens in Horn advocates levels of anxiety result from

an objective demand interpreted as threatening by an individual. Horn highlights that anxiety is viewed as feelings of nervousness and tension, which is linearly associated with levels of arousal. Anxiety can be further sub-divided into somatic and cognitive anxieties. Somatic anxiety refers to the bodily symptoms of autonomic reactivity; butterflies, sweating, increased heart-rate and shaking. Cognitive anxiety refers to the negative concerns about performance, lack of concentration and poor attention. Levels of anxiety can affect athletes individually, there not a single optimal level of anxiety, the effects of anxiety on performance is largely attributable to whether the athlete perceives anxiety to be facilitating or debilitating.

Stress

Stress can be described as both an environmental variable and an emotional response to a specific situation. Much like anxiety, the effects of stress on performance is down to how the athlete perceives this stress. Selye in Horn highlighted that not all stress is negative, eustress (good stress) and distress (bad stress). Environmental stresses often deemed as distresses are somewhat unavoidable unpredictable, therefore the sports psychologist has very little control over their effects on performance. Emotional stresses however, can be improved, the athlete can be thought how to better 'cope' with stresses where they may perceive an imbalance between the demands of the situation and his or her response capabilities.

Psychological Skill Training Program

The PST program will focus on optimising performance by improving self-efficacy and emotional control. To improve these psychological skills, the athlete will complete sessions using goal setting, imagery and relaxation. The program will follow an educational approach as advised by Gill and Horn. The program consists of three main phases: Educational Phase - developing the understanding and importance of PST and how it can affect performance. Acquisition Phase - Athletes learn how to sued PST methods and how best to implement them. Practice Phase - devote time and effort to PST and complete training in both competition and practice. Fournier et al., reported that four gymnasts out of nine improved on the vault by 10% and seven out of nine on the asymmetrical bars improved by 10%. These findings support the use of PST programs to optimise performance within gymnastics.

The first mental skill to be used within the program is goal setting. To fully educate the athlete on how goals should be implemented, both short and long term goals will be discussed. The athlete will be informed of the benefits of setting 'smarter' goals, and will be educated on the use of outcome, process and performance goals and a mixture of these will be used to best improve performance. The coach will be fully involved in the goal setting process, especially when process goals are used, the coach will provide the relevant technical information and needs analysis for each piece of apparatus. The athlete will be set goals to; perfect each individual piece of equipment (process goal), win minor practice competitions (outcome goal) and to achieve a point boundary for competitions (performance goals).

Imagery sessions

The imagery sessions will incorporate internal (imagination) and external (video demonstration) of performances. All sessions will focus solely on optimal performances, participant will be encouraged to use imagery in real time and in slow motion, slow motion imagery will be encouraged especially when there is a certain technique which the athlete is performing incorrectly, this will allow them to imagine performing the skill correctly employing all the teaching points. The athlete will be encouraged to develop a competition-specific session. This session will be practiced intensely prior to and during competition.

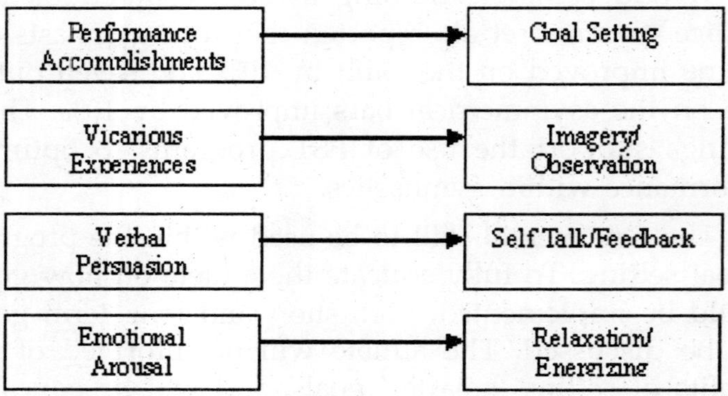

Fiugre 2: Building self-confidence, PST skills and the PST methods employed

Relaxation sessions

The third mental skill to be employed throughout the PST program is relaxation. This will be delivered via a three-stage approach. The first stage which will focus on the use of Progressive Muscular Relaxation (PMR) this allows the athlete to feel what it is like to be completely relaxed and free from the aforementioned muscular tension. The athlete will be asked to practice the Centring technique which helps control breathing. This will be performed while the athlete is warming up for training sessions so that it becomes habitual when they warm-up for a major competition. Once these skill have been perfected participants will be asked to monitor their own tension levels pre and post relaxation sessions by responding to verbal descriptors, the athlete must scale their feeling from 0 (very tense) to 10 (very relaxed). Such a strategy will allow the athlete to be aware of their tension levels (self-reliant), and subsequently employ PMR or centring to reduce high levels of anxiety.

Rationale for Goal Setting

The most commonly used tool used by sports psychologists is goal setting. Setting goals provides this focus and directed attention by agreeing a timed end point to their action. Researchers and practitioners in both sports and organisational literatures have argued that a combination of both short term and long term goals is most effective for improving performance and changing behaviour, short term goals should be enforced to directly reach the long term goal of the client/performer.

The goal-training condition reported higher free throw efficacy when compared to the no-goal condition. Some suggest that in sports which are highly complex (gymnastics) process goals should provide the framework for improving technical aspects of difficult skills. The support for the use of process goals is also evident in it is suggested that process goals are more beneficial for increasing self efficacy as they are more controllable and flexible, this allows the coach/psychologist to mould goals so that the athlete constantly achieves their goals. This constant achievement will improve self-efficacy via increasing the performance accomplishments.

Rationale for Imagery

According to Bandura 'vicarious experiences' is the second most powerful technique to improve self-efficacy (See figure 1). The tools utilised sports psychologists to promote these vicarious experiences are imagery and observation, Horn suggests that motivational general-mastery (MG-M), a form of imagery which focuses on effective coping and mastery of challenging situations, is most effective for improving self-efficacy. Callow, Hardy and Hall found that MG-M imagery significantly improved sport confidence in two out of three elite badminton players, and it stabilised the other players confidence. Callow and Hardy used seventy-six subjects to whether external imagery (observation) would improve gymnastic performance to a greater extent than a combination of internal visual imagery and kinaesthetic imagery. Performance was significantly higher within the external imagery group as opposed to the internal visual groups. Therefore, for the imagery sessions within the PST program a mixture of internal and external imagery will be used as proposed by Callow and Hardy.

Imagery techniques have been used within clinical psychology to induce relaxation. In a study investigating the use of imagery in elite athletes, it was noted that imagery not only 'psyched up' the athlete, but helped maintain composure during competition. Martin, Moritz and Hall suggested that imagery which focuses on feelings such as relaxation, stress, arousal and anxiety could be used as an effective tool to control emotions. In addition to using imagery to regulate anxiety, athletes can also use imagery within practice to pre-plan and rehearse their emotional responses prior to competition.

Rationale for Relaxation

High levels of somatic and cognitive anxiety are detrimental to performance, within a sport such as gymnastics, where movements have to be executed with finesse and composure excessive anxiety will undoubtedly hinder performance. Athletes in closed skill sports (such as gymnastics) report more concerns about anxiety management than other athletes. Relaxation is often cited as the most important skills to learn. The ability for an athlete to control anxiety can be the difference between good and poor performance, within gymnastics it is vital that the athlete can overcome the debilitating effects of anxiety.

Relaxation not only improves emotional control within athletes, according to Bandura 'emotional control' directly affects the self-efficacy of the athlete. Although relaxation and energizing techniques are classified as the fourth most useful tool for improving self-efficacy (See figure 1), relaxation techniques were incorporated within the PST program for the positive effect on anxiety control.

Monitoring PST Program

Assessing the progression of the athlete during a PST program is essential. The two main psychological skills which will be improved within this program are anxiety and self-confidence. Anxiety levels and self-confidence will be measured using the CSAI-2-R. To help understand the mood state of the athlete the Positive and Negative Affect Schedule (PANAS) will also form part of the assessment.

In order to asses the multidimensional aspects of anxiety Martens et al., developed the Competitive State Anxiety Inventory-2 (CSAI-2). The 27 item measure was constructed with three subscales: cognitive anxiety, somatic anxiety and self-confidence. The CSAI-2 represents the best validated psychometric instrument with which to quantify competitive anxiety. Some found significant psychometric weakness for the CSAI-2 and revised each subscale to improve the psychometric properties for cognitive anxiety, somatic anxiety and self-confidence, it was concluded that the CSAI-2-R should be administered in place of the CSAI-2.

Time and Implementation

Throughout the Educational and Acquisition phases the athlete will be required to spend increased time with the sports psychologist. When developing new psychological skills there performer and psychologist must work together to ensure techniques such as goal setting and imagery can be fully effective in optimising performance. Once in the Practice phase of the PST the psychologist and athlete can reduce the time and frequency of sessions. Therefore the Educational and Acquisition phases of the PST will be completed during the off season/pre-season when physical training time and frequency is low. Sessions within the practice phase can be reduced to 15-30mins for 3-4 sessions per week in some instances.

It's all in the Mind

The increased stress of competitions can cause athletes to react both physically and mentally in a manner, which can negatively affect their performance abilities. They may become tense, their heart rates race, they break into a cold sweat, they worry about the outcome of the competition, they find it hard to concentrate on the task in hand. This has led coaches to take an increasing interest in the field of sport psychology and in particular in the area of competitive anxiety. That interest has focused on techniques which athletes can use in the competitive situation to maintain control and optimise their performance. Once learned, these techniques allow the athlete to relax and to focus his/her attention in a positive manner on the task of preparing for and participating in competition.

The 4C's

Concentration, confidence, control and commitment (the 4C's) are generally considered to be the main mental qualities that are important for successful performance in most sports.

— Concentration - ability to maintain focus
— Confidence - believe in one's abilities
— Control - ability to maintain emotional control regardless of distraction
— Commitment - ability to continue working to agreed goals

The techniques of relaxation, centering and mental imagery can assist an athlete to achieve the 4C's.

Concentration

This is the mental quality to focus on the task in hand. If the athlete lacks concentration then their athletic abilities will not be effectively or efficiently applied to the task. Research has identified the following types of attention focus:

— Broad Narrow continuum - the athlete focuses on a large or small number of stimuli
— Internal External continuum - the athlete focuses on internal stimuli (feelings) or external stimuli (ball)

The demand for concentration varies with the sport:

— Sustained concentration - distance running, cycling, tennis, squash
— Short bursts of concentration - cricket, golf, shooting, athletic field events
— Intense concentration - sprinting events, bob sleigh, skiing

Common distractions are: anxiety, mistakes, fatigue, weather, public announcements, coach, manager, opponent, negative thoughts etc. Strategies to improve concentration are very personal. One way to maintain focus is to set process goals for each session or competition. The athlete will have an overall goal for which the athlete will identify a number of process goals which help focus on specific aspects of the task. For each of these goals the athlete can use a trigger word (a word which instantly refocuses the athlete's concentration to the goal) e.g. sprinting technique requires the athlete to focus on being tall, relaxed, smooth and to drive with the elbows - trigger word could be "technique".

Athletes will develop a routine for competition which may include the night before, the morning, pre competition, competition and post competition routines. If these routines are appropriately structured then they can prove a useful aid to concentration.

Confidence

Confidence results from the comparison an athlete makes between the goal and their ability. The athlete will have self-confidence if they believe they can achieve their goal.

When an athlete has self confidence they will tend to: persevere even when things are not going to plan, show enthusiasm, be positive in their approach and take their share of the responsibility in success and fail. To improve their self confidence, an athlete can use mental imagery to:

— visualise previous good performance to remind them of the look and feel
— imagine various scenarios and how they will cope with them

Control

Identifying when an athlete feels a particular emotion and understanding the reason for the feelings is an important stage of helping an athlete gain emotional control. An athlete's ability to maintain control of their emotions in the face of adversity and remain positive is essential to successful performance. Two emotions which are often associated with poor performance are anxiety and anger.

Anxiety comes in two forms - Physical (butterflies, sweating, nausea, needing the toilet) and Mental (worry, negative thoughts, confusion, lack of concentration). Relaxation is a technique that can be used to reduce anxiety.

When an athlete becomes angry the cause of the anger often becomes the focus of attention. This then leads to a lack of concentration on the task at hand, performance deteriorates, confidence in ability is lost which fuels the anger - a slippery slope to failure.

Commitment

Sports performance depends on the athlete being fully committed to numerous goals over many years. In competition with these goals the athlete will have many aspects of daily life to manage. The many competing interests and commitments include: work, studies, family/partner, friends, social life and other hobbies/ sports Within the athlete's sport commitment can be undermined by:

- a perceived lack of progress or improvement
- not being sufficiently involved in developing the training program
- not understanding the objectives of the training program
- injury
- lack of enjoyment
- anxiety about performance - competition
- becoming bored
- coach athlete not working as a team
- lack of commitment by other athletes

Setting goals with the athlete will raise their feelings of value, give them joint ownership of the goals and therefore become more committed to achieving them. All goes should be Smarter.

Many people (coach, medical support team, manager, friends, etc.) can contribute to an athlete's levels of commitment with appropriate levels of support and positive feedback, especially during times of injury, illness and poor performance.

Mental Models - Noticing Distinctions

There is no denying it; some people are just much better at some things than others. No matter how much effort you put in, no matter how much practice, there just seems to be an insurmountable gap between them and us. In general if someone is a professional sportsperson they have the luxury of time and resources that amateurs do not have, but even then there are vast differences between the skills even of world-class athletes. It cannot just be practice, although this clearly has a major impact, perhaps it is talent? Yet some may argue that it is talent that gets you noticed, and gives you the opportunity. You have to somehow turn that talent into enhanced skill. So what is the difference that makes the difference?

Consistency

One of the key attributes of world-class athletes is consistency, the ability to perform at a top level of skill in every situation. Milton Erickson, a psychiatrist who was a pioneer in the use of Hypnotherapeutic methods in sport, worked with a number of world-class athletes. In one story relating to a tournament golfer Erickson is asked to assist in improving the golfer's consistency across all holes throughout a round. He seemed to always play the first hole perfectly, and then deteriorate. The question, for

Erickson was: if you can play the first hole perfectly, then can you do as well on the next? He put the golfer in a trance and told him "You will play only the first hole, that is all you will remember, and you will be alone on the golf course". The golfer, needless to say, played an excellent round in his next tournament.

The secret to Jonny's conversions

This is one of the things that set Jonny Wilkinson above his peers, consistency. He is feared by opposing teams for his ability to turn pressure into points, and he is able to do it under the most stressful conditions. How does he do this? In fact his approach is not too dissimilar from that taken by Erickson. You only have to watch him prepare for a kick; he uses the same ritual every time.

He places the ball carefully, the same way that he has so many times before. Shutting out the cheers and jeers of the crowd, he stands up, and walks just the right amount of paces backwards. Then takes a single sidestep. But he is not yet ready. Standing with his feet a shoulder width apart, he clasps his hands in front of himself, staring at them for what seems like an age. Finally looking towards the posts, tilting slightly upwards, he pulls his head back just a little, as if the target somehow magnifies in his vision. He focuses, and there he sees her, sitting right in the middle, in the crowd, between the posts. Then he feels it; he knows that he is ready. And the rest is history.

By following this series of steps, the same steps each time, he is able to get himself in the zone and shut himself away from all the pressure and noise. He has a single focus of attention, the process of kicking a rugby ball over the bar and between the posts, he is alone and it seems that for him, this is the only kick that matters. If you have a chance to watch him, you may also notice the defocusing of his eyes, and the flattening of his face, as he stares at his hands, the way looks up at the posts, bringing them closer in his mind, visualising the ball going up, and then down between them.

However Jonny attributes his success to one fact above all, that he is able to visualise a woman sitting in the crowd behind the posts, directly in-between them. He has named her Doris. He aims for Doris, and invariably collects the three points on offer. Essentially, Jonny Wilkinson hallucinates during his kicking process. Hallucination, along with a number of other phenomena that Jonny exhibits - single focus of attention, defocusing of the eyes, disassociation - are signs of trance. When he is at his most accurate, most elegant and most efficient, Jonny is in a brief, specifically directed trance.

If we wish to replicate Jonny's consistency we not only have to practice constantly, modeling his style and specific movements, we have to understand his mental processes as well. As Annett 1995 suggests, "The key to cognitive motor learning lies in elucidating the way in which learned skills are represented in memory". Often it is the mental processes that are the difference that makes the difference. These processes are skills, and skills can be learnt.

Acquiring Mental Skills

The good news is that just like their physical counterparts, mental skills can be developed and perfected. The acquisition of physical skills can be thought of as a three-phase process:

— Cognitive (focusing on the nature of the task)
— Associative (develops proprioception - learning to feel if our movements are correct)
— Autonomous (making this an unconscious process)

Mental skills can be thought of as developing in the same way. Skill acquisition essentially begins in the cognitive stage with the process of modeling the skill required. This is a straightforward matter when this skill is physical and can be observed and taught. In particular the use of videotapes and computer software can assist is establishing the finer nuances, which perhaps the performer did not even know about. Yet when the skill has mental components, or is a purely mental skill, you can only achieve so much by observation, the way to really understand the breakdown of the strategy is to ask. And of course you have to ask the right questions.

Bandler 1982 tells of a time that he was asked to assist a Baseball player raise his game. Not knowing much about baseball, he watched a lot of videos of the top hitters and observed a pattern of behaviour that could only be attributed to mental processes. He interviewed a number of them and found out that as the ball was thrown towards them they were using a mental process of slowing down the ball, and making it much bigger. This made it, for them, easier to hit.

Now of course the ball did not actually slow down or increase in size, and equally they did not go through this process consciously. But this process did exist and it did seem to be the difference between the top hitters and the player that wanted to improve. In real terms, these players were exhibiting the signs of trance: time distortion and hallucination, being two indicators. So Bandler taught this player to go into trance, and make the ball bigger, and go slower. He connected this to standing on the plate. The player improved his game and became a top hitter.

The difference that makes the difference

Not all mental strategies are connected with trance, but many are. Hypnosis has, for a long time, been utilised in improving sports performance, and research is now catching up. Alternative models are suggesting that (alert) hypnosis should be induced before or during performance. Practically, of course, we are not all hypnotists and inducing trance does require special skill and training. Anyone can learn self hypnosis, and we have seen that some sportsmen use alert trance as part of their mental strategy for success. We need not focus on trance in our modeling of mental processes however, as it will come as a by-product, if we get it right. The key elements of such modeling concerns the way in which we represent skills internally.

What you hear, see and feel is important

We may make the assumption that experience is stored internally in the three main sense systems (Visual, Auditory, Kinaesthetic), and that by modeling and replicating this structure, we can have access to the same experiences as someone else. In this way we have more chance of developing the same mental skills. Understanding how someone represents skills internally then is essentially a case of asking the following two questions repeatedly:

— What do you See, Hear and Feel, inside, when you are about to (perform whatever physical skill)?

— What do you do then?

These questions address two aspects of internal strategy, the key representations associated with the skill, and the order in which things happen.

For example Jonny sees Doris, he hears nothing and he feels that it is right. Then he kicks. For some athletes it may be that having a thumping soundtrack playing in their head gives them just that extra push, but it may not start until they hear the gun or get a specific feeling in their stomach of excitement. If these strategies are successful, then they constitute part of the whole that makes up a specific skill, and such mental strategies may tip a performer into the world-class arena.

The key to modeling the mental structure and process is to notice finer and finer distinctions. For example, when Jonny sees Doris, is she in focus or out of focus, does he wait until she is in focus and then he knows that it is the right time? Without asking, we will not know, but if we can find a successful performer in our sport, and understand the order, structure and distinctions in their mental strategy, then we will have a model of the psychological underpinning of whatever skill we are working on.

Try this with your athletes

By way of example you may like to try the following exercise on yourself, or with your athletes. Pick a time in the past when you were highly motivated. Go back and see what you saw, hear what you heard, feel what you felt. Imagine you have a control panel in which you can adjust the representation. It has the following controls: Volume, Brightness, Contrast, and Focus. Adjust them up and down until you feel totally motivated and utterly compelled. Write down the numbers on each control knob. Now think of something that you do not want to do and make a representation of you doing it. Set all the controls to those of your most compelling motivation. How does that make you feel?

The key to modeling internal process is to understand not only at the general level of what it is that the expert sees, hears and feels internally, but also the fine distinctions that they make in these representations. It may be that you can take these basic building blocks and subtly modify the distinctions to suit your own representations, improving perhaps at the micro level, whilst adopting at the macro level the winning strategy.

Towards autonomous installation

Having broken the mental processes of the expert on a specific skill down into a number of representations in a specific order we then need to install it in ourselves and in our athletes. This is the process of Association. It is important to remember the aim of our modeling, to learn a whole skill. So the mental processes that we have elicited must be connected with the physical aspects of the skill, and should go hand in hand with the practice of that skill. During coaching sessions the mental and the physical aspects must be practiced and seen as two sides of the same skill.

We do have an additional advantage in the learning of mental skills: they can be practiced and refined almost anywhere. Even on the bus. There is enormous value in repetition, and mental skills can be repeated far more and much more quickly. There is a view that the brain learns quickly, not slowly. We can take advantage of this by repeating and practicing the skill mentally at a much faster rate than we would perform it in practice.

Practice makes permanent

By constant repetition, these mental skills and strategies will become unconsciously installed. Additionally in moving to the autonomous stage, we can benefit from hypnosis, which can quickly install processes directly in the unconscious. Accelerated learning works in this way, and many sportsmen can see immediate benefits in their game after just one or two sessions of hypnosis. Understanding mental processes is just as relevant for the occasional squash player as for an international sportsman.

5

Exercise-related Behaviours

Physically active lifestyle plays a great role in maximising and maintaining both physical and mental health. Specifically, participation in physical activity programs has been linked to improved health status for many different physiological and psychological conditions, including cardiovascular disease, hypertension, diabetes, obesity, osteoporosis, depression, and anxiety.

As children grow and develop it is important for them to increase their level of self-determination. For young children, it is appropriate for parents, caregivers, teachers, and professionals to make decisions and direct children to leisure opportunities. Parents make decisions for their children based on what they have deemed appropriate for their child and within the capabilities they believe the child possesses. The role of parents and teachers is to assist children with exploration of multiple leisure options, gauging interests, and creating opportunities to learn skills and behaviors in the activities preferred by the child.

Self-determination Theory

Self-determination theory is one contemporary framework that is increasing being used to understand exercise motivation and adherence. Specifically, self-determination theory proposes that behavioural regulation towards an activity can't be amotivated, extrinsically motivated, or intrinsically motivated. These overall classifications of motivation differ in the extent to which they are self-determined (autonomous), because they represent different degrees of internalisation of external values and goals.

Specifically, amotivation represents the lack of both extrinsic and intrinsic motivation and is characterised by the lack of value for an activity, or the belief that the activity will not result in desired outcomes. Extrinsically motivated, behaviours are divided into four different types of behavioural regulation: external, introjected, identified and integrated. External regulation represents behaviours that are regulated through external means, such as rewards or fear of punishment (e.g. exercising because of pressure from significant others). Introjected regulation refers to behaviours that are partially internalised, but they are not fully self-determined.

These behaviours are performed to gain social approval and self-worth or to avoid internal pressure and negative feelings (e.g. exercising to avoid feelings of guilt). Identified regulation represents a relatively self-determined regulation because the outcomes of the behaviour are highly valued (e.g. exercising to improve physical fitness), and the behaviour is performed with no pressure even if it is not particularly enjoyable. Finally, integrated regulation represents the most self-determined form of the internalisation process. It refers to behaviours that are performed out of choice to harmonise and bring coherence to different parts of the self.

For example, some individuals might view exercise, together with healthy eating and adequate rest, as important components of a healthy lifestyle. However, even at the higher end of the self-determination continuum, behaviours are engaged in for instrumental reasons, and thus they are extrinsically regulated. Only when individuals are intrinsically motivated towards an activity is the behaviour considered to be fully self-determined. When intrinsically motivated, individuals enjoy the process of engaging in the activity (e.g. exercising because it is fun) rather than the outcomes associated with the latter. In conclusion, intrinsic motivation, integrated regulation and identified regulation represent self-determined (autonomous) motivational regulations, whereas introjected and external regulation represent low self-determined or controlling motivational regulations.

According to Vallerand, the different motivational regulations can directly predict a wide variety of behavioural, cognitive and affective outcomes. In a comprehensive review of self-determination research across a wide variety of life contexts, Vallerand outlined that self-determined motivation regulations are related to more adaptive outcomes compared with less self-determined regulations or amotivation.

Self-determination theory has recently been used by researchers to study motivation in exercise contexts. The results have been similar to those found in other life contexts in that self-determined motivation to exercise has been associated with more positive behavioural, cognitive and affective outcomes, compared with controlling motivational regulations or amotivation. For example, in terms of self-reported behaviour, Ingledew, Markland and Medley examined the relationship between different exercise motives and the stages of behavioural change proposed by the transtheoretical model.

In the context of exercise adoption, the transtheoretical model argues that individuals move through five stages of behavioural change, starting from being physically inactive and ending up as regular exercisers. Ingledew et al. found that extrinsic, especially body-related, motives were more important in the early stages of behavioural change, whereas enjoyment (an intrinsic motive) was important for progression to regular exercise patterns. However, Ingledew et al. used a descriptive questionnaire that measures motives for exercise, but not the underlying motivational regulations that underpin exercise behaviour.

In contrast, Mullan and Markland assessed the variations in four motivational regulations (intrinsic motivation, identified, introjected and external regulation) across the different stages of change. Mullan and Markland found that those individuals who reported that they exercised infrequently (preparation stage) had significantly lower scores on intrinsic motivation and identified regulation to exercise than individuals who indicated that they exercised regularly but for less than 6 months (action stage), and those who exercised regularly for 6 or more months (maintenance stage).

No stages -of change differences were found in introjected regulation and external regulation. This is surprising given that controlling behavioural regulations are more likely to be associated with maladaptive behavioural outcomes. Unfortunately, amotivation was not assessed by Mullan and Markland. Clearly, more research is needed to examine whether there are significant variations in self-determination among the different stages of change. Such research is important to understand why as well as how individuals move across different stages of exercise behaviour.

One of the greatest challenges facing researchers and clinicians alike is how to prevent relapse for those individuals who have recently started exercising. There is a clear need to use theoretical frameworks to study relapse behaviour, as previous research studying relapse in exercise settings has been mainly a theoretical. Self-determination theory can provide a potentially useful theoretical framework. For example, Mullan and Markland suggested that controlling exercise regulations may lead to a greater number of relapses from exercise compared with more self-determined types of exercise regulation. This is probably because those who are self-determined engage in exercise because they find it fun or because they consider it personally important.

Therefore, they are less likely to experience motivational setbacks than individuals who exercise out of feelings of guilt or other extrinsic reasons. In line with this argument, Ryan, Frederick, Lepes, Rubio and Sheldon showed that adherence to an exercise programme was associated with enjoyment and competence motives (i.e. intrinsic motives) as opposed to body appearance motives (i.e. extrinsic motives). However, this study did not assess the motivational regulations that underpin exercise behaviour. Clearly, more studies are needed to examine whether different types of exercise regulation with varying degrees of self-determination can predict relapse from exercise. This is important in view of the high relapse rates of exercisers.

Exercise-related cognitions

Intention to continue exercise is an important outcome variable when studying exercise behaviour. Indeed, a meta-analysis by Hausenblas, Carron and Mack showed that there was a moderate effect site between intention and behaviour in exercise settings. For the purposes of the present study, the question is whether amotivated, controlling and autonomously regulated motivation will differentially predict intention to continue exercising. Currently, there is some support for the positive role of self-determined motivation in predicting intentions of children to be physically active.

In a recent meta-analysis of a small number of studies, Chatsisarantis, Hagger, Biddle, Smith and Wang found that intentions to be physically active were negatively correlated with amotivation and external regulation, and positively associated with introjected regulation, identified regulation and intrinsic motivation. However, all studies in this meta-analysis were carried out with children or with sport participants. More research is needed to examine whether the findings from this meta-analysis will apply to adult exercisers. This is particularly important in view of the high drop-out rates from exercise programmes.

Another cognitive variable, which is a key predictor of exercise behaviour and adherence, is self-efficacy. In the context of exercise, self-efficacy has often been operationalised as barriers self-efficacy, which has been defined as the belief individuals have about their ability to overcome commonly identified barriers to regular exercise. To the knowledge, there has been no research examining the relationship between barriers self-efficacy and exercise motivation using a self-determination theory framework. The researchers aim was to examine this relationship, bearing in mind the important role of barriers self-efficacy in predicting exercise behaviour. From a conceptual standpoint, self-determination theory suggests that people with high perceptions of autonomy (self-determination) feel that they have a sense of choice and control of their behaviour.

As a consequence, great self-determination to exercise should positively predict self-efficacy to overcome barriers to regular exercise. At this point it is important to differentiate between the need for competence and self-efficacy. Bandura viewed self-efficacy as a domain-specific perception of competence and an instrument for goal attainment, as opposed to an innate psychological need that transcends contexts. Furthermore, according to Deci and Ryan, self-efficacy theory focuses on the satisfaction that results from the outcomes that competence might yield. In contrast, self-determination theory views the experience of competence per se as a source of satisfaction and a contributor to wellbeing over and above any satisfaction resulting from the outcomes that competence might bring.

Self-evaluations

The physical self plays an important role in daily functioning and well-being. This is reflected in the consistently high correlations between aspects of the physical self, such as body image, with global self-esteem. Furthermore, research has shown, that physical self-worth, a global indicator of feelings about salient aspects of the physical self, is significantly related to emotional adjustment and positive affect, even when global self-esteem and social desirability are statistically controlled. Self-determination theory discusses the relationship between global self-esteem and motivated behaviour and suggests that true self-esteem (a type of self-esteem that is stable and secure) may be developed through engaging in behaviours that are autonomously regulated, and that engender feelings of competence and relatedness.

However, the theory does not discuss the relationship between physical self-worth and motivated behaviour. Nevertheless, the self-determined motivational regulations may be positively related to physical self-worth. For example, engaging in exercise to achieve personally important goals is more likely to lead to feelings of accomplishment and subsequently to high physical self-worth, as opposed to engaging in exercise to avoid feelings of guilt or to appease significant others.

The results of this study showed that autonomously regulated exercise motivations (i.e. intrinsic motivation and identified regulation) discriminated between those with high and low physical self-esteem, whereas controlling exercise regulations (i.e. introjected and external regulation) did not. However, this study was conducted with young female` exercisers and the generalisability of the findings to other populations has yet to be tested. Clearly, more research is needed to examine the extent to which different types of exercise motivation may be differentially related to the physical self.

Another construct related to the physical self is social physique anxiety, which has been defined as the apprehension that some individuals have about displaying their body in social settings. Social physique anxiety is often salient in exercise classes where the body is "on display". Very few studies have examined the relationship between extrinsic/intrinsic motivation for exercise and social physique anxiety. Frederick and Morrison found that exercisers with high social physique anxiety were more likely to report extrinsic motives for exercising, such as appearance, than exercisers with lower social physique anxiety. Similarly, Crawford and Eklund found that motives to improve toning and physical attractiveness (i.e. extrinsic motives) were significant and positive predictors of social physique anxiety. However, since the previous studies were not based on the self-determination theory framework, the motives they assessed did not represent the whole continuum of self-determination.

It is important to extend this research by looking at how social physique anxiety relates to self determined, controlling and amotivated behaviours. Self-determination theory does not directly discuss such links. However, Deci and Ryan talked about the struggle for body control (which is undeniably embedded in the concept of social physique anxiety) and argued that this struggle is the outcome of deficiencies in self-determination. It is therefore reasonable to assume that if individuals exercise due to enjoyment or because they value the benefits of exercise, they are less likely to be focused on how their bodies appear to others. Therefore, exercise regulated by intrinsic or identified motivation should help individuals to reduce their preoccupation with appearance-related factors. In contrast, individuals whose exercise motivation is regulated by controlling motivation, such as the need to obtain social approval or avoid social disapproval, are more likely to report social physique anxiety symptoms in an exercise setting.

Age, Sex and Motivational Regulations

With regard to exercise relapse; approximately 90% of the participants selected the, first two (i.e. "no relapse", "1-3 relapses") of the five available relapse categories. As a consequence, researchers created a new binary variable ("no relapse", "one or more relapses") that served as the dependent variable in a binary logistic regression. Although one might consider the cut-off point between the two categories as stringent, one should bear in mind that they excluded from the analyses those individuals who indicated uncontrollable reasons for relapse. In the logistic, regression, as well as in the other regression analyses reported below, statistically controlled for age and sex due to the age and sex differences that have been reported in the literature with regard to both the independent and dependent variables of this study.

The number of relapses in the past 5 years due to controllable reasons was positively predicted by external regulation and negatively predicted by identified regulation. In relation to the stages of change, a multivariate analysis of variance indicated significant differences between the three stages of change (preparation, action, maintenance) in exercise motivation. No cut-off values exist for partial eta-squared, but a value above 0.06 is considered a moderate effect size and a value above 0.14 is considered a large effect size. Follow-up univariate analysis indicated significant differences in all types of exercise motivation.

All differences among the three stages of change were in the expected direction with the exception of introjected regulation. Cohen's *d* index was calculated to provide an effect size estimation of the mean differences. According to Cohen, *d* values of 0.2, 0.5 and 0.8 indicate small, medium and large effect sizes respectively. A post hoc Tukey test revealed that the participants in the maintenance stage had significantly higher intrinsic motivation (d= 1.10), identified regulation (d= 1.12) and introjected regulation (d=0.56), and significantly lower external regulation (d = 0.83) and amotivation (d = 0.50), than those in the preparation stage. Furthermore, the participants in the maintenance stage reported higher introjected regulation (d=0.41), identified regulation (d=0.53) and intrinsic motivation (d= 0.66), and lower external regulation (d = 0.43), than those in the action stage. Lastly, identified motivation was significantly higher in the action stage than in the preparation stage (d=0.55).

A separate one-way analysis of variance showed no significant age differences across the three stages of change ($F_{2,357} = 2.65$, $P > 0.05$, partial $\eta^2 = 0.02$). Lastly, a chi-square analysis showed that there were more males than females in the maintenance stage ($\chi^2 = 8.07$, d.f. = 2, $P < 0.05$).

Multiple hierarchical regression analyses were employed to examine whether the different motivational regulations could predict exercise-related cognitions and physical self-evaluations. The results showed that all regressions were significant.

With regard to the cognitive variables, intention to continue exercise in the next 6 months was negatively predicted by amotivation and positively predicted by introjected regulation and identified motivation. In addition, barriers self-efficacy was significantly predicted by sex, with males having a higher efficacy to overcome barriers than females. The motivational variables explained a much greater proportion of variance of the dependent variable compared with sex and age. More specifically, high barriers self-efficacy was predicted by high introjected regulation, identified regulation and intrinsic motivation, and low external regulation.

Two variables related to physical self-evaluations were assessed in this study: physical self-worth and social physique anxiety. Physical self-worth was significantly predicted by sex and intrinsic motivation. Sex explained a considerable amount of variance of physical self-worth, with women having lower scores than men. The motivational variables added an approximately equal amount of explained variance of physical self-worth. As expected, intrinsic motivation positively predicted physical self-worth.

With regard to social physique anxiety, it was significantly predicted by age, with younger participants displaying significantly higher social physique anxiety than older ones. Furthermore, sex was a significant predictor, with women having higher scores than men. The motivational variables increased the explained variance of social physique anxiety, although more variance was accounted for by sex and age. Specifically, social physique anxiety was positively predicted by introjected regulation and negatively predicted by intrinsic motivation.

Self-determination Theory in Exercise Domain

Many researchers and professional organisations identify physical education as a potentially important component in efforts to improve children's health, but physical education classes alone are not sufficient to meet the recommended physical activity requirements for children. From this perspective, it is important to investigate ways to design physical education class environments that will facilitate the adoption of physically active lifestyles. Specifically, the relationships among key motivational constructs and engagement variables were investigated using a structural equation model. The model was generated based on self-determination theory. It was hypothesised that a pattern of positive relationships would exist among perceptions of the mastery climate, levels of self-determination, and attitudes, and that those three variables would be predictors of perceived competence.

A Test of Self-determination Theory in the Exercise Domain, is a study of Jemma Edmunds, Nikos Ntoumanis and Joan L. Duda. The first aim of this study is to explore how satisfaction of the three psychological needs relates to the type of motivational regulations guiding exercise behaviour. Furthermore, they examine the extent to which psychological need satisfaction and motivational regulations can predict exercise behaviour.

Physical inactivity now constitutes one of the major behavioural risk factors to health in modern society. In view of this evidence, promoting physical activity is clearly an increasing public health priority. Physical activity engagement involves a complex interaction between biological, environmental, social, and psychological influences. Examining the motivational determinants of exercise behaviour has become a prominent topic in exercise psychology. One theoretical approach to human motivation that is receiving increasing attention in the exercise domain is self-determination theory.

Essentially, SDT proposes that human motivation varies in the extent to which it is autonomous or controlling. Behaviours and actions that are autonomous are initiated freely and emanate from within oneself. In contrast, when behaviour is controlled, it is regulated by an external force. The individual in this instance feels pressured to engage in the behaviour. Based on these distinctions, SDT proposes that three forms of motivation exist; namely, intrinsic motivation, extrinsic motivation, and amotivation, which, based on the level of autonomy associated with them, lie oft a continuum ranging from high to low self-determination, respectively.

Intrinsic motivation constitutes the most autonomous form of motivation, and refers to an inherent tendency possessed by all humans to seek out novelty and challenges, to extend and exercise their capabilities, to explore, and to learn. An individual who pursues a goal or activity because it is enjoyable or intrinsically captivating would display intrinsic motivation.

Not all human behaviours can be considered enjoyable, however. To understand how such behaviours are regulated, SDT proposes extrinsic motivation as an additional motivational force, and a process called internalisation. Extrinsic motivation refers to behaviours that are carried out to attain outcomes unrelated to the activity itself. Internalisation refers to an inherent tendency possessed by all humans to integrate the regulation of extrinsically motivated activities that are useful for effective functioning in the social world, but that are not inherently interesting.

SDT further proposes that the extent to which extrinsic motives are internalised can vary. A multidimensional conceptualisation of extrinsic motivation is hypothesised to exist, consisting of external, introjected, identified, and integrated regulations. These regulations lie on a continuum from lower to higher self-determination and reflect the extent of the internalisation process.

External regulation can be defined as exercising to either appease an external demand or to attain a reward. An example of an external regulation in the exercise domain is "I exercise because my friends and family say I should." Introjection, which is a slightly more self-determined form of extrinsic motivation, involves internalising the behaviour's regulation, but not fully accepting it as one's own. It is a relatively controlling form of regulation in which behaviours are performed to avoid negative emotions, to support conditional self-worth, or to attain ego enhancement. Identified regulation reflects a more autonomous form of extrinsic motivation and reflects participation in an activity because one holds outcomes of the behaviour to be personally significant, although one may not enjoy the activity itself. For example, an individual who exercises because he or she values the benefits of exercise would display identified regulation in this domain.

In addition to specifying the different types of motivational regulations that may guide behaviour, SDT also details specific conditions that are responsible for more or less self-determined motivation. Specifically, SDT assumes that all humans possess three basic psychological needs; that is, the need for competence, autonomy, and relatedness. The need, for competence implies that individuals have a desire to interact effectively with the environment, to experience a sense of competence in producing desired outcomes, and to prevent undesired events.

The need for autonomy reflects a desire to engage in activities of one's choosing and to be the origin of one's own behaviour. Finally, the need for relatedness involves feeling connected, or feeling that one belongs in a given social milieu. Essentially, SDT suggests that the most self-determined forms of regulation will guide behaviour when the needs are satisfied. In contrast, low self-determination is a consequence of a thwarting of the three basic needs.

According to Deci and Ryan, SDT also specifies that differential levels of psychological need satisfaction in a given domain will result in diverse cognitive, affective, and behavioural consequences. Furthermore, need satisfaction has been postulated to influence outcomes indirectly via the promotion of different types of motivational regulation. It is assumed that intrinsic motivation will engender the most positive consequences, followed by identification.

However, some research findings in physical activity settings —as well as in other domains, such as politics and education—have been less conclusive regarding the positive implications of intrinsic motivation compared to other self-determined forms of regulation. Wilson et al. provided evidence suggesting that among participants recruited to engage in a 12-week structured exercise programme, identified regulation was a stronger predictor of self-reported exercise behaviour than was intrinsic motivation, although both regulations predicted exercise behaviours, exercise attitudes, and physical fitness. In addition, introjected regulation has been shown to be correlated positively with strenuous exercise behaviour in some studies, but not in others.

Ryan proposed that the characteristics of the situation in question will determine the extent to which intrinsic and internalised extrinsic regulations will produce positive behavioural outcomes. With respect to the latter, in contexts in which the activities undertaken are important, but may lack in intrinsic appeal, it is assumed that the innate tendency to internalise the role of such activities will be witnessed. In view of the considerable value that society bestows upon exercise for health aesthetic gains, research demonstrating that introjected and identified regulations positively predict exercise behaviour may indicate that, for some individuals, exercise engagement is maintained via the process described by Ryan. That is, exercise behaviour constitutes an externally motivated activity that requires internalisation to initiate and sustain action.

An additional tenet of SDT relevant to the current investigation concerns the social context in which individuals operate. According to SDT, autonomy-supportive contexts are conducive to need satisfaction and ensuing self determined motivational regulations. Such contexts are characterised by the minimisation of controls by significant others, the understanding of other people's perspectives, and the provision of choices that guide and facilitate the decision-making process.

Supporting these propositions, Wilson and Rodgers found that among female students and staff enrolled in a team-based intramural physical activity event, perceived autonomy support from friends was associated positively with intrinsic motivation and identified regulation. Furthermore, Standage, Duda, and Ntoumanis recently demonstrated that, among secondary school physical education students, an autonomy-supportive climate was related positively to satisfaction of the need for competence, autonomy, and relatedness, which, in turn, predicted greater self-determined motivation. However, as far as the present authors are aware, no study has considered the implications of an autonomy-supportive environment provided by an exercise class leader.

The present research study also examines whether, as assumed in SDT, an autonomy-supportive context provided by an exercise class leader corresponds to greater intrinsic motivation and identified regulation via the support provided for the three basic psychological needs. Based on the propositions of SDT and previous research in the physical, educational, and political domains, the researchers hypothesise first that positive relationships will be observed between psychological need satisfaction and identified and intrinsic motives; and a negative link will emerge between psychological need satisfaction and introjected and external regulations. Second, identified and introjected regulation and intrinsic motivation are expected to predict exercise behaviours positively and to mediate the relationship between psychological need satisfaction and exercise behaviours.

In turn, external regulation is hypothesised to predict exercise behaviours negatively and to mediate the relationship between inadequate psychological need satisfaction and more negative behavioural outcomes. Third, it is predicted that perceived autonomy support (PAS) provided by the exercise class leader will be related positively to satisfaction of the three basic needs and self-determined motivation. Finally, PAS is also hypothesised to predict intrinsic motivation and identified regulation via satisfaction of the basic psychological needs.

Method

Participants (N = 369; 173 male, 192 female, 4 unspecified) ranged in age from 16 to 64 years (M = 31.86, SD = 11.28). The majority (88.7%) of the participants were White. One hundred six of the participants reported taking part in regular exercise classes, and thus constituted the subsample with which they examined relationships between PAS, need satisfaction, and motivational regulations. The subsample ranged in age from 16 to 62 years (M = 30.24, SD = 10.32).

An a priori power analysis, conducted using GPower, ensured that these sample sizes were sufficient to yield adequate statistical power for all statistical procedures planned and subsequently conducted in the current study. More specifically, to detect a significant finding (at the.05 level) at a desired power level of.95, a minimum of 143 participants was required for analyses conducted on the total sample, and 41 for the substudy analyses.

Measures

Psychological need satisfaction was measured via the 21-item Basic Need Satisfaction at Work Scale, adapted by the authors to make it relevant to the exercise domain. This 21-item scale is based on a 15-item measure developed by Kasser, Davey, and Ryan to tap reported autonomy, relatedness, and competence in the work' domain. In the development of the original 15-item measure, some items were taken from the Intrinsic Motivation Inventory, support for which has been garnered in the physical domain. The 21-item Basic Need Satisfaction at Work scale exhibited alphas of.73 for competence,.84 for relatedness, and.79 for autonomy in a sample of U.S. workers.

The 21-item scale utilised by Deci et al., includes six items that measure competence, eight items that measure relatedness, and seven items that measure autonomy need satisfaction. Following the stem "Please indicate how true each of the following statements is for you, given your experiences of exercise," participants responded to each item on a 7-point scale ranging from 1 to 7.

Behavioural Regulation in Exercise Questionnaire. Participants completed the BREQ, which is a 15-item self-report measure assessing the reasons why people exercise. The BREQ includes scales assessing external, introjected, identified, and intrinsic regulations. Following the stem "Why do you exercise-" participants responded to each item on a 5-point scale ranging from 1 to 5. Previous research supports the BREQ's multidimensional four-factor structure, the invariance of this factor structure across gender, and the internal consistency of each subscale.

Godin Leisure Time Exercise Questionnaire. The GLTEQ was used to assess self-reported exercise behaviour. The GLTEQ contains three questions assessing the frequency of mild, moderate, and strenuous exercise engaged in (for a minimum of 15 min) during a typical week. Exercise behaviour scores can be calculated by multiplying weekly frequencies of strenuous (e.g., running, vigorous gym workout), moderate (e.g., easy cycling), and mild activities (e.g., easy walking) by 9, 5, and 3 METS (units of metabolic equivalence), respectively. An overall exercise behaviour score is calculated by summing the weighted product of each question as follows: (mild x 3) + (moderate x 5) + (strenuous x 9). Based on its correlations with objective indicators of exercise and physical fitness (e.g., exercise monitor and maximal aerobic capacity test scores), a previous study has concluded that the GLTEQ is a reliable and valid measure of leisure time exercise behaviour.

Perceived autonomy support. PAS from the exercise class leader was measured using a short (6 items) version of the original 15-item Health Care Climate Questionnaire. The original scale assesses participants' perceptions of the degree of autonomy support provided by a relevant health care provider and includes items such as "I feel that my health care provider provides me with choices and options." In the current study, the term "my health care provider" was replaced with "my exercise class leader," and participants were asked to respond to items in reference to the exercise class in which they participated most commonly. Participants responded to each item on a 7-point scale ranging from 1 (strongly disagree) to 7 (strongly agree). Previous studies using the original HCCQ revealed a one-factor solution measuring PAS and an alpha value of.95.

Procedure

The current research was approved by the ethics subcommittee of a university in the United Kingdom. Participants were recruited in a number of different settings, including sports clubs, public leisure centers, private fitness clubs, shops, and supermarkets in the West Midlands, UK. Participants were approached by the first author, who explained the purpose of the study, and were asked if they were willing to complete a multisection questionnaire packet. Those who agreed to take part provided their informed consent.

The first section of the questionnaire assessed psychological need satisfaction via exercise, motivational regulations, and exercise behaviours. Those participants who reported taking part in regular exercise classes completed an additional section of the questionnaire tapping PAS provided by the exercise class leader in the class in which they participated most commonly.

Total and strenuous exercise behaviours

Separate regression analyses were carried out to predict total and strenuous self-reported exercise from psychological need satisfaction and motivational regulations. Mild and moderate exercise were not examined because they did not correlate with the needs or the, regulations. Preliminary MANOVA revealed significant age and gender differences in exercise behaviours: age, $F(6, 686) = 8.51$, $p =.00$, Pillai's trace =.14; and gender, $F(3, 361) = 4.38$, $p =.01$, Pillai's trace =.04. In view of these results, as well as the fact that the existing literature has linked these characteristics to exercise behaviour, they controlled for their influence in the first step of the regression. By doing so, we could determine whether the theoretical constructs embedded in SDT accounted for additional variance in exercise behaviour above and beyond important demographic variables.

Needs were entered in the second step of the regression, as they are postulated to affect behavioural outcomes indirectly via motivational regulations, which were entered in the final step.

As seen in Table 2, 18% of the variance in total exercise behaviour was explained by this model. Two of the variables contributed independently to the prediction of total exercise behaviour; namely, age and introjected regulation. Six of the variables contributed independently to the prediction of strenuous exercise behaviour: gender, age, competence, external regulation, introjected regulation, and identified regulation. This set of predictors predicted 32% of the variability in strenuous exercise behaviour.

SELF-DETERMINATION THEORY FRAMEWORK

This framework is the study of Nikos Ntoumanis (University of Birmingham). This study examined whether contextual and personal motivational variables, taken from self-determination theory, could predict student cognetive and affective experiences in school physical education (PE). A theoretical framework that is being increasingly used to study motivation in PE is self-determination theory. SDT distinguishes among three types of behavioural regulation with varying degrees of self-determined motivation: intrinsic motivation, extrinsic motivation, and amotivation. Intrinsic motivation represents the highest degree of self-determined motivation and refers to situations in which individuals freely engage in activities that they find interesting and enjoyable and that offer the opportunity for learning.

In contrast, extrinsic motivation is evident when individuals perform an activity because they value its associated outcomes (eg., public praise, extrinsic rewards) more than the activity itself. Three types of extrinsic motivation have been measured in classroom education and in PE. These are identified regulation, introjected regulation and external regulation. Identified regulation represents behaviours with high degree of self-determined motivation. Individuals with high identified regulation have internalised the value of certain behaviours that they perform out of choice but without necessarily enjoying them.

For example, some students may participate in PE because they value the importance of exercise for their health. Introjected regulation describes extrinsically motivated behaviours which have been only slightly internalised and which are performed out of feelings of guilt or shame. For example, some students may participate in PE in order not to let their parents down. Last, external regulation represents the lowest degree of self-determined motivation and, refers to behaviours carried out in order to attain tangible rewards (e.g., social status among peers) or to avoid punishment.

The third type of behavioural regulation described by Deci and Ryan is amotivation. Whereas both intrinsic motivation and extrinsic motivation represent different degrees of volition, amotivation represents the absence of motivation. Amotivation is evident when individuals lack the intention and willingness to engage in a particular behaviour. It often results from feelings of incompetence and uncontrollability and is frequently linked up decisions to drop out of PE or school altogether.

The antecedents and outcomes of the different types of motivation have been described by Vallerand in his model of motivation. According to this model, a number of social factors (e.g., autonomy-supportive or controlling teaching styles) can impact on the various types of motivation via the satisfaction of the fundamental human needs for competence, autonomy, and relatedness. Social factors that satisfy these needs Will promote self-determined forms of motivation. In contrast, social factors that undermine these needs will result in controlling motivation and amotivation. In turn, the various types of motivation can predict a number of cognitive, affective, and behavioural outcomes. Usually, intrinsic motivation and identified regulation predict the most positive outcomes, whereas amotivation and external regulation predict the most negative outcomes.

An important behavioural outcome that has been assessed in classroom education and sport is persistence (or drop out). For example, Vallerand et al., found support for a motivational model of high school drop out in a sample of 4,537 Canadian students. The results of structural equation modeling analysis showed that the degree of autonomy support provided by parents, teachers`, and the school administration influenced students' reported satisfaction of their needs for competence and autonomy (relatedness was not assessed). In turn, these two need satisfaction variables positively predicted an index of self-determined academic motivation. Finally, the more self-determined the students were the less likely they were to intend to drop out of high school. These behavioural intentions positively predicted (β =.24) students' actual drop out behaviour a year later.

Two studies have replicated the prospective design used by Valleranil et al. to examine drop out behaviour (or persistence) in youth sport. Pelletier et al. used a prospective 2-year design to examine persistence in competitive swimming in a sample of predominantly adolescent Canadign swimmers. The results of structural equation modeling analysis showed that swimmers' perception of coaches' autonomy support positively predicted self-determined motivation (intrinsic motivation and identified regulation), and unexpectedly, introjected regulation. In contrast, swimmers' perception of coaches' controlling style predicted swimmers' amotivation, external regulation, and introjected regulation.

Self-determined motivation predicted participation in swimming at two follow-ups (10 and 22 months later). Introjected regulation was a positive predictor of persistence at 10 months, but not at 22 months. External regulation and amotivation were negative predictors of persistence at the second follow-up and both follow-ups respectively. Last, mean comparisons between persistent and drop-out swimmers showed that the former, compared with the latter, had higher intrinsic motivation and identified regulation and lower external regulation and amotivation. No differences in introjected regulation were found. Pelletier et al. did not assess the three psychological needs postulated by SDT to mediate the effects of social factors on motivational regulations. Furthermore, autonomy support is only one aspect of the means by which coaches influence athletes' motivational experiences and behaviours.

In a subsequent study, Sarrazin et al. also tested a motivational model of drop out of sport (handball) with a sample of 335 French female adolescents. This study integrated aspects of SDT and achievement goal theory. Sarrazin et al. examined the social factor of motivational climates, that is, whether coaches are perceived to evaluate and reward their athletes on the basis of task (self-referenced) or ego (comparative) competence criteria. The results of structural equation modeling analysis showed that a taskinvolving motivational climate was more conducive to the satisfaction of the three psychological needs compared with an egoinvolving climate. Of the three need satisfaction variables, autonomy (and, to a much lesser extent, competence and relatedness) predicted an index of self-determined motivation.

In turn, the latter negatively predicted behavioural intentions to drop out of handball. Twenty-one months later, 22% of the handball players dropped out of their sport. The path from behavioural intentions to drop out behaviour was moderate (β =.55). Comparison of mean scores between persistent players and drop outs showed that the former perceived the motivational climate as being more taskinvolving, experienced greater satisfaction of their three psychological needs, and reported higher intrinsic motivation and lower amotivation and intentions to drop out.

The studies by Pelletier et al. and Sarrazin et al. are interesting because they clearly show the importance of contextual and personal motivational factors in predicting drop out behaviour in sport. However, it is important to assess multiple outcomes, and not only intention and behaviour, in order to have a more comprehensive understanding of how personal and environmental factors affect individuals' motivational experiences. Furthermore, both studies, as well as the study by Vallerand et al., relied exclusively on self-reports which inadvertently inflate common method variance.

Admittedly, from a theoretical viewpoint, self-reports are more appropriate. This is because SDT argues that student perception of significant others' autonomy support is a more important determinant of their motivational experiences compared with "objective" measures of autonomy support. Furthermore, self-reports are needed to assess students' motivational regulations as well as the degree to which their needs have been satisfied. However, in terms of student behaviour, some more "objective" measures (e.g., teacher ratings) can be used.

In sum, the primary purpose of the present study was to expand on previous studies on dropout by looking at multiple antecedents of self-determined motivation and how the latter can predict a number of important consequences, including dropping out of or participating in optional PE programmes. More specifically, although most of the past research has restricted the examination of sociocontextual antecedents of motivation to autonomy support (or the lack of it), this study also assessed the extent to which PE teachers emphasised task-involving criteria for success and promoted cooperative learning.

Research by Ntoumanis has shown that the emphasis PE teachers place on individual improvement criteria (e.g., mastering new or difficult skills) can result in student competence need satisfaction reducing the controlling nature of interpersonal ability comparisons. In addition, the promotion of learning via student cooperate can result in stronger feelings of relatedness, among students. In terms of the motivational outcomes assessed, besides intention and behaviour which were measured in previous studies on drop out, this study also assessed levels of negative affect, concentration in the class, and effort. These variables were chosen because they have been shown to be indicators of student interest and investment in learning.

An SDT-based motivational model was tested that hypothesised that the degree to which PE teachers supported their students' needs would predict the latter's need satisfaction. The indicators of need support were autonomy support, teacher emphasis on individual improvement criteria, and promotion of cooperative learning. It was also hypothesised that student need satisfaction would predict an index of self-determined motivation. In turn, it was expected that self-determined motivation would negatively predict negative affect and positively predict student levels of concentration and effort in the class as well as their intentions to participate in optional PE. Last, it was expected that behavioural intentions would positively predict actual behavioural choices.

In terms of mean differences between participants and nonparticipants, it was hypothesised that the participants would rate their past experiences in compulsory PE as more adaptive. More specifically, it was expected that the participants would report that their teachers used more task-involving criteria for success, and were more autonomy supportive compared with the teachers of the nonparticipants. Furthermore, the participants were expected to report greater need satisfaction, more self-determined motivation, and less controlling motivation and amotivation compared with, the nonparticipants. Last, the participants were predicted to report more adaptive affective, cognitive and behavioural experiences in compulsory PE.

Method

Participants

The participants were 460 (girls n = 145; boys n = 315) British 15-year-old school students from eight schools in the north of England. Almost all students were Caucasians. As explained in the Procedure below, follow-up information regarding participation status was obtained from 302 of those students. With the exception of the confirmatory factor analyses that used the full sample, all other analyses reported in the Results section used the subsample of 302 students.

Measures

Learning Climate Questionnaire. The short form of the LCQ (6 items) was used to measure student perceptions of the autonomy support provided by their PE teachers. The wording of the items was adapted to be applicable to PE classes. An example item is "My PE teachers encourage me to ask questions." Each item was measured on a 5-point scale (1 = strongly disagree; 5 = strongly agree). Williams and Deci reported that an exploratory factor analysis of the long form of the LCQ (15 items) produced one factor that had a Cronbach's alpha coefficient of.96.

Perceived Motivational Climate in Sport Questionnaire-2. Two facets of a task-involving motivational climate were measured with a PE adaptation of the PMCSQ-2. These facts were the emphasis by the PE teachers on individual criteria for student improvement and the extent to which the teachers promote cooperative student learning. An example item of the former factor is "In this PE class, the PE teacher makes sure students improve on skills they're not good at." An example item of cooperative learning is "In this PE class, students help each other learn." Both factors were measured on 5-point scales (1 = strongly disagree; 5 = strongly agree). Evidence for the validity of the PMCSQ-2 has been provided by Newton et al. In the same study, both factors were shown to have adequate internal reliability coefficients.

Basic Need Satisfaction Scale. This is a 21-item questionnaire that taps perceptions of competence (6 items), relatedness (8 items), and autonomy need satisfaction (7 items). The scale was used by Deci et al. to measure need satisfaction at work, but it was modified in the present study to assess need satisfaction in PE. Example items are "I feel that I can make a lot of inputs to deciding what to do in PE" (autonomy), "I really like the students I exercise with in PE" (relatedness), and "I have been able to learn interesting new skills in PE" (competence). All factors were measured on 7-point scales (I = not at all true; 7 = very true). Deci et al. reported adequate alpha coefficients for the three factors with a U.S. sample; however, with a Bulgarian sample, the alphas for relatedness and autonomy were low (a =.57 and a =.57, respectively).

Self-Regulation Questionnaire. To measure the different types of motivation postulated by SDT, a questionnaire presented by Goudas et al. was used. This questionnaire adapted to PE the Self-Regulation Questionnaire, which measures intrinsic motivation, as well as identified, introjected and external regulations in the classroom. Furthermore, Goudas et al. adapted to PE the Amotivation subscale of the Academic Motivation Scale. The students in the present study responded to 20 items measured on scales ranging from 1 (strongly disagree) to 7 (strongly agree). Each item followed the stem "I take part in PE..." Example items are "because PE is fun" (intrinsic motivation), "because I want to improve in sport" (identified regulation), "because I would feel bad about myself if I did not" (introjected regulation), "so that the teachers will not yell at me" (external regulation), and "but I cannot see what I am getting out of PE" (amotivation). The adapted SRQ has been used in various studies in PE and has been shown to have clear factor structure and high internal reliabilities with the exception of introjected regulation whose alpha coefficient is usually slightly below.70.

Negative affect in PE. Four adjectives that measure negative affect (e.g., "disappointed," "embarrassed") were used to assess typical negative affect experienced by students in PE. These adjectives were taken from Ebbeck and Weiss. Each adjective was assessed on a 5-point scale ranging from 1 (never) to 7 (always). Participants responded to the stem "In this PE class I feel..." Ebbeck and Weiss have provided psychometric evidence for the use of these items in youth sport.

Concentration in the PE classes. Three items were written in the present study to measure students' concentration in PE classes. An example item is "In PE, I concentrate on the skills/tasks I have to do." Each item was assessed on a 7-point scale (I = strongly disagree; 7 = strongly agree).

Intention to participate in optional PE. Two items were written in the present study to measure students' intention to participate in optional PE classes in the following school year. An example item is "I intend not to do PE next year." Each item was assessed on a 7-point scale (1 = strongly disagree; 7 = strongly agree).

Teacher rating of students' effort. The PE teachers were asked to provide an overall rating of each student's levels of effort in PE. For each student, one PE teacher provided a single rating on a 7-point scale (1 = no effort at all; 7 exceptionally high levels of effort). The PE teachers were told that an objective of the study was to assess how hard the students try to improve their skills and whether they "give their beat" during PE lessons.

Procedure

Informed consent was obtained from the participants and the head teacher of each school. The questionnaires were administered at the start of a PE lesson. Prior to questionnaire administration, the students were told that their responses would be kept confidential add, that hey could decline to participate or withdraw at any time. The questionnaires were administered in late spring and early summer to 460 fifteen-year-old students. In the fall of the same year, the schools were contacted and were asked to confirm whether the students had enrolled on an optional Year 12 PE programme.

In Great Britain, after the age of 16 years, participation in PE is optional. Academic-that is, science-based PE programmes offered by some schools to 16-year-olds were not targeted, because the purpose of this study was to focus on health-enhancing physical activity programmes. To protect anonymity, the students were matched on the basis of their dates of birth, gender, and school identification. It was possible to obtain information for 302 students, of whom 171 chose to enroll in an optional PE programme. There are various reasons that it was not possible to obtain information for the remaining

158 students': (a) Some students dropped out of school altogether; (b) others relocated to a different part of the country; and (c) some students moved to a different school in the same area, but the new school declined to provide the necessary information.

Results

Confirmatory factor analysis using the full sample of 460 participants was carried out for all scales to examine their factorial structure. To evaluate model fit, the two-index presentation strategy was used. According to this strategy, the standardised root-mean-square residual (SRMR) should be used along with one or more incremental or absolute fit indices to evaluate the fit of the confirmatory factor model. Hit and Bentler found that, among all fit indices, the SRMR (a) is the most sensitive to misspecification in both simple and complex models and (b) is less sensitive to sample size and violations of distributional assumptions. According to Hit and Bentler, a value close to.08 for SRMR, combined with a value close to.95 for the comparative fit index (CFI) and a value close to.06 for the root-mean-square error of approximation (RMSEA), is indicative of good model fit.

For brevity reasons, the results of the confirmatory factor analyses are not presented here but are available on request. All scales were found to have satisfactory fit indices with the exception of the Need Satisfaction scale whose fit indices were very poor: Sattora-Bentler χ^2 (186, N = 460) = 838.60, p <.001; SRMR =.11; CFI =.70; RMSEA =.10. Inspection of the modification indices and the standardised loadings suggested the removal of all negatively worded items. Therefore, these items (3 from each BNSC subscale) were excluded from any further analyses. The revised Need Satisfaction scale had a satisfactory model fit: Sattora Bentler χ^2(186, N = 460) = 838.60, p <.001; SRMR =.06; CFI =.93; RMSEA =.06.

Descriptive statistics and internal reliability coefficients for the 302 participants are presented in Table 5. The descriptive statistics and alphas for the full sample of 460 students were almost identical and are not presented here. According to Table 5, the participants' mean scores were slightly above the midpoint for all variables with the exception of amotivation, external regulation, introjected regulation, and negative affect: The teachers' average ratings of student effort were moderate to high. The alpha coefficients for all the subscales were satisfactory with the exception of competence need satisfaction and introjected regulation, whose reliabilities were marginal.

The intercorrelations (Table 6) among the need support factors and among the need satisfaction factors were moderate in size. Of the three need satisfaction variables, competence had in general the highest correlations with the need support factors. The three need satisfaction variables were positively correlated with self-determined motivation regulations and negatively with amotivation and external regulation. Negative affect was correlated positively with amotivation and external regulation and negatively with self-determined motivation regulations. The opposite pattern of relationships was observed between concentration, future intentions, participation status, and the motivational regulations.

Motivational model of participation in optional PE

A motivational model of participation in optional PE classes was constructed on the basis of Vallerand's model of motivation and previous work by Pelletier et al., Sarrazin et al., and Vallerand et al. The model postulated that need support by PE teachers would relate to students' satisfaction of their psychological needs, which in turn would predict self-determined motivation. The latter was hypothesised to predict positive motivational consequences, such as high levels of concentration in the class, effort (as rated by the PE teachers), and intention to participate in optional PE classes in the following school year. Positive intentions were hypothesised to predict actual behavioural decisions to participate in optional PE.

A consideration in the present study was the ratio of the number of participants per estimated parameter. According to Bentler and Chou, a ratio of 5:1 is considered as a minimum. To achieve this ratio, it was decided to collapse some scales. Following the example of Deci et al. and Gagnd, an overall need satisfaction factor was postulated underpinned by the three composite scores representing the three psychological needs. Furthermore, in the same way, an overall need support factor was created whose indicators were the three composite scores reflecting the extent to which the PE teacher supported students' autonomy, gave emphasis to individual criteria for improvement, and promoted student cooperative learning. Following the example of many previous studies an overall self-determination index was created with four indicators. Higher scores on this index reflect higher levels of self-determined motivation.

The proposed model was tested with EQS 6.1 using structural equation modeling with robust maximum likelihood estimation method. The ratio of sample size to estimated parameters was approximately 6:1 which is considered acceptable. The results of the structural equation modeling analysis revealed that the hypothesised model fit the data relatively well but there was room for improvement: Sattora-Bentler $\chi^2(204, N = 460) = 393.42$, $p < .001$; SRMR =.07; CFI =.91; RMSEA =.06.

The modification indices suggested the addition of a path from teacher ratings to participation status which seemed appropriate. Furthermore, it was suggested that covariance links should be added between the errors of autonomy support and need for autonomy, and between the errors of cooperative learning and relatedness need satisfaction. These covariations were added in the model because links between the two sets of variables have also emerged in studies by Ntoumanis and Standage et al. After implementing the changes suggested by the modification indices the model fit improved: Sattora-Bender χ^2 (201, N = 460) = 332.15, p <.001; SRMR =.07; CFI =.94; RMSEA =.05. No other changes suggested by the modification indices made theoretical sense.

An alternative model was also tested; it included autonomy support; cooperative learning; improvement; and autonomy, relatedness, and competence need satisfaction instead of the generic need support and need satisfaction factors. The model postulated a path from autonomy support to autonomy, from cooperative learning to relatedness, and from improvement to competence. The three need satisfaction factors were hypothesised to predict self-determined motivation. The ratio of participants to estimated parameters was very small (3.25:1). With the exception of the paths from autonomy and relatedness to self-determined motivation, all other paths were significant. However, the model did not fit the data well: Sattora-Bentler χ^2(768, N = 460) = 1142.61, p <.001; SRMR =.09; CFI =.88; RMSEA =.05. No changes suggested by the modification indices made theoretical sense. Therefore, the model was not explored further.

Coaching Behaviour

Sports coaches are expected to conform to ethical standards in a number of areas: humanity, relationships, commitment, co-operation, integrity, advertising, confidentiality, abuse of privilege, safety and competence.

Coaches must respect the rights, dignity and worth of every human being and their ultimate right to self-determination. Specifically, coaches must treat everyone equitably and sensitively, within the context of their activity and ability, regardless of gender, ethnic origin, cultural background, sexual orientation, religion or political affiliation.

The good coach will be concerned primarily with the well-being, safety, protection and future of the individual performer. There must be a balance between the development of performance and the social, emotional, intellectual and physical needs of the individual.

A key element in a coaching relationship is the development of independence. Performers must be encouraged and guided to accept responsibility for their own behaviour and performance in training, in competition, and in their domestic, academic or business life.

Coaches are responsible for setting and monitoring the boundaries between a working relationship and friendship with their performers. This is particularly important when the performer is a young person. The coach must realise that certain situations or friendly words and actions could be misinterpreted, not only by the performer, but also by outsiders (or other members of a squad or group of performers) motivated by jealousy, dislike or mistrust, and could lead to allegations of misconduct or impropriety. The relationship between coach and performer relies heavily on mutual trust and respect. This means that the performer should be made aware of the coach's Qualifications and experience, and must be given the opportunity to consent to or decline proposals for training, performance or competition.

Coaches should clarify in advance with performers (and/or employers) the number of sessions, fees (if any) and method of payment. They should explore with performers (and/or employers) the expectation of the outcome of coaching. Written contracts may be appropriate in some circumstances. Coaches have a responsibility to declare to their performers and/or employers any other current coaching commitments. They should also find out if any prospective client is receiving instruction from another teacher/coach. If so, the teacher/coach should be contacted to discuss the situation.

Coaches should expect a similar level of reciprocal commitment from their performers. In particular, the performer (parent/guardian in the case of a minor) should inform the coach of any change in circumstances that might affect the coach/performer relationship. Coaches should receive appropriate acknowledgment for their contribution to the performer's progress and achievement. Where money is earned from performances, it is reasonable to expect the coach should receive an appropriate share of the rewards. Such apportionment with any attendant conditions should be agreed in advance (in writing) to avoid any misunderstanding.

Coaches should communicate and co-operate with other sports and allied professions in the best interests of their performers. An example of such contact could be the seeking of:

— educational and career counselling for young performers whose involvement in sport impinges upon their studies

— sport science advice through the British Association of Sport and Exercise Sciences (BASES)

Coaches must communicate and co-operate with registered medical and ancillary practitioners in the diagnosis, treatment and management of their performers' medical and psychological problems.

Coaches must not encourage performers to violate the rules of their sport. They should actively seek to discourage and condemn such action and encourage performers to obey the spirit of the rules. Coaches must not compromise their performers by advocating measures that could constitute unfair advantage. They must not adopt practices to accelerate performance improvement that might jeopardise the safety, total well-being and future participation of the performer. Coaches must never advocate or condone the use of prohibited drugs or other banned performance enhancing substances.

Coaches must ensure that the activities, training and competition programs they advocate and direct ore appropriate for the age, maturity, experience and ability of the individual performer. Coaches must treat opponents with due respect, both in victory and defeat, and should encourage their performers to act in a similar manner. A key role for a coach is to prepare performers to respond to success and failure in a dignified manner. Coaches must accept responsibility for the conduct of their performers and discourage inappropriate behaviour in training, competition, and away from the sporting arena.

Advertising by sports coaches in respect of qualifications, training and/or services must be accurate and professionally restrained. Coaches must be able to present evidence of current qualifications upon request. Evidence should also be available to support any claim associated with the promotion of their services. Coaches must not display any affiliation with an organisation in a manner that falsely implies sponsorship or accreditation by that organisation.

Sports coaches inevitably gather a great deal of personal information about performers in the course of a working relationship. Coach and performer must reach agreement about what is to be regarded as confidential information (i.e. not divulged to a third party without the express approval of the performer). Confidentiality does not preclude the disclosure of information about a performer to persons who can be judged to have a right to know. For example:

— Evaluation for competitive selection purposes
— Recommendations for employment
— In pursuit of disciplinary action involving performers within the sport
— In pursuit of disciplinary action by a sports organisation against one of its members
— Legal and medical requirements for disclosure
— Recommendations to parents/family where the health and safety of performers might be at stake
— In pursuit of action to protect children from abuse

The sports coach is privileged to have regular contact with performers and occasionally to travel and reside with performers in the course of coaching and competitive practice. A coach must not attempt to exert undue influence over the performer in order to obtain personal benefit or reward. Coaches must consistently display high personal standards and project a favorable image of their sport and of coaching to performers, their parents/families, other coaches, officials, spectators, the media and the public.

Personal appearance is a matter of individual taste but the sports coach has an obligation to project an image of health, cleanliness and functional efficiency. Sports coaches should never smoke while coaching. Coaches should not drink alcohol so soon before coaching that it would affect their competence to coach, compromise the safety of the performers or obviously indicate they had been drinking (e.g. smell of alcohol on breath).

Within the limits of their control, coaches have a responsibility to ensure as for as possible the safety of the performers with whom they work All reasonable steps should be taken to establish a safe working environment. The work done and the manner in which it is done should be in keeping with the regular and approved practice with their sport as determined by the NGB.

The activity undertaken should be suitable for the age, physical and emotional maturity, experience and ability of the performers. Coaches have a duty to protect children from harm and abuse. The performers should have been systematically prepared for the activity and made aware of their personal responsibilities in terms of safety. Coaches should arrange adequate insurance to cover all aspects of their coaching practice.

Coaches shall confine themselves to practice in those elements of sport for which their training and competence is recognised by the appropriate NGB. Training includes the accumulation of knowledge and skills through formal coach education courses, independent research and the accumulation of relevant verifiable experience.

The National Occupational Standards for Coaching, Teaching and Instructing (and/or the approved NGB coaching awards) provide the framework for assessing competence at the different levels of coaching practice. Competence to coach should normally be verified through evidence of qualifications. Competence cannot be inferred solely from evidence of prior experience.

Coaches must be able to recognise and accept when to refer performers to other coaches or agencies. It is their responsibility, as for as possible, to verify the competence and integrity of any other person to whom they refer a performer. Coaches should regularly seek ways of increasing their personal and professional development.

Coaches should welcome evaluation of their work by colleagues and be able to account to performers, employers, NGBs and colleagues for what they do and why. Coaches have a responsibility to themselves and their performers to maintain their own effectiveness, resilience and abilities. They should recognise when their personal resources are so depleted that help is needed. This may necessitate the withdrawal from coaching temporarily or permanently.

6

Psychological Side of Injury

Some of the injuries were explainable. These injuries were unpredictable and could happen to anyone at any time. In order to ensure that they were, however, we needed to talk about injuries in general and how to deal with them. If these athletes were injured, it would not be the last time they would be, so the sooner they learned the lessons on how to deal with injuries the sooner they would learn how to cope, recover and get back running in the fastest time possible.

How do Athletes Deal with Injury

An injury can be a traumatic experience for some runners. Some runners because each runner has a unique personality and because of that will deal with an injury in his or her own unique way. For athletes who are open to accepting an injury and sincerely want to get better and return to running there are some guiding principles to consider and should be tried when dealing with an injury. If an athlete is not currently injured, they should keep these principles in mind for the future in case he or she is ever faced with one.

An athletic injury is on a smaller scale similar to the process of dealing with a death, or a significant loss. That is because as athletes our training schedule, our competitions, our training group and our coaches shape our very existence. It is a significant and important part of our lives. When this is taken away all of a sudden, many athletes cannot cope and deny that there is anything wrong. The emphasis on certain important competitions, or goals that have been set are so powerful as to cause the athlete to think they have to keep going and push through the injury. This only makes things worse of course.

Emotional Phases of Injury

As in death there are 5 phases that an individual will normally go through until the injury is accepted and corrective action can take place:

1. Denial and isolation - the refusal to recognise the injury, and the difficulty of not being able to talk about it to anyone or to reject advice given. The athlete feels alone in his or her struggle.
2. The second stage is anger, where the athlete feels a need to punish, to get even, to make others hurt as much as he or she does, all of the punitive kinds of reactions are present.
3. The third stage is bargaining - "I will do anything to get to Toronto"; "Please let me run, I do not want to let the school team down".
4. The fourth stage is depression - the "all is lost" stage, when the feelings of loss and gain are confused. The past looks good and the future cannot be tolerated. The hurt is intolerable so that the world looks lonely and desolate. "I will miss the competition" - "I will be left behind", "I will never get back in shape". There is nothing to look forward to, this is a bleak stage indeed, but it is a stage.
5. The final stage is acceptance, which is one of facing the reality of the situation - being willing to deal

with this reality, moving on to the future, and making a plan to get better and sticking with it until the injury is healed.

Manage the Emotional as well as the Physical Issues

An injured athlete may spend considerable time in each of the 5 phases or minimal in each one. It depends on the maturity, and sensibility of the individual. In our sport we are faced with a 10 year, 10,000 hours of dedicated practice, development program. So an injury early on is not going to have much affect on performances 10 years down the road.

There is plenty of time to recover and carry on and be a very successful athlete. So the trick is for the athlete to understand what he or she will go through with an injury and to come to acceptance as quickly as possible. Then work with the coaches on dealing with both the psychological and physical issues involved with getting over the injury. By being aware that athletes having these feelings of denial, depression, anger, etc. helps considerably in the process.

The feelings are very normal and not to be feared or ignored. By dealing with emotions, using common sense and really wanting to heal an injury, even in the event of an upcoming major competition, the athlete will recover much quicker and be back in action doing what he or she loves and enjoys. Makes sense to me. Hope all athletes dealing with injuries see it the same way.

Wishing yourself a Speedy Recovery

It is a fact of sports, competitive or not, that sportspeople get injured. Traditional medicine recommends rest and relaxation with gentle exercise during the recovery process, and this is sometimes a difficult regime to stick with. It is clearly important to speed the recovery process as much as possible, and the evidence drawn on above suggests that hypnosis may be utilised as part of treatment during a recovery period.

Underlying psychological Sauses

Sports injuries are generally physical in nature; most do not have an underlying psychological cause. Hypnosis and has been shown to be of value in the treatment of asthmatics and is often employed in dealing with so-called psychosomatic illness. Physical symptoms of illness and injury sometimes have an underlying psychological cause. This underlying issue usually has a positive intention, known as secondary gain. This can be seen, for example, in cases in which pain recurs predictably before competition or in stressful situations. The mind has a way of protecting us from things that it thinks may not be beneficial, and often pain is a positive message of warning from our unconscious.

Physiologically the pain seemed to be caused when exercise caused the muscle to expand beyond the capacity of the muscle compartment. However the pain did not occur every time he exercised the leg, this pointed to an underlying psychological cause. Under hypnosis the athlete revealed that there was an event in their past that seemed to seed times when there was an onset of the pain. Specifically the pain seemed to occur when he believed that someone was outperforming him. The secondary gain here is that the pain gives the athlete an excuse for not performing as well as his competitor.

There are a number of ways of resolving problems with secondary gain. It is essential first of all to recognise the intention as valuable and positive, and perhaps then to look for other ways of achieving the same result without the symptom of pain. Liggett, in this case, installed a post hypnotic suggestion that the athlete would make comparisons with his own past performances, rather than with other peoples, in future. This reduced the psychological element of his pain, and although the physiological aspect was still present the intensity of the pain reduced to a level that no longer impeded his performance.

As well as addressing the psychological aspects of injury, the power of the mind can be brought in to play in the healing process itself. The body has a remarkable capacity to heal itself, as it demonstrates in the rapid healing of a deep cut, a broken bone or a torn ligament. The role of the mind in this process is still very much debated.

Conceptualising the Body-Mind

When we learn a skill and perform it perfectly, is it our body or is it our mind that is responsible for this perfect performance? Our body is extremely capable, it can jump, sprint, run, swim; our mind is also extremely capable, it can read, learn, absorb. When you are driving a car and you get a while down the road and you cannot remember how you got there, or when you are pole vaulting or making a perfect pass and you are not focussing on every little detail, is it your mind or your body that is taking control of your automatic processes? Our fascination with distinctions between mind and body stems back at least as far as the philosopher Descartes who showed quite convincingly that since he thought, he must exist who knows? No matter, never mind. Since then philosophers, psychologists, neuroscientists and others, in the western world at least, have been obsessed with charting the functions of the mind and the body as separate entities.

Doing this creates a few problems. For example how do you explain the ways in which the mind and the body communicate? The eyes take in light reflected off of an object, the rods and cones at the back of the eye translates this into electro-chemical signals which activate a part of the brain, and this makes us think of the colour red. How? How are the mind and body connected?

Explaining this is not an issue in cultures with beliefs outside of the western medical tradition. People who have strong beliefs in the power of Shamanism, Tai Chi, Acupressure, Yoga etc. talk of the body-mind as one entity, and they have no problems in modelling the way in which the body-mind functions, heals, evolves. Deepak Chopra posits that it is through the endocrine system and neuropeptides that the body and the mind meet and shows compellingly how appropriate channelling can lead to spontaneous cures for desires such as cancer and diabetes.

We do not necessarily have to turn to Aruyvedic meditation or Chi Gung to explore ways of mind-body healing. A fascinating study demonstrated the benefit of hypnosis in bone healing. In a group of people with fractures they showed a significant increase in speed of both anatomical and functional fracture healing over a control group with similar injuries. Sunnen gives an outline of the ways in which hypnosis can be used in both the physical and mental aspects of cancer care. It is clear then that there is a good deal of evidence that the body-mind has the ability to heal itself. There are a number of models of how it does this, and a variety of approaches, self and hetero-hypnosis is one method of accessing the body-mind directly and accelerating the healing process.

Accelerating the Physical Healing Process

In many cases it seems to be sufficient to have a positive attitude, it has often been noted that those most likely to recover from serious injury need to first feel that they can. Not only did this dancer recover but actually improved and reached an extremely high standard, such that a one act ballet was created with him in mind as the principal ballerina. Research, anecdote and experience point to a few key things that can be done to speed up the healing process:

— The first is to recognise that there may be a psychological aspect to the pain or slow recovery rate. Identifying and dealing with the secondary gain is essential in the recovery process

— Secondly it is important to be positive about the powers of the body-mind to self heal. Rather than suggesting that the injury may heal, you need to suggest that it will heal, better than before, and rapidly

— Thirdly self or hetero-hypnosis can be used to reduce stress and induce relaxation. Positive self healing suggestions can be most effectively made under hypnosis

— Finally the use of guided imagery and metaphor has been shown to be extremely successful

A powerful metaphor that have used successfully in dealing with injuries is to visualise the affected part and associate it with a colour. Usually things in the body come in pairs visualising the healthy part would usually give a different colour, the colour of "healthy and healed". The final part of this self-healing process is to enter a meditative or hypnotic state and to visualise some mechanism of re-colouring the injured part with the healthy colour. This could be through imagining a spray gun or a paintbrush for example.

Repeating the healing metaphor over a period of time, and having a positive attitude, will, in my experience, speed up the recovery process. Whatever the mechanism, it is clear that hypnosis is a powerful addition to the more traditional approaches to healing, and deserves to be explored and utilised much more.

Minding the Injury

Every athlete, regardless of his or her skill level, will go through a grieving process after incurring an injury - without exception. In 1969, Kubler-Ross first outlined the stages of grief a person goes through when facing a serious or career ending injury, death or serious disease prognosis. An understanding of the four stages of managing grief: denial, anger, depression and acceptance will help you in supporting the athlete through them.

Denial

At the beginning, the athlete cannot believe the injury is severe or that it will impact their ability to continue with their sport. They may still believe in the myth that "no pain means no gain". If so, they have been living under a rock for quite some time. Pain is an indicator that something has gone wrong and needs immediate attention. The realisation that the pain is stopping them from participating leads to the next stage.

Anger

Denial quickly turns to anger as the reality of the situation settles in and the athlete is forced by the circumstances to alter or even stop their participation in their sport. Recovery is often not an easy path and the athlete becomes frustrated and more irritated with the pace of the rehabilitation process. At this point, the coach is in an ideal position to be a sounding board for the athlete's exasperation, and help ease their aggressiveness toward the athletic trainers who are trying to get them back in shape. Realising the athlete is angry at their loss of ability to perform, their loss of power over what has happened to them and the current situation they now find themselves in are important points to keep in mind while dealing with the individual.

Depression

Self worth becomes an issue at this point in the process and depression sets in due to the reality of the situation now being fully realised. The athlete begins to feel as though he or she has no physical or emotional control. The team continues onward without them, which leaves a void in their life and this leads to feelings of isolation, further self-doubt and lowering of their self-esteem. Hope for a successful outcome becomes cloudy and they may not see any good coming from the rehabilitation process.

You as the coach will have the most difficult time during this stage as the athlete may stop going to rehab, to team practices or even talking to you. You must continue talking to them by providing encouragement. Explain to them the progress they have made and keep them engaged in their recovery. Once they have completed the journey through this stage, they enter the final one, acceptance and recovery begins in earnest.

Acceptance

Acceptance of the full enormity of the circumstances they find themselves in begins the physical and emotional healing process. Once this stage is entered an attitude change is noticed and the real work towards full recovery begins.

Not one of the four stages of grief will be lit up with flashing lights and banners waving in the air. They are gradual movements into and through each one. There may even be periodic lapses back and forth into previous stages. So expect these setbacks. In many cases, they are only temporary. However, if extremes in mood are continuous and seem to remain locked into one part of the process it is incumbent upon you as their coach to recommend they seek additional professional assistance in managing the problem.

In each instance recognition of the particular stage of grief is a key factor in providing assistance toward the full recovery of their athletic prowess. Effective communication by the coach, providing education as to what is happening to their body, supporting the recover and cooperatively setting goals will help ensure positive progress is made after the injury.

So how do you go about this important task?

Here are a few suggestions to follow. Bear in mind this is not about counselling, these are simply suggestions that may provide you with a little extra information to help get over the rough spots. In most cases, we are not trained mental health counsellors or athletic trainers so act with common sense and do not go beyond your educational training specialty. Remember the axiom of 'Do no harm'.

Communication skills are vital throughout the rehabilitation process and being a good and active listener will aid you and your athlete tremendously. Actively engaging in the conversation by rephrasing their uncertainties about the future, their worries, and goals into your own words demonstrates you are interested in their concerns and more importantly have heard what the athlete is saying to you.

Maintaining eye contact is a simple part of good communications and should be used whenever speaking to someone, regardless of the situation. Providing an environment that is conducive to communications by ensuring privacy, low noise and no interruptions is essential. Place the phone on the answering service, turn your computer to energy save mode, and put a note on the door announcing that you are not to be interrupted.

Once in an environment that supports open communication, use good judgment in what you say to the injured athlete. Being timely, i.e. are they ready to receive the information about the injury, can be of importance depending on their state of mind. That is where knowledge of the stages of grief enters into the picture.

Communication includes both oral and written information and instructions for the management of the rehabilitation process. Encouragement for their efforts indicates your attentiveness and concern for their well-being and successful return to the sport.

Setting goals with the athlete is also important in the recovery process as it gives them a buy in to the program. They now have control over their future and a mutual understanding of the importance of how these goals fit into the large scheme of the training.

Coach and athlete should have the same goals, if not the coach will have to reach a consensus on them in order to proceed or failure will result. Monitoring of the goals and recording progress at each stage of the training is a roadmap that can be referred to as the journey continues. Each objective reached along the way is positive reinforcement that the program is working and that progress is being made by the athlete. Support throughout the entire rehabilitation period comes from a variety of sources, family, friends, team-mates, church, athlete training partners and you, their coach. Positive comments about the progress and the recovery will help the athlete reach their goals faster.

Finally

Designing an interesting but challenging program is in the best interest of the athlete. If it is boring, no matter how good it may be compliance will surely be lacking. This is where the athlete and you have to be together on what is best for their safe return. Every athlete has their favourite exercises so include them in the training schedule. Follow these suggestions and it will not be long before you have a healthy athlete back on the field again.

Mind over Injury

Physical factors involved in injury prevention are becoming increasingly well characterised as the process of fitness improvement and skills development becomes better understood. However, looked at the prediction and prevention of injury from a psychological approach and found from a study of 470 rugby players that social support; type of coping and previous injury all interacted to maximise the effect of life stress and injury. The second part of the study looked at stress management strategies as an intervention to reducing injury among players identified in the first part as having an 'at-risk' psychological profile for injury - numbering 48 in total. The experiment ran for a whole season with half of this number randomly assigned to a control group. The outcome from those in the intervention group was a significant reduction in lost time due to injury and a reduction in worry.

Time of Training Relates to Time of Performance

Researchers looked at the effect of time of training on time of competition by preparing a group of 8 cyclists in two different ways for a 16.1km time trial started at 07:00hrs. In time trial 1 the cyclists underwent a 30min sub-maximal session at 60% VO2peak at 07:00hrs and in time trial 2 at 12:00hrs the day before separate time trials. The outcome was that time trial 1 was completed in 1672+/- 135s while time trial 2 in 1706 +/- 159s.

The physical / physiological data from the quicker time trials following the 07:00 previous day preparation outing showed elevated work-rates, lactate accumulation and heart rate relative to the time trial completed after the 12:00hrs previous day outing. These data suggest that performing exercise at the same time in the day(s) before competition benefit the cyclist. Only one point appears unclear from the paper in relation to the recovery period following the 12:00hrs outing - this was 18.5hrs rather than 23.5 hrs before the 07:00 time trial. Could the shorter recovery have been a contributing factor to the slower time trial?

Cycling is Best for Anaerobic Capacity Assessment

Comparing and contrasting the effectiveness of laboratory measurements provides potentially useful information. A study that compared treadmill running to cycle ergometry for estimations of anaerobic capacity (AC) was based on the examination of 10 untrained, 10 aerobic-trained and 10 anaerobic-trained (400m sprinters). The tests comprised measurement of VO2max, individual aerobic threshold (IAT) to determine aerobic power and finally from a series of sprints at increasing speeds the work output was calculated. The results indicated absolute values of AC below those measured by cycle ergometry and it was proposed that a factor not taken account of was the horizontal work done while running on a treadmill. Also a factor could be the duration of each sprint test. Finally, the critical velocity was higher than the IAT that must therefore lead to an underestimation of the AC value. The treadmill test allowed for differentiation between the groups but does not assign correct AC values.

Men and Women are Different!

An interesting paper continued the theme that was raised last month on different responses to exercise between male and female athletes. The study used two different running tests - firstly - graded exercise to exhaustion to determine maximal aerobic flow, velocity at lactate threshold and velocity at the half way point between these two measures and, secondly - a constant all out run at the delta 50 to determine time to exhaustion at this intensity. 8 male and 8 female middle distance endurance-trained athletes participated in the tests. The outcome was that the female athletes all perceived exercise as being harder, felt they could endure less and had higher heart rate values than males for a given absolute velocity whereas there were no differences for a given relative velocity.Interestingly female athletes perceived exercise as lighter and felt that they could endure more than the males for a given absolute time period whereas at a percentage time relative to the final time of exhaustion there was no difference.

Aerobics Energy System

A number of papers have been reviewed in general physiology in relation to oxygen consumption and recovery. The first looked at a group of competitive collegiate level footballers and the impact of pre-season training and in-season adaptations based on the Wingate test and other appropriate measurements before and during the season. The authors conclude that no change in power performance measures were observed at any time whereas the extent of muscle de-oxygenation between the start of the season and 11 weeks into the season was measurably reduced during intense exercise and that oxygen recovery kinetics improve dramatically during the competitive season - meaning shorter rest spells were necessary.

A study of cyclists indicates that this type of improvement may be largely attributable to adaptations in the peripheral circuit rather than to central adaptations following intensive exercise bouts in well-trained endurance athletes. To help identify appropriate test measurements to support such aerobic development a paper found that in general sub-maximal indices of aerobic fitness including oxygen uptake and power output are more useful measures of actual cycling performance than VO2max and peak power output.

Recovery and Fatigue in Power Workouts

Moving away from exercise predominantly involving the aerobic energy system researchers have looked at factors affecting fatigue and the recovery of power. The study used a group of 13 men performing isotonic knee extensions at the fastest rate they could until velocity reduced by 35%. In this time power was reduced by 42% and maximum voluntary contraction (MVC) by 26%. Power recovered by 5 minutes whereas MVC only recovered to 85% of baseline even after 10 minutes rest. Peripheral factors were again concluded to be the limiting factor. The implication of this information on planning a power training session are interesting since although potentially useful power work can be performed maximally after 5 minutes recovery the ability to express MVC will be depressed for longer.

Shoe technology better than nature?

One or two middle distance and endurance runners spring to mind when barefoot running is mentioned. A recent study looked at the mechanical comparison of barefoot versus shoe running. The primary findings based on a study of 35 subjects running for 4 minutes at 3.33m/s (or around 8 minutes / mile) were that barefoot running reduces contact and flight time as well as attenuating impact peak force. Barefoot running at this pace also lead to higher breaking forces and pushing impulses - perhaps not as energy efficient at this pace as when running in appropriate running shoes.

Nutrition Cornucopia

Fuelling the system is critical to support all long-term training and so a study of eating disorders and risk factors in 283 elite Spanish female athletes provides extremely useful and meaningful information. Taken from 20 different sports the athletes were questioned with various well-accepted methods to establish that the proportion suffering from some form of eating disorder was 5-times that of the general population. Key factors identified included exposure of body form in public as a general factor and specifically pressure from coaches seems to be a risk factor for bulimia.

Looking at an array of recent papers on specific dietary components or supplements revealed a whole series of interesting evidence: The first paper sought to establish a relationship between controlled caffeine consumption at different levels and hydration levels on the basis that caffeine is touted as a diuretic that may impair performance. The study could find no evidence that caffeine acts chronically as a diuretic.

The next looked at glucose feeding during endurance cycling and confirmed that over a 75 minute ride at 80% VO2max that glucose ingestion during exercise can spare endogenous protein and carbohydrate, in fed cyclists, without glycogen depletion. Clearly this would ultimately allow the cyclist to continue for longer at this intensity.

Vitamin C supplementation was shown to attenuate exercise induced protein oxidation in a manner proportional to dose. Sparing protein oxidation may be beneficial to endurance athletes - the truth behind the legend as to why some east African endurance athletes are believed to consume large quantities of oranges prior to training bouts and why oranges are also a favourite half-time food for soccer players?

Specific supplementation with L-carnitine receives massive promotion in the gym environment promising to do everything for you except perhaps your training sessions. Much of its claimed physiological benefit seems to centre on enhancement of fat burning. A recent paper that looked at combining L-carnitine with L-tartrate actually found no impact on fat burning whatsoever but did appear to increase carbohydrate oxidation in males but not significantly in females.

Amino Acids - Vital to Life and Performance

Finally, two massively informative review papers have appeared from different groups looking at dietary supplementation with minerals and their effect on sports performance and a second on nutrient administration and resistance training. In this issue we will focus on the latter and cover the former next month. Resistance training clearly acts to improve hypertrophy (build muscle) and to increase muscle strength and ultimately, with correct practice, enhance power and explosivity. The study has reviewed the literature with a clear emphasis on amino acid supplementation and has produced a proposal for a series of guidelines as follows:

— Resistance training modestly stimulates protein synthesis and further stimulates protein breakdown resulting an overall negative protein balance after exercise

— As the training status of an individual progresses, the magnitude of changes seen in protein synthesis and breakdown diminishes after each exercise bout as well as a diminished increase of protein synthesis after each subsequent exercise bout

— Infusion or ingestion of amino acids is an effective way to increase amino acid concentrations at rest or after resistance exercise

— Availability of amino acids after resistance exercise increases protein synthesis

— Essential amino acids do appear to play a primary role in protein synthesis and adding carbohydrate to them may enhance this effect

— Ingestion of carbohydrate alone after resistance exercise causes marginal improvements in overall protein synthesis while maintaining a negative net protein balance. No studies have found carbohydrate to be detrimental and it may be useful to enhance palatability; however the additional caloric burden may not be desired

— A small dose of essential amino acids after resistance exercise has been found to stimulate protein synthesis to a similar degree when compared to studies that used much larger doses of both amino acids (EAA, NEAA, or both) or that were combined with carbohydrate

— Ingestion of amino acids after resistance exercise has been shown at many different time points in several studies to stimulate increases in muscle protein synthesis, time points in several studies to stimulate increases in muscle protein synthesis, cause minimal changes in protein breakdown and increase overall protein balance. It has not been conclusively determined what time point is optimal. Similar changes have been found for studies that have administered amino acids alone or with carbohydrate immediately upon completion of an acute exercise bout, 1 hour after completion, 2 hours after completion and 3 hours after completion. Interestingly, ingesting nutrients before the exercise bout may have the most benefit of all the time points

— It is possible for the mechanisms involving amino acid transport and protein synthesis to be overwhelmed with extremely high, continuous levels of amino acids. The likelihood of this occurring is rare even upon considering the highest of protein intakes among individuals

— An optimal dosage in which to ingest amino acids at this time does not exist. Studies using similar techniques while resistance training have used 6g EAA only, 6g EAA + 6g NEAA, 12g EAA only, 17.5g whey protein, 20g casein protein, 20g whey protein, 40g mixed amino acid, 40g EAA only all with similar increases in protein synthesis and protein balance. Athletes who desire to increase muscle mass or are involved in power sports should consider consuming protein supplements that will provide amino acids in similar amounts used in these studies

— Intact proteins or combinations of them that are commonly used in popular protein supplements appear to elicit similar increases in protein balance after resistance training as compared to other studies using free amino acids.

From these primary findings, it is hoped that athletes, coaches, nutritionists and researchers will be able to provide clearer advice and recommendations when consulting themselves, their players, clients, or research participants in regards to optimal administration of nutrients while participating in a resistance training program.

7

Stress and Sports Injury Rehabilitation

Physical factors are obviously the primary cause of injuries in sports and exercise for instance, a poor tackle in football, an awkward landing in gymnastics or poor warm-ups in sprinting. However, psychological researchers are continuing to show that thoughts, perceptions and aspects of personality may be linked to the incidence of injury.

Stress and Athletic Injury

Past research has seen the relationship between athletic injuries and psychological factors as essentially stress-related. In this sense, stress is predicted to produce increased state anxiety and consequently alterations in attentional focus and muscular tension. It is important to note that stress does not exist outside the individual not all people respond negatively to potentially stressful situations; one person may view a championship match as exciting and exhilarating while another becomes anxious and chokes. This will usually depend on the individual's personality traits and the coping response present.

In situations seen as stressful, athletes will often report attentional narrowing and excessive muscular tension, which are thought to increase the chances of sustaining an injury. Having a flexible attentional focus is an important attribute in many fast sporting activities that require both narrow and broad focus at different times during play.

Stress can cause attentional narrowing which results in important peripheral cues being missed. For example, the football player that only attends to the ball may fail to withdraw from an unrealistic challenge (rather than stay on his feet) in which his opponent is obviously going to meet the ball first. This can result in a late tackle and/or injury. A significant body of past evidence also supports the notion that stress can cause increased muscular tension, which disrupts coordination and increases the risk of injury. A figure-skater who becomes tense during a difficult routine might lack coordination due to muscular tension and fall, injuring an ankle.

Threatening Situations

One important model that highlighted the stress-injury relationship cited both situational factors (i.e. importance of situation) and personal characteristics (i.e. personality traits) as important determinants of outcome. This model cited the interaction between factors as crucial and provided an impetus for future research. An athlete who tends to view situations as threatening (high trait anxiety), who has a history of life stressors (major life-changing events and daily hassles) and has poor coping resources (lacks social support, etc.) is considered to be more likely to experience a negative stress response and consequently is more prone to athletic injury. Although the relationship between stress and injury is complex, one say that used a large sample size 452 athletes showed that as predicted, athletes with more life stress, little social support and poor coping skills were associated with more days of non-participation due to athletic injury.

Personality Research

Some researchers are quick to associate personality traits with athletic injury. In general, research concerning the measurement of personality in the sport and exercise field has been controversial, plagued by inappropriate and inconsistent methodologies and grossly over-generalised application of results.

Unfortunately, many psychologists have adopted one of two bi-polar stances that either ascribe great significance to the role of personality or virtually no significance at all. Many contemporary researchers, however, are beginning to take the middle ground and suggest that the truth lies somewhere between these two polarised positions. Despite this, the research findings to date are difficult to interpret due to inconsistencies, with the relationship between personality and injury remaining unclear. It would seem unlikely that a personality profile that characterises 'injury-prone' athletes actually exists, although some studies have identified patterns/trends that appear to warrant further investigation.

One recent study identified injured college gymnasts as possessing emotional instability, emotional disturbance, stress proneness and lack of self-control. This finding appears to support the stress-injury model previously discussed. Other research has shown a readiness to take risks as characteristic of injured athletes, although this is not sufficient to establish a causal relationship between such traits and injury. The relationship between personality and injury should be viewed with caution. Some recent reviewers emphasise that personality characteristics appear to either buffer or exacerbate the stress response which is proposed to be the mechanism linked to injury. If personality is linked to injury it is likely through indirect means.

Attitudes and Injury

In work with injured athletes, some sport and exercise psychologists have proposed that certain attitudes might predispose athletes to injury. According to this research, the attitudes that coaches often try to instil in their athletes can actually backfire with regard to injury risks. For example, the 'no pain, no gain', and 'give 110%' attitudes might unwittingly lead to athletes taking undue risks. In many sports, participants need to be assertive and play hard, but within safe limits, employing appropriate techniques and strategies. This doesn't just apply to contact sports since many other exercisers attempt to go through the pain barrier and as a result suffer overuse injuries or over-train.

Weinberg and Gould perfectly illustrates why giving 110% does not always produce the best performances. The study concerned 400m runners who were first asked to run all-out during a timed trial (giving 110% effort). A few days later the same runners were asked to complete a second run, this time at 95% of their capacity. Interestingly, runners' times were quickest in the 95% effort. The result was due to increased muscular tensions in attempting to run beyond capacity which interfered with the necessary relaxed coordination of working muscles.

A second identified attitude associated with injury is the notion of 'worthlessness'. When an athlete sustains a minor injury that requires both treatment and rest, he/she may feel 'worthless' from not being able to contribute to winning. If the coach reinforces this feeling by unconsciously conveying the wrong message, the performer might easily decide to play through the injury to remain part of the team. There are times when the coach must insist on the player receiving treatment and sitting-out the competition for the benefit of all concerned. In such cases the coach can reassure the player that his/her contribution to the team will be greater with early treatment and quick recovery rather than with more lengthy rehabilitation periods caused by playing on through injury. Coping with stress

The most consistent psychological factor related to injury seems to be stress. It therefore follows that the ability to cope with stress can act as an essential buffer to reduce the likelihood of injury. Although the causes of stress can reside both inside and outside the sporting arena, and the coping mechanisms used by athletes appear to vary considerably, one of the fundamental and simplest buffers to stress appears to be social support from significant others. This can mean numerous sources such as coach, parents, partners, sport psychologist, etc. and can involve a variety of different approaches from formal counselling to simply being there to listen.

An in-depth review of coping and exploration of coping responses is beyond the scope of this article, but such approaches as stress-inoculation training, cognitive affective stress management, and systematic desensitisation, employing such applied techniques as progressive muscular relaxation, meditative relaxation, and cognitive restructuring are commonly cited in applied sport psychology texts. However, there are some simple approaches that can help athletes deal with stress at the competition site itself.

The actions and behaviour of coaches can psychologically impact on athletes so try to maintain consistent behaviour. The coach can actually transfer tension and nervousness to the athlete by behaving differently than when in practice situations.

The coach should try to help athletes embrace the challenge and see pressure situations as exciting and a chance to excel, rather than fearing the consequences of poor performance. To this end, it is important to promote focusing on the present and on what needs to be done (being instructional, not emotional) rather than on past events or on worrying about what might happen in the future the 'what if...' scenario.

Setting-up simulated practice situations that incorporate pressure is a good way of familiarising the athlete with likely competitive conditions. Also, plan in advance the strategies and tactics to be employed as this can help reduce the uncertainty which is often a root cause of anxiety. When athletes feel stressed they often rush their actions. Try to encourage them to take their time. It is good to practise simple activities such as breathing control as a means of refocusing on the task in hand and remaining calm during breaks in play.

Physchology of Sports Injury

Should distance runners concentrate on their bodily sensations, or try to think of something else? Distance runners and their coaches recognise the importance of developing an aerobic base and then implementing progressive overload training in 'safe doses' in order to allow the necessary adaptations to occur. Those working in sports medicine, however, acknowledge that problems can arise when the overload principle is applied too rapidly and the loads exceed the athletes' capabilities. This might include overtraining and running too many miles per week, or too much work conducted on hard surfaces. These precursors to injury are quite obvious, although when athletes become so focused on their goals the path towards injury may only be retrospectively recognised.

Which is better, association or dissociation?

A groundbreaking American study of elite and college distance runners that was mainly concerned with the psychological profiles of athletes triggered a great deal of research by sport and exercise psychologists. This happened because of the different types of attentional strategy used by the two groups. The elite runners tended to use a strategy called association, which involves monitoring sensory inputs and focusing attention internally on bodily sensations such as muscular strain, breathing, etc. in order to set an appropriate pace and potentially avoid pain.

In contrast, the non-elite runners were more likely to try to direct attention away from bodily physiological signals by distracting themselves. Although many different dissociation strategies exist, the idea is essentially to shift attentional focus from an internal to an external perspective, although internal dissociation can occur. For example, an athlete may complete a training run while listening to music on a personal stereo system. The music can capture attention and help distract it from inner feelings, such as pain and discomfort.

Following the initial research findings, psychologists have spent many hours attempting to discover if association is indeed related to higher levels of performance, and as such is a better strategy for distance runners to use. Although research results have been mixed, the current general consensus is that:

1. Association is related to faster running times than dissociation;
2. Regardless of level of performance, it appears that runners use more association in competition and dissociation in training and
3. Elite runners seem to have flexible attentional strategies that allow them to change focus during races as required.

Dissociation, Pain and Injury

Considerable evidence exists to link dissociation strategies with increased pain tolerance during endurance tasks. Essentially, theorists suggest that by attending to an external stimulus, our limited attentional channels become flooded with this information and consequently physiological sensations can be blocked-out temporarily. In support of this, many experimental studies that have asked participants for their ratings of perceived exertion during sub-maximal exercise trials have shown that, at given intensities, lower ratings are found when participants dissociate. However, since dissociation apparently involves blocking-out potentially important warning signals (physical pain) some researchers have suggested it is a risky strategy that could increase the chances of sustaining an injury. In one study say that a runner who had sustained fractures to both fibulas and subsequently suggested that this could have been avoided if the athlete had not tried to dissociate from the pain. Unfortunately, such speculation does little to advance our scientific understanding of any relationship between dissociation and injury.

Although relatively few research studies have been conducted, there is little support for the notion that dissociation is related to injury. One study found that dissociation scores in both marathon runs and in training did not correlate with history of running-related injuries. In contrast to expectations, four marathon runners who stopped running during the race due to injury were actually using association in the miles immediately prior to getting hurt. In two follow-up investigations no relationship was found between injury rate and dissociation strategies, although injury prevalence was greater in those who ran more races and were more competitive.

Motivation rather than pain relief

Some elite runners do appear to use dissociation some of the time, but current research involving marathon runners suggests this is safe and unrelated to injury. It has been argued that the type of cognitive strategy used has little to do with pain relief and is more closely linked to motivation. Take the example of elite marathon runners who apparently use more association in competitive runs rather than in training. In competition, runners will be pushing themselves towards the upper limits of endurance and are more likely to experience pain. If dissociation is used for pain relief and blocking-out aversive stimuli, one might have expected greater use of this strategy in competitions, but the opposite appears to be true. In fact, evidence suggests that dissociation is a limited pain reliever that is most effective in mild and moderately painful situations. It seems that when physiological inputs begin to increase towards higher intensities, they demand attention and cause a shift from an external to an internal perspective. Simply stated, although you may temporarily 'switch-off' from pain, as soon as it exceeds a specific threshold dissociation strategies are no use.

Association, pain and injury

Careful examination of early research suggests that elite marathon runners were well aware of the pain (in fact they associated to it) but chose to continue running. This may well be competitiveness but, interestingly, it has been implicated in relation to injury. Perhaps of greatest significance is one study that assessed attentional strategy and then evaluated its relation to injury after a four-month period. Importantly, after controlling for running addiction, competitive and goal-oriented motivation, history of injury, miles and days of running per week, and number of races and marathons, association still predicted injury while dissociation was unrelated. Runners may use associative strategies by redefining incoming physiological inputs as a coping strategy, expecting the sensations and focusing on the actual sensations (stripping away emotional content) which can render the state less aversive. This tough-minded approach can allow the runner to continue through pain but the drawback would appear to be increased risk of injury. This finding bolsters previous research that has also linked association with injury rates.

Psychological Rehabilitation Techniques

Although the process of rehabilitation has traditionally been viewed as 'physical' in nature, it is now considered a multi-faceted process involving not only the services of surgeons and physiotherapists but also exercise scientists, dieticians, athletic coaches and sport psychologists.

Over the last decade, researchers have become increasingly interested in the psychological impact of injury and how athletes react to being hurt. This has spawned an advancement of knowledge about the psychological adjustments made by athletes during times of injury, and the subsequent impact of these on mental state and adherence to rehabilitation programmes. Although ideally the psychological support of injured athletes should be provided by psychology professionals, in practice it is very often administered informally by physiotherapists. Although physiotherapists generally consider psychological components of injury as important, recent research suggests that most feel limited in their abilities to deal with these concepts and consider additional training as necessary. Further, a related study of patient perspectives indicated that injured athletes felt that physiotherapists and other members of the healthcare team had not consciously considered the emotional impact of their injuries.

With serious injuries that are likely to result in a significant period of time out of the sport, athletes will often experience emotional disturbances. Researchers suggest that athletes often follow a five-stage process following injury:

— Denial;

— Anger;

— Bargaining;

— Depression;

— Acceptance and reorganisation.

After the initial shock is over, many athletes tend to play down the significance of the injury. However, as the injury becomes more apparent, shock is often replaced by anger directed internally toward themselves or externally towards other people. The responses can vary in intensity depending on situational and personal factors but can be especially strong in individuals whose self-concept and personal identity are based on being 'an athlete'. The loss of identity due to an inability to perform can cause much distress.

Following anger, the injured athlete might try bargaining/ rationalising to avoid the reality of the situation. A runner may promise herself to train extra hard or to be especially pleasant to those around her if she can recover quickly. By confronting reality, and cognitively realising the consequences of the injury, an athlete can become depressed at the uncertainty of the future. It must be noted, however, that depression is not inevitable and has not always been observed during the grief reaction in research studies.

Finally, the athlete moves towards an acceptance of the injury and focus is directed to rehabilitation and a return to sports activity. This stage tends to mark the transition from an emotional to a problem-coping focus as the athlete realises what needs to be done to aid recovery. The timescale for progression through these stages can vary considerably and setbacks during rehabilitation can lead to further emotional disturbance. In cases of very serious injury and ones in which the emotional reactions are prolonged, the skills of a clinical psychologist might be required.

Fear of Re-injury

A number of other reactions to injury can be caused by being sidelined and having plenty of time to worry. In one study, researchers found evidence that fear of re-injury, anxiety, and questioning of their own abilities to recover were say by a significant number of injured athletes. More recent research, which investigated the subjective experiences of patients following anterior cruciate ligament (ACL) reconstructions, highlighted fear of re-injury as having associations with those who did not adhere to the rehabilitation programme. This fear may be linked to a reduction in self-motivation for such patients and avoidance rather than approach behaviours. Thus, what appears to be lack of motivation on the part of the injured athlete might actually be a symptom of emotional distress. Although these findings only represent qualitative data, there are implications for future researchers to establish if interventions to reduce this fear of re-injury might improve the adherence to rehabilitative programmes.

Adjusting to Injury

In reality, although some athletes experience negative emotions during the adjustment process, most cope without great difficulty. Positive adaptation can be helped by reducing the uncertainty surrounding rehabilitation and the recovery process. Psychologists recognise uncertainty as one of the major triggers for anxiety, but by educating the patient about the injury and what to expect during the rehabilitation phase this uncertainty can be reduced. Although individuals differ in the way they cope with injury and how much information they require, it is probably best to prepare the athlete for the difficulties of the process. Other applied sport psychologists take a similar approach to athletic counselling and suggest that by acknowledging the difficulties, the athlete is less likely to be deterred by unforeseen occurrences.

Sport and exercise psychologists Robert Weinberg and Daniel Gould suggest that providing the injured athlete with an approximate timescale for achieving certain goals during rehabilitation is important. For example, knowing that if things go well and compliance with the rehabilitation programme is maintained, that by week 4 (as appropriate) exercise cycling could be possible, to help to maintain a patient's motivation. During my own rehabilitation a number of clear targets helped me keep positively striving for progress. These included regaining full range of motion at the joint, walking without a leg-brace, swimming, cycling, running on a trampette, running on grass and returning to competitive action (the dream goal).

These markers are good examples of what psychologists call intermediate goals - the stepping stones that pave the way to achieving the dream goal. This approach can help combat any feelings of self-doubt that can arise from only focusing on the long journey towards a dream goal. Intermediate goals provide direction for the day-to-day efforts of the injured athlete. Physiotherapists can also help to provide short-term goals in the form of daily exercises that should be performed by the athlete. Goal achievement is especially good for increasing an athlete's self-confidence.

Picture a Staircase

You can get a clearer idea of how this process works by picturing a staircase where each step reflects an important marker for rehabilitation and the top of the stairs is the dream goal. In order to engage patients in this process it can be helpful to ask them to record and chart their progress. Their self-confidence can be enhanced by knowing how far they have already moved towards the dream goal. Thus, monitoring and evaluation of goals are important, as is re-setting goals that are too easy or too difficult to achieve in a given timescale. The importance of the psychological appraisals that athletes undertake regarding progress should not be underestimated. A recent study showed that therapist support and progression of exercises were identified as being important determinants of attendance at physiotherapy sessions. Furthermore, a study of athletic trainers involved in the rehabilitation of athletes identified differences between athletes who coped either more or less successfully with their injuries. Results revealed that a willingness to listen, maintaining a positive attitude and intrinsic motivation distinguished those who coped more successfully from their less successful counterparts.

Identifying Poor Adjustment

Being able to detect those athletes who are not adjusting to their injuries at an early stage can help to establish the necessary support. Poor adjustment can manifest itself in non-compliance or adherence to rehabilitation programmes, with some athletes doing too little while others may push too hard. Physiotherapists have identified non-compliance as a significant problem preventing effective and efficient recovery from injury. One study identified a number of key characteristics in athletes who experienced difficulties in adjusting to their injuries. These included:

— Feelings of anger and confusion;
— Obsession with the question of when one can return to sport;
— Denial (considering the injury to be no big deal);
— Exaggerated bragging about accomplishments;
— Rapid mood swings;
— Withdrawal from significant others;
— Fatalistic thinking (whatever I do, things are not going to improve);
— Dwelling on minor physical complaints.

It is necessary to be particularly aware of athletes who almost obsessively ask about returning to their sport. Having a desire to recover is healthy but some athletes over-estimate their capabilities and risk re-injury by over-stretching themselves. During attendance at knee clinics I came across a good example of this - a skier who had suffered an ACL injury and had undergone a reconstruction. Having reached the stage of being able to cycle for the first time in the presence of a physiotherapist, this athlete over-estimated her recovery progress. The first cycling session lasted just 10 minutes and was apparently taken as the green light for resuming more intense training. Without consulting her physiotherapist, the skier completed a 20-mile outdoor cycle ride only a few days after the initial cycling session. The predictable result of skipping the steady progressions caused increased swelling and a loss of range of motion at the joint, and rehabilitation was inevitably prolonged.

Optimists and Pessimists

The process of adjustment can be helped or hindered by the injured athlete's own personality. Some people perceive uncontrollable negative events as internal, stable and global. Such thinking has been called a pessimistic explanatory style and some people are more prone to it than others. Contrast these feelings with a more optimistic approach and you can clearly see the barriers to progress and the psychological damage that is being self-inflicted in the former example.

Forms of pessimistic thinking can be dismantled by rational analysis through helping injured athletes to explore their own feelings and the meanings they attach to their current situation. Verbal encouragement can help and reframing negative statements made by the athlete into more optimistic positive ones that are rehearsed and spoken by the athlete as part of his or her own internal dialogue can lead to more positive approaches to rehabilitation. For the athlete to rehearse regularly this can be shortened to: 'keeping to the programme will lead to full range of motion'. This self-talk is instructional and motivational instead of being negative. Rehearsal is the key to success and over time the injured athlete will start to harbour more positive beliefs and expectations. These established techniques - goal-setting and self-talk - are two of the most important in the rehabilitation process. These techniques have been shown to be positively associated with adherence to rehabilitation programmes and with faster healing times.

The psychological impact of injury can affect an athlete long after the body has successfully healed. For this reason the role of a trainer or coach is particularly important in the progression from the rehabilitation clinic to full competition. Both the performance and self-confidence of the athlete will likely be lower than pre-injury and this can be tackled by implementing a steady process of goal-setting and achievements to build both factors. On occasions, the circumstances surrounding the initial injury might cause negative memories and expectations that need to be worked through with a sport psychologist.

Athletes can Avoid Stress

Stress is experienced when an individual feels that they cannot cope with a situation with which they are presented. If an athlete is in a stressful situation then their athletic performance, whether this be in competition or in training, will be effected. The coach can limit the effect on performance of competitive anxiety by assisting the athlete to identify an appropriate coping strategy.

Tips to Avoid Stress

Aim to exercise regularly. Exercise dissipates the adrenaline that builds up in stressful situations and leaves us feeling with a sense of achievement and control.

Eat healthily. Ensure you are getting adequate vitamins and minerals in your diet. One recommendation that very few of us manage is to eat 5 servings of fruit and vegetables daily.

Make sure you are getting enough sleep. People need varying amounts ranging from 5 or 6 hours to 10 hours a night. By trial and error you will know how much sleep YOU need to perform at your best. Learn to think clearly and set yourself realistic goals and objectives. Work through one problem at a time in a logical way.

If you feel a panic or anxiety attack coming on, think through the problem by breaking it down. Imagine the worst that can happen. Nine times out of ten it then appears less serious. Say no to tasks and projects you cannot take on. People will not think any less of you. After all they haven't got ESP. Remember that you are human and mistakes are inevitable. Learn to view mistakes as learning opportunities and problems as challenges.

Practice positive visualisation. Think about a time or a place when you were relaxed and at peace. It could have been on a holiday or a day off. Try to recreate the situation again in your mind, thinking about the sights, sounds and smells you experienced. Visualise yourself back into the scene. You will find that after 5 to 10 minutes you feel much more relaxed as your brain doesn't know the difference between imagining a situation and actually being there. Some people call it day dreaming but visualisation is a very powerful tool in reducing stress and anxiety.

Take time out for yourself. Make sure you are doing some things in your life because they are important to you, rather than because you ought to or should do. You deserve to take a break occasionally, don't feel guilty enjoy it.

Accept your strengths and weakness and like yourself anyway. If you don't like yourself you can't expect anyone else to. Understand also that you can't change anybody else - only yourself. Practice physical relaxation techniques. Progressive relaxation contracting and relaxing all the body parts is a very effective way of reducing tension.

Sports Massage is an alternative method of helping to relieve tension and to relax you.

When you can manage your emotions, you can perform at your best

At the top level it is not your physical or technical expertise, which separates you from the competition but your mental toughness. To be outstanding you have to hold your nerve, perform under the most intense pressure, and consistently turn it on even when you do not feel at your best. Mental toughness is what made Michael Jordan and Pete Sampras so special. These athletes knew their real battle was not so much on the court, but inside their heads. You absolutely must manage your mental side if you want to be the best. Given that mental strength is so vital, then why is it so neglected in training routines? If you are one of those athletes who spends all your training time on technique and fitness while paying no attention to your mental side, you are doing yourself a serious disservice. We know from countless studies that mental skills are acquirable and you can, with practice, learn to perform mentally. You can improve your confidence, concentration, motivation and anxiety levels if you chose to.

Four Important Principles

Feelings affect your performance. Whether you are aware of them or not, how you feel affects how you perform. Feelings are based on what you imagine or interpret from an event and not from the event itself. Two players appearing in the Wimbledon final for the first time will imagine different things about the match. One might imagine she would be unable to play well in such a big final. This player is likely to feel nervous and uncertain and her performance will be poor.

The other might imagine it as the experience of a lifetime for her to go out and enjoy. She might feel liberated and relaxed and her play is likely to reflect these emotions. The same event evokes two different responses, which result in two very different performances. The message here is very simple, learn how to change your interpretations and you learn how to manage your emotions. When you can manage your emotions you can perform at your best.

The mind and the body are inextricable linked, how you feel physically affects how you feel emotionally. This means that we can improve our mental performance using physical interventions and vice versa. You operate within a system and your performance is just a symptom or outcome of how your system operates. The parts of your system are all interrelated. A cricket player's confidence may be affected by his technique, which may be affected by his fitness, which may be affected by his lifestyle which may be affected by his time management.

It is always more potent to look to remedy the underlying causes of a problem than the symptom itself. If Alan Shearer is not scoring goals, the problem might lie not with him but with the midfield who are not creating chances for him. You can divide mental skills training into two approaches, individual work and group work. A standard programme for both may last for a minimum of six weeks with sessions of 60 to 90 minutes.

8

Sport Specific Psychology

Psychology of Motivation

Cognitive psychology theorists endeavor to study and to fully conceive the nature of motivation or desire. People do one thing in order to achieve a specific goal; however understanding that doing one thing is necessary to achieve another thing is insufficient for a person to start doing the "one thing". This fact leaves nothing else but to bring out the idea of desire. Therefore, the knowledge, or the cognition, about particular characteristics of actions and objects is required but is not enough to motivate a person to start doing relevant things. Another important component is person's personal desire coming from within a person; otherwise the nothing will be done.

In order to achieve some C, a person has to do a particular action B, but, as mentioned above, the person needs to wish this C in order to get to action B. These are the basic concepts of the folk psychology, that try to explain the nature of motivation. On one hand, these concepts as well as the "scientific" terms of this branch are incompatible with genuine psychology. They also fail to explain the real procedures of behavior, although they seem quite satisfactory and sufficient. These folk concepts are mainly different from Maze's theory. On the other hand, however, there truly are similarities in this folk "purpose" or "desire" concept and Maze's understanding of nature of motivation.

The main differences between the folk cognitive psychology concept and Maze's instinctual theory are the following; folk psychological concept of desire suggests that the mechanism from its inception till the achievement is mental. In other words, a person fully understands actions, means, their goals, and ends. What Maze offers, is that processes in a person behavior are "neutral". What he meant is a human has certain centers in his or her brain, which are responsible for things like thirst, hunger, self-defense, sex, and others. And so whenever a person's get excited, the person immediately receives a signal and does everything necessary to satiate the need.

Of course, people would not defend themselves when are thirsty, rather they would try to get something to drink, which means that they understand what is going on, but have no control over the phenomenon. Folk psychology, on the other hand, suggests that people consciously motivate themselves to get a drink, but Maze offers another view, which completely satisfies the needs of the science to explain human behavior. Of course both folk psychology and Maze's theory claim that a person does one thing in order for the other thing to happen, but the approaches and mechanisms are completely different.

Top 7 Exercise Motivation Secrets

Let's face it, we all know we need to exercise. Many of us know how to exercise. How many books and videos do you own? How many gym memberships have you had in your life? You may even be an expert on the perfect exercises for your body. But you're not doing it! Why? Well the problem isn't lack of knowledge, it's lack of motivation. Does this sound familiar?

What can you do? Focus less on gaining more knowledge, and more on getting and staying motivated. As you become more consistent and start seeing results, you will be able to apply all that knowledge. Here are seven secrets to getting and staying motivated:

Secret One: Find Your "Why"

In order to be successful at any endeavor, we must have a good reason for doing it in the first place. Exercise is no exception. What will get you up in the morning on those cold, dark days when you just want to stay in bed? Many people say "because I want to lose weight" or "I want to be fit". While these are good goals, they are not good enough reasons for long term success. You must dig deeper. What is important to you? What do you value in life? Answer these questions, then see how a regular exercise program can support your values.

Secret Two: Make a Commitment

Once you find your "why", it's time to make a commitment. Here is a definition of commitment you may not have heard: a commitment is the ability to carry out a worthy decision, even when the excitement of making that decision has passed. Read that definition again, and really understand it. How many times have you been excited to start an exercise program, only to become bored or distracted by other things? As soon as the excitement passes, so do your exercise plans. Be sure you are ready to commit, and if you are not, then commit to not exercising. That way you can let go of the guilt and commit when you are ready.

Secret Three: Set Daily, Measurable and Realistic Goals

If your only goal is to lose 40 pounds it will be a while before you feel successful. After all, it can take a while to see such results. Rather, set daily measurable, achievable goals that allow you to feel successful every day. Keep a weekly diary and set goals each day for what kind of exercise you will do, how long you will workout, how hard you will exercise, etc.

Secret Four: Keep Track of Your Progress

After you set your goals and write them down, you want to also chart your progress. Be sure to write down your daily achievements to compare to your goals. This will become extremely motivating as you see yourself meeting your goals. With consistent exercise, you will also see your workouts becoming easier and your ability to work harder and longer. This often happens faster than visible results on your body, such as weight loss or definition. Many people become frustrated and quit exercise right before big changes are about to happen, because they don't see the results on their bodies. Seeing measurable progress on paper will keep you motivated while you work towards the bigger goals you have set for yourself.

Secret Five: Get Objective Feedback

You may know what a good workout feels like - you have that endorphin "high" after exercise, or you have energy to spare all day long. But do you know what an effective workout feels like? It is hard to know how effective your workout is every day without waiting for weeks or months to see the results. What if you could see day after day how many calories you burned, or what your heart rate was each workout? Using a heart rate monitor can tell you if you are working too hard or not hard enough. What about calories? An accelerometer can tell you all day long how many calories you are burning and keep you motivated to move! When you look for ways to add activity to your day it becomes a fun game and you can instantly see the results.

Secret Six: Avoid the "All or Nothing" Mentality

Have you had plans to exercise five times one week and the first day something happened and you didn't exercise? When this happens, many people give up on the rest of the week This is known as the All or Nothing Mentality. Keep away from this - it doesn't work. If you approach your exercise and nutrition program in that manner, you set yourself up for failure. Allow for flexibility in your exercise plans and know one missed day is not a setback.

Secret Seven: Be Accountable!

About 95% of all participants in an exercise program will stop exercising. Why? No support. Research has shown that exercisers with some kind of support system have a better chance of continuing exercise. You need someone who will also hold you accountable for your exercise. Working with someone like a personal trainer, a coach or a mentor will give you the support you need and you can work together to identify barriers to keeping your commitment and develop strategies to overcome these obstacles. Most people need far more support, follow up and accountability than they think to start and maintain an exercise program.

In the interest of avoiding the all or nothing mentality, don't try to implement all these secrets at once. Pick one or two and when you have those working, add another secret. Just like results from exercise, building motivation and consistency will take time. Fitness is not just about reaching a destination, it is a journey where you will learn much about yourself and grow from your experiences. Keep your short term goals in mind, and enjoy the journey to reaching your ultimate goals.

Tips on How to Keep the Commitment

Psychologists tell us, when starting something new like a

new fitness plan, we become enthusiastic initially. Then we go through four phases before the new activity becomes internalised and part of our normal routine.

Be Prepared to Experience Four Phases

The four phases we experience when making a commitment to a fitness plan are Form, Storm, Norm, and Perform.

Form Phase

The excitement of beginning a new program is the unmistakable sign of the Form Phase. After making the initial commitment to a fitness plan, sticking with the plan the first couple of weeks should be easy.

You may even feel you can handle more training than your plan suggests. Don't do this! Not only does over-training risk injury, it jeopardises your continued motivation over time.

One main mental deterrent can occur in this phase - waiting for all the lights to turn green before beginning. While preparation is positive, pick a start date, go for it, and don't look back.

Storm Phase

The Storm phase follows a few weeks later. When we learn the program is hard work (on some days), and we just don't want to train - this is the storm phase. It happens to everyone. Be prepared.

In the Storm Phase, we begin to create excuses (conscious and subconscious) for missing workouts. This is by far the toughest phase to master.

How should you get through this phase? Mentally prepare ahead of time.

The Storm phase is a natural phase that everyone experiences. And the key to overcoming it is to make the commitment now to press through the Storm Phase when it occurs - and it will occur. Don't let this natural human emotion deter you from your fitness goal.

Consistency is a must for a lifetime of fitness. Following a well designed, comprehensive, reasonable fitness plan will improve appearance, make you feel better, and produce fitness gains rapidly.

Seeing positive results from your effort will increase positive self image, and create even more motivation to continue for the long term.

Norm Phase

The Norm phase is adapting to your fitness training commitment by learning that you can press through the tough days when you do not feel like training - and still get in a great workout.

Every successful, long-term training individual knows - feeling bad at the beginning of the workout, often means this will be the best workout of the week.

Perform Phase

The Perform Phase is achieved when fitness training becomes internalised, and fitness training becomes a part of who you are. The Perform Phase occurs when you have experienced the first three phases and begin to train consistently.

Repetition eventually becomes habit, and that should the ultimate goal of every fitness plan. Training can't be a choice. Fitness training is just something that you do. It must become a part of who you are.

During the first eight weeks of beginning a new fitness plan, you will not only be making positive physical changes, but there are also many positive mental benefits.

Don't make the mistake of thinking that you will bypass the first three phases and go straight to the Perform Phase. This is a huge mistake. This thinking will set you up for failure. When this happens, the Storm Phase seems forcefully to pop up and pull the person back into this phase.

The Strategy that works

The best strategy is simply to be mentally prepared to experience all four phases ... in advance. Identify the phase you are currently experiencing, and with maturity and confidence, work through the mental aspects of fitness training by sticking to the plan even on the tough days. This is the real test! When you reach the Perform Phase, maintaining the fitness plan is much easier. But you can't achieve this level until the first eight weeks are completed and fitness training begins to become apart of who you are.

The Take Home

Mentally, prepare in advance for the four stages that everyone experiences as they begin a new fitness plan.

Sport Specific Psychology

Golfing addiction is not a new thing - at one time in it's early history the game of golf was even banned for a while by the King of Scotland, as golfers had become so obsessed with the game that they neglected their archery practice. Although the addiction that we may all have with the game is psychological, the role of psychology is more about your golfing performance, about how you approach the game, prepare for it, and how you deal with pressure.

There are millions of people addicted to golf. Why? Golf can be played on a beautiful course with as many people as you like, and in very pleasant weather. Golf is very gentle on your body, and is truly the sport of a lifetime.

Golf has many physical benefits and is a very efficient way to stay in shape, and has many physical benefits. With golf, you will get the most out of a round if you walk the course; this will also burn a number of calories and improve your cardiovascular health.

Carrying your clubs will strengthen your upper body and actually hitting the ball improves your hand to eye coordination.

Golf can be played by yourself or with as many friends as you like. You can also chat and visit between each hole while you are waiting on others to finish their holes. Or if you enjoy playing by yourself, you can enjoy the great outdoors, at your own pace.

Professional golfers make the game look easy. Their swing seems as fluid and effortless as running water, and they look as thought they are on a leisurely stroll as they pound drives more than 300 yards and hit high soft iron shots. The truth is they young professionals are strong and fit enough to make a complicated athletic move look simple.

Few amateurs can devote that amount of time, energy, and money to their golf games, but that shouldn't stop them from making positive changes in their games by improving their strength and conditioning. Golf is a game of balance, discipline, and touch.

Enhancing and improving those specific shills, requires a balanced regimen with four important components: strength, flexibility, endurance, and diet.

The Mental Game

The one time that you need to have a clear mind is when you are standing over the ball ready to hit. Before and after that you need to control your thoughts. In fact a clear thought out round can really help you relax and have a more enjoyable round.

Warming up and streching can help you get into the golf mind set. It will also get the blood flowing. Before Bob Power tee off on the first hole he take two clubs and swing them about 20 times in a full easy golf swing. This gets the muscles loose and the blood flowing.

Before each shot stand behind the ball and think about where you would like to hit it. Pick a spot in the fairway or on the green where you will target your shot to. Think about and even try to envision the shot as you stand behind the ball. When you set up to hit clear your mind, swing easy and commit to the shot. If your shot does not work out the way you wanted spend a very little time in analysing the shot. If you know what you did wrong then fine, but if you don't know what happened, forget it. Your not going to figure it out on the course anyway. Try not to get frustrated it' onlygoing to spoil your next shot or your entire round.

As you walk to your ball after you have hit it try to take in the surroundings and enjoy the time you have on the course. Try to get as much relaxation out of your round as possible. Enjoy the people you are with or enjoy the personal alone time you have, it's precious.

As you approach the ball try to decide in your mind where you are in yardage from the green. There are usually markers on the fairways or makered with colored stakes on the edge of the fairways. Knowing how far you are from the green will help you think about what type of shot and what club you will use.

Thinking about your round, or the next shot can really help you lower your score. A little forethought will help you be honest with yourself and help you avoid those shots that you are not capable of. Playing within your strenghts is not coping out, but it is accepting your own capabilities

Psychology and Tenpin

Sports psychology is often quoted as making the difference between someone who is good and someone who is a champion, giving you that little extra edge to put you ahead of your opponent. All good sporting performances come from being well prepared, mentally as well as physically. To be the best requires you to use the skills that you have as effectively as possible.

Often athletes who are fit and talented do not achieve their best possible performances because they have not developed the necessary mental skills. Maybe their concentration lapses at vital moments, they lack motivation or find it hard to perform under pressure.

Sport psychology is about helping athletes tap their potential and achieve the performances they dream about. Setting goals is an important starting point. All good athletes set goals and develop targets and plans to achieve their goals. Effective goal setting comes from making your goals positive, specific, actionable and flexible. The goals also need to focus on what is important, and involve short and long term goals. You have to focus.

The mental side of bowling will be obvious to many of you. In a sport where games are won or lost by very small margins, your psychological state of mind can often be the difference between winning and losing. There are many aspects of sport psychology that can be applied to tenpin. The first will allude you to is the concept of motivation.

Motivation

Staying motivated is important if you are going to make use of all the bowling science information that is provided on this site. It will keep you training when things don't seem to be going right. It will maintain your focus when your opponents seem to be on a roll.

Cricket Psychology

An excellent cricket tip picked up is the power of visualisation. It is a skill which is often neglected by cricketers. For batsmen, bowlers and fielders at any level of the game it is an important skill that should be mastered.

Visualisation or guided imagery is a very powerful technique that can help increase both your efficiency and effectiveness in achieving your cricket goals, whether it would be scoring one hundred runs, playing a perfect cover drive or taking that vital wicket or catch.

All top class athletes utilise visualisation to mentally rehearse what they have to do and how they are going to achieve it. By doing this they train their minds and bodies to actually perform the skill as effectively and efficiently as possible.

For example, before batting Ricky Ponting will have visualised every stroke and shot in his many inning's this season which have netted him an average of over one hundred so far this season.

When you begin to use visualisation techniques, you want to mentally create a vivid scene in you mind of your wanted outcome. You want this scene to be as detailed and clear as possible, you need to be able to see, feel and smell your success.

Actually visualise your success, picture yourself taking that critical wicket or scoring that winning run. Visualise whatever you want your desired situation to be, how it feels, what your emotions are, imagine being in the situation and succeeding.

Make visualisation a daily activity, to go alongside your other cricket training. By succeeding in your mind you will become more passionate about your cricket and you will work harder, pushing yourself to do whatever is necessary to achieve success.

When using visualisation never ever consider failure or giving up as this will likely be the eventual outcome. Always have a positive mental attitude and draw on your success as inspiration however small they may be.

Dream big and aspire to succeed at the highest levels, be patient, work hard and persevere there is nothing except yourself stopping you from achieving your goals in cricket.

Tennis Psychology

The field of tennis psychology is not just common advice and tactical or mental tips. It is based on general and sports psychology and then applied to tennis specifically. There are many common elements in the psychology of tennis which can be found in other sports too. An athlete that wants to perform at his peak needs to learn:

1. How to refocus

Many players start the match with good concentration but they drop their level of concentration because of disturbing outside events, pressure situations, emotional reactions to various events and so on. A player needs to learn how to quickly and effectively refocus to be able to play his best tennis.

2. How to control his arousal - to manage his intensity and body energy

A player's arousal can be too high or too low and in both

cases he is not able to play his best tennis. Arousal affects his body and mind abilities - a player may have too much muscle tension and his decisions are usually not tactically intelligent. Learning to find the "ideal state" is the key in controlling one's arousal and one of the most important aspects of tennis psychology.

3. What elements of the tennis game can a player control

A player may get upset about an event that he cannot control or even influence. For example - the noise of the planes flying over the court, windy conditions, court conditions, his opponent's luck and so on. By being focused on these events he wastes his energy which could be used on elements that he can control - his attitude and effort, how he intends to play, ...

4. How to control his thinking

Negative thinking affects players much more than they are aware of. It affects body abilities in two ways - being aware of them (feeling tension) and being unaware (the pendulum experiment); moreover it evokes negative feelings - emotions that cloud the player's judgment and affect his body abilities - again.

By being more and more aware of what he is thinking a player can then change his thoughts to a more positive and solution based thinking. The awareness of our thoughts is quite a challenge in the psychological approach to tennis.

5. How to use imagery

Imagery or visualization is extremely useful in almost all aspects of the tennis game. A player can improve technique, strategy, physical abilities and his mental preparation of certain events. Another use of imagery is when a player misses a shot and then quickly sees in his mind how he hit the ball correctly. Using imagery is an incredibly efficient technique, not only in the psychology of tennis but in everyday life too.

6. How to build confidence

Confidence is one of those elements where tennis psychology can help really quickly and with very simple tools. A player who is not confident will hesitate in his decisions, will be afraid to take risks and his shots will usually miss by just a little. Doubt can be seen in reality as small misses that happen regularly. When a player builds his confidence he is able to play at his best and doesn't lose his hope when a big challenge appears.

7. How to find and get rid of limiting beliefs

Limiting beliefs are one of the most limiting and troublesome aspects of human's psyche. They are mostly deep in the subconsciousness and are sometimes hard to find. A limiting belief for example is when a player believes that he is not good in tie-breaks and he will then self-sabotage himself in those crucial moments to prove himself right. Having no limiting beliefs means that the player is in total acceptance of everything that happens. Outside events are just events with no meaning. The player accepts them and deals with them.

8. How to empty the mind - Inner Game principles to enter the zone

There are three main principles of the Inner Game - quieting the mind, non-judgment and trusting the body. The player must first learn to apply them in training. And when he experiences these effects in training he knows what to look for in the match. He then plays the inner game - how to perform at his peak. These are the fundamentals of tennis psychology and by understanding these principles and applying them daily a player develops mental toughness. He knows how to apply the tools and as a very positive side effect gains a lot of self confidence.

9

Pre-game Mental Preparation

One of the tenants in sports psychology is that consistent mental preparation and pregame focus leads to a greater consistency in performance. The hallmark of champion athletes is their ability to perform consistently every performance. You should take advantage of having a consistent pregame routine to help get into a mindset for success. You can find examples from many important tasks - in almost any career - that use prepatory routines - from a pilot going through a preflight checklist to a surgeon preparing for surgery. Although sports is not brain surgery, it is very important to have a mental routine to prepare you for what's to come.

Pregame mental preparation during your normal warm up is an excellent time to apply some of the mental game strategies you have learned in the last few weeks as a subscriber to my newsletter. Think of your routine as your final mental tune-up prior to competition. It has four important purposes: (1) to get physically ready, (2) to focus the mind, (3) to instill confidence, and (4) to help you trust your ability. Some sports psychology experts would say that sport is an "escape" from the daily hassles of life. The structure of sports allows you to become fully immersed in the experience and not be self-conscious.

However, want to point out that a pregame routine or ritual is not the same a a superstitious ritual.

Superstitious rituals - eating a ham sandwich before every game, wearing the same shirt under your jersey, talking to your bat - are not the same as pregame routines.

Athlete superstitions are based on the notion that if a certain behavior once brought you good luck, repeating that behavior will bring you more luck. Superstitious rituals have been around since the dawn of sports, and as irrational as they may seem, they sometimes promote a sense of confidence or control. But do they really generate confidence, or are they just wacky habits?

Pregame routines help athletes prepare mentally and physically for competition - in a rational, systematic and meaningful way.

Athletes use superstitions because they think it brings them luck or controls the future. If a lucky shirt works, some athletes will wear it until the first loss. It's hard to argue with Tiger Wood's success on Sunday wearing a customary red shirt, for example. Unlike pregame routines, superstitions are not based on science or reason. Sound mental preparation strategies create the proper mindset for success and are based on reason and science. Don't rely on lucky superstitions to bring you success.

Step 1: Make the Transition from Life to Sports

The warm up or pregame routine is a time to begin focusing on your sport. Think of your routine as a transition from the office, school, or normal activities to competing in sports. Some athletes contemplate about life issues when they play sports, and this affects their focus and performance. Use the pregame routine to let go of daily hassles, deadlines and chores - to become fully engaged in your sport.

Your mental game strategy is to "park" any troubles that are occupying your mind for the duration of your competition. Make a written list of the life issues on your mind, and make a commitment not to think about them while you're engaged in sports. You can't possibly change your life while you're on the field for three hours, so the best option is to temporarily shelve those problems.

Step 2: Review and Commit to a Game Plan or Strategy

You should set a game plan before entering competition, because athletes don't always make the best decisions under pressure. Ideally, you should decide on a game plan prior to your pregame warm up. For example, you should study the course or track, and decide on the best plan of action, given the conditions.

Step 3: Be Responsible for Your Self-Confidence

Confidence is a long-term project, and develops from years of practice and play. Most athletes should have a good foundation of confidence - one based on past successes and practice. However, some athletes doubt themselves at the worst possible time - during the pregame warm up. Others wait for something good to happen before they feel confident. Use positive self-talk and use this to help you feel deserving - that you have paid the dues. Be aware of any last-minute doubts and shoot these down quickly.

Task 4: Gear Your Mind to Focus on Execution

A priority for your mental game is to prepare to focus on the process - and on the here and now - instead of outcomes or results. Focusing on results only serves to place expectations on your performance. In your warm up routine, spend a few minutes to set simple objectives for the game, round or match. Make sure these objectives focus your attention on what your want to accomplish and on your execution.

In addition, keep your mind focused on the warm up and preparing yourself for competition. This is not the time to dwell on outcomes, compare your game to the opposition, or wonder who will be watching the game. Bring focus and intensity to your pregame routine, so you'll be dialed in when the whistle blows.

Task 5: Rehearse Your Performance

Your warm up routine is a good time to rehearse your performance and gain confidence in your game. The nature of the rehearsal will depend on your particular sport and learning preference (visual, kinesthetic, auditory). For example, a golfer can review his game plan for playing the golf course, including targets and clubs to use from the tee and into greens. A baseball player can rehearse pitches he will see and how he will get a hit. A gymnast can rehearse her beam routine, and feel or see successful execution.

The pregame warm up or routine is not the appropriate time to continue working on technique or mechanics! The purpose of practice is to improve your game for the future. The warm up is about preparing to perform your best. You have already put in the practice, trust what you have trained, and now it is time to perform! Prepare to play well with the game you have that day!

Performance in Batting Practice does not Mean Squat

Too many athletes worry about the quality of their warm up. If they perform poorly in the batting cage, on the practice range, or on the court before competition, they worry that performance in a game will also be sub-par. In other words, the warm up becomes a trial or test for the real game! And this affects their mindset in the game!

Keep in mind that the purpose of a warm up or pregame routine is to get ready to play - mentally and physically. You don't have to win warm ups or perform your best in the pregame! Some athletes worry when a warm up performance is not up to standards, especially when the athlete has perfectionist tendencies. This can lead to doubt, and cause athletes to undermine their own confidence.

Modifying Beliefs that Hurt your Composure

What are unhealthy beliefs or irrational beliefs and how are they relate to your sports performance? Irrational or unhealthy beliefs are thoughts, feelings, ideas, attitudes, or ingrained ways of behaving that are self-defeating and often not based on reality. No matter how much visualisation and goal setting you do, these beliefs will hold you back from achieving your potential in sports.

Many irrational beliefs are born out of expectations, while others come from perfectionistic ideals. These beliefs athletes hold tightly to are automatic scripts that are kept in one's head about how life "should" be. Irrational beliefs can also be ineffective, habitual responses you learn to use to protect your ego when faced with trying situations. These beliefs will keep you stuck from progressing in your sport.

How do irrational beliefs undermine your composure? The best way can highlight how self-defeating irrational beliefs are is to use an example. The classic example of irrational beliefs is the athlete who has strict perfectionistic ideas about his sport.

The perfectionistic athlete believes that he or she should and must perform perfectly to win or play well.

For perfectionists, this is an unrealistic demand they place on themselves, which causes additional expectations about performance.

Top Four Irrational Beliefs in Sports:

1. *Perfectionism.* An unrealistic expectation of performing perfectly, leading to excessive pressure and frustration when not performing to one's expectation.
2. *Self-Conscious Behavior.* This is a belief that you are the focus of people around you, which is born out of social approval.
3. *Over-Generalisation.* Athletes use past events, sometimes a single event, to define expectations for future performances. It then becomes a self-defeating prophecy about what should happen in future performance, such as "I never swim well in this pool."
4. *Negative Self-Labels.* Labels, you give yourself, are the most destructive and hard to overcome beliefs of any beliefs. These are judgmental self-labels you use to define yourself as an athlete. Some labels that are common with perfectionist athletes are: choker, butterfingers, or loser.

How does an athlete overcome these unhealthy beliefs? Let me first say that it is a huge step just to recognise and identify these beliefs even exist. However, in order to improve your mental game, you must begin to change these beliefs and adopt new healthy ones. This can be a difficult task if the belief is one that you have held onto all your life. For you to change any belief system, you must begin by questioning yourself about these beliefs - sort of a personal rebuttal to your own ineffective beliefs. For example:

— *Unhealthy belief*: "If I don't finish first in the race, I am a loser."

— *More productive belief*: "Losing a race does not mean I am a loser. I am not perfect and cannot expect to win every race I enter. I accept this. My goal is to race up to my ability."

You have to look honestly at the beliefs that stifle your potential and keep you stuck in old patterns. Once you identify just how limiting some beliefs are, it is easier to accept that change is necessary. Once you decide to make positive changes that positively affect your mental game and performance, then you can take the final step of modifying your beliefs to enhance your confidence and composure.

WINNING UGLY: USE WHATEVER WORKS TO WIN

Many athletes work with have a great practice game, but cannot perform up to their ability in competition. Often, they try too hard to be perfect in games. This is very characteristic of an athlete who works a lot in practice trying to perfect his or her jump shot, pitching motion, or swimming technique. In competition, this athlete focuses so much perfect technique that he or she cannot play to win.

This attitude is great for developing sound mechanics, but can often lead to a mental game breakdown in competition - worrying too much about how to win the right way instead of the functional way.

The successful tennis player and coach Brad Gilbert wrote a tennis book called "Winning Ugly." In his book, he stressed the importance of athletes putting aside the correct way of winning for the functional method of winning.

Perfectionists and athletes who are stuck in a practice mindset have trouble with a winning ugly mindset or performing functionally - they become too obsessed with perfect technique or an error-free performance. What is winning ugly? Winning ugly is the ability to abandon the right way or perfect way to perform for the functional way - the ability to get the job done any way you can.

Some athletes get stuck on making their performance look pretty or perfect and this can actually hurt your chances of winning. Some of my golf students, for example, are happier shooting 72 while hitting the ball well instead of shooting 70 and scraping the ball around, but scoring well. This does not seem rational to me because the goal in golf is to shoot the lowest score!

Some basketball players, for example, get too obsessed with looking pretty and hitting pretty shots. This is fine if they are hitting every shot in a game, but a miss can cause them to pass the ball instead of keep shooting. A focus on style and form is not the best mindset if you want to score your best. You have to stop worrying about how it looks and instead focus on the goal to get the ball in the hoop any way you can that day.

A good example or winning ugly is the University of Florida Football team this season. Florida has found a way to win several close games this season, including last Saturday in Tallahassee, and Arkansas 38-28 Saturday night. Late-game heroics have kept the team in the national championship picture.

All great teams find a way to win and win ugly if necessary - they are able to get the job done and win with whatever works. Florida has definitely qualified for that this year. With their most recent win over Arkansas 38-28 Saturday, Florida has won five games by seven points or less.

The Gators are a team that avoids the pitfalls of perfectionism. They do not worry about who was favored or by how much. The only thing that matters is the final score and a "W" in the win column when talking about winning ugly. Perfectionism in team sports is the belief that everything must go according to a well-conceived plan that looks and feels perfect. For many athletes and coaches perfectionism can cause problems.

Sometimes a coach can become obsessed with his knowledge and game plan, the perfect play call, and the pretty pass for the touchdown - when he still got the desired outcome, a win. You can see the problems this might cause for a QB. Self-doubt will creep in. He will be second-guessing himself instead of letting his instincts take over and running for the touchdown.

In the end, the only thing that is important is the outcome after you hit the locker room. How you achieved the outcome - pretty, ugly, or perfect is unimportant. Athletes sometimes strive too much for perfection and not enough for a positive result.

Three tips for avoiding the perfectionism trap and adopting the get-it-done mentality:

1. Do not have any preconceived notions on how many points your team should or needs to score to win or how you need to win. Focus on execution and generating good outcomes instead of the perfect play or shot.
2. If you coach, let players play the game you trained them to play. Do not over coach. On those times when a contest is very tight, your players must rely on their instincts, and the hours of training you have spent with them. Trust in the abilities of your players to perform.
3. Sports is not like Hollywood. Your performance does not happen according to a perfect script in sports. Whatever play is working, no matter how it looks or

what other people may think about your strategy, use what ever works to win.

Helping Young Athletes Perform with Less Distractions

Today to more and more unsportsmanlike acts by over-concerned sports parents in youth sports. Coach-parent disputes about playing time and coaching methods are now being scrutinised in the media. And unfortunately sports parents are made to look like monsters. Last week Fox News asked me to comment on a very visible dispute between a coach and youth sports parent in Minnesota.

The dispute started between a coach and sports parent when the parent complained to the coach about his son's playing time. The sports parent, Wade Campbell, asked his son's coach why his son was not getting enough playing time, and the coach replied "your kid hurts us," according to Campbell. To make a long story short, Campbell son's coach ended up filling a police report stating that Campbell had driven to his house and threatened to shoot him. Campbell was arrested based on the coach filing a report.

Disagreements between coaches and concerned parents are playing out all over the country and this is nothing new. But they are gaining momentum with the media.

Although this was an extreme case of a sports parent gone mad, this situation highlights how the parent/coach relationship can get out of control. Sports parent or coaches can avoid communication breakdowns and altercations at the start of the season - thus helping kids have a better sports experience and be able to perform with less distractions.

As a young athlete, you don't know how to react to this type of behavior - if you should feel embarrassed, feel proud, or cheer a parent on. At the very least, can say that it becomes a massive distraction for athletes when they have to worry if a parent is going to behave well during the game or when a child feels embarrassed by a parent's behavior. There are a few steps parents and coaches can take to improve communication and reduce miscommunication on the sidelines, thus helping young athletes have a better experience.

For parents, before signing your child up with a team it's appropriate to do your research. Interview or observe the prospective coach in action. When you interview the coach, ask questions that are important to you. You might ask about his/her coaching philosophy, how he/she views playing time, practice guidelines, and how he/she motivates his or her athletes. It is a good idea to attend one or two practices to see the coach in action. This will also give you the opportunity to meet other parents and get their views on the coach.

If you are a youth coach, it's a good idea to discuss with your players and their parents about what you expect from them and what they should expect from you in the coaching process. Lay down the law about playing time, practice, and game time behavior (this is a big one).

Be clear with where you stand with playing time, your coaching philosophy, and your motivational style of coaching. If you coach your own children on the team, explain how you will treat them in relation to the other kids, as parents are often concerned about coaches who play favorites. You should also listen carefully to the demands of parents and decide whether their child will be a good fit for the team or not.

For young athletes, it's important you talk with your parents and coaches about all these issues. Discuss with your parents how you feel about their behavior at games and what your biggest distractions are. Young kids should discuss their motivation for participating in sports too so parents understand their motives. Do you play for fun, to make friends, enjoy competition, to get a trophy, or some other reason?

From a performance perspective, athletes and parents should follow these guidelines to improve the sports experience and help kids have more fun:

1. The main goal is to feel confident about the game or competition. If you discuss the game, remember to be positive about past experiences and successes. Don't dwell on past mistakes or losses. Stay away from the subject of avoiding mistakes from previous games.
2. Keep your emotions in check. As a parent, be a good role model for composure. As an athlete, you want to stay composed and calm as well. If parents show that they are jittery, nervous or worried about the game or competition, a child or teen will likely be affected by these feelings.
3. Don't over-analyse before the game, focus too much on technique, or analyse past performances. Less is better before a game. Keep comments brief, supportive and positive.
4. Leave the coaching to the coach during games. Parents should show their support for the coach's decisions. Don't talk about how you'd like the coach to manage the team or how you disagree with some of his decisions before a game. This will undermine your athletes' confidence and trust. They need to enter the game trusting their coaches. If you disagree with a coach's decision, you should approach the coach at the right time and place — after the game or over the phone when cooler heads prevail.

Mental Traps of Perfectionism in Sports

It seems that more and more of my mental coaching students are held back by perfectionistic tendencies. They want to perform perfectly and this actually causes more tension and anxiety. Perfectionism can be both a good trait and a bad trait to your performance. The key is to understand what is functional and what is harmful about being a perfectionist or having perfectionistic tendencies toward your sport.

Don't interpret in the wrong way ... Lots of successful athletes have had to overcome perfectionism. There are some advantages of perfectionism such as having a strong work ethic, commitment to your goals, and a willingness to learn and improve, which often disguise this mental roadblock to success. It can also help you achieve a few goals quicker.

However, perfectionism presents more disadvantages than advantages when you enter into competition. For example, trying to be too perfect with your performance is one mental barrier. Your very first step in tweaking out the disadvantages of perfectionism is to identify the behaviors that hold you back from success.

What mental barriers keep you blocked from success?

1. You try too hard to win and thus get in your own way with tension and fear. You fear not winning after putting in a massive amount of "investment" in sports.
2. You become easily frustrated when you do not perform up to your expectations and then try even harder to not fail. Perfectionists often have very strict and high expectations that are very difficult to achieve.

3. You have low self-confidence in competition because you are more comfortable in practice and more anxious in games.
4. Wanting badly to win creates a tentative mindset because you are afraid to make mistakes because you believe you can't make mistakes and still win.
5. You might feel as if your self-esteem is threatened when you do not perform up to your own expectations because you define yourself based on your success (or failure) in sports.
6. You have difficulty playing relaxed, free, or effortless (you perform too cautiously) and lose trust in your abilities.
7. You have a fear of making mistakes in front of your coach and what might happen (what ifs) such as getting yanked from the line up and can't play freely.

Why do so many athletes have perfectionistic behaviors or tendencies. Why this is... Do some sports instill perfectionism or are perfectionists drawn to certain sports? The real culprit is fear of failure...

Athletes who are perfectionistic do not perform up to their potential primarily because of fear of failure. Why? Since perfectionists are so highly motivated and often have lofty goals for themselves, this causes a strong need to win or succeed in sports.

However, the hallmark sign of perfectionism in sports is that perfectionists spend a lot of time training and practicing to become successful, but often under perform in competition.

It is ironic that the athletes who want to win the most and train the hardest are often those who are the most likely to be mentally stuck in fear of failure. Perfectionistic athletes often lose sight of the real objective when they practice - to use their training as a vehicle to perform well in competition.

They become so engrossed in training and practice that perfecting their technique or working hard in practice becomes the primary goal instead of performing with confidence in competition. And when they do compete, they believe anything less than perfect execution or winning is deemed as failure due to extremely high standards or expectations.

How do you know if you have fear of failure?

The number one sign is when you have difficulty taking your "practice game" to competition. You might have a high level of self-confidence when you train or practice, but this type of confidence is not the same as having a high level of self-confidence on game day. Low self-confidence on game day is a huge barrier for athletes with fear of failure. Fear of failure overcomes any confidence that was developed through practice or training!

Another sign that you have fear of failure is when you want to win or succeed so badly that this leads to cautious performances because you are so afraid to make mistakes and not win! I will also add that you probably focus too much on results or outcomes, which leads to anxiety or tension during competition.

Another big challenge for perfectionistic athletes who have fear of failure is that they care too much about what others think. For some reason, they want to impress others or gain the respect of others.

And in many cases they do not want to disappoint others. For example, they make false assumptions about what others might think, such as "my parents will not drive me to practice if I don't perform well."

If you can identify with any of the above mental game traps of perfectionism or fear of failure, here is a good start to helping you perform better ... Learn to give yourself permission to make mistakes. Since you think anything less than a flawless performance is a failure, you have to modify your expectations.

You have to accept that you are human and you will have bad days just like everyone else. It may help to give yourself permission to make mistakes. You're not perfect and even the best athletes in the world make mistakes. Learn to live with winning ugly or performing well even when you are not perfect!

Mental Game Coaching

Mental Game Coaching is that the segment of sports psychology that concentrates specifically on helping athletes break through the mental barriers that are keeping them from performing up to their peak potential. By focusing on the mental skills needed to be successful in any sporting competition, mental game coaching seeks to achieve the overall goal of performance improvement.

Improve Focus and Deal with Distractions

Many athletes have the ability to concentrate, but often their focus is displaced on the wrong areas such as when a batter thinks; "I need to get a hit" while in the batter's box, which is a result-oriented focus. Much of my instruction on focus deals with helping athlete to stay focused on the present moment and let go of results.

Grow Confidence in Athletes who have Doubts

Doubt is the opposite of confidence. If you maintain many doubts prior to or during your performance, this indicates low self-confidence or at least you are sabotaging what confidence you had at the start of the competition. Confidence is what a core mental game skill because of its importance and relationship to other mental skills.

Emotional control is a prerequisite to getting into the zone. Athletes with very high and strict expectations, have trouble dealing with minor errors that are a natural part of sports. It is important to address these expectations and also help athletes stay composed under pressure and when they commit errors or become frustrated.

Find the right zone of intensity for your sport

Intensity in a broad sense to identify the level of arousal or mental activation that is necessary for each person to perform at his or her best. This will vary from person to person and from sport to sport. Feeling "up" and positively charged is critical, but not getting overly excited is also important. You have to tread a fine line between being excited to complete and not getting over-excited.

Help teams develop communication skills and cohesion

A major part of sports psychology and mental training is helping teams improve cohesion and communication. The more a team works as a unit, the better the results for all involved.

Improve or balance motivation for optimal performance

It is important to look at your level of motivation and just why you are motivated to play your sport. Some motivators are better in the long-term than others. Athletes who are extrinsically motivated often play for the wrong reasons, such as the athlete who only participates in sports because of a parent. You need to adopt a healthy level of motivation and be motivated for the right reasons.

Develop confidence post-injury

Some athletes find themselves fully prepared physically to get back into competition and practice, but mentally some scars remain. Injury can hurt confidence, generate doubt during competition, and cause a lack of focus. I help athletes mentally heal from injuries and deal with the fear of re-injury.

To develop game-specific strategies and game plans

All great coaches employ game plans, race strategies, and course management skills to help athletes mentally prepare for competition. This is an area beyond developing basic mental skills in which a mental coach helps athletes and teams. This is very important in sports such as golf, racing, and many team sports.

To identify and enter the "zone" more often This incorporates everything do in the mental side of sports. The overall aim is to help athletes enter the zone by developing foundational mental skills that can help athletes enter the zone more frequently. It is impossible to play in the zone everyday, but you can set the conditions for it to happen more often.

Not every person who plays a sport wants to "improve performance." Sport psychology is probably not for recreation athletes who participate for the social component of a sport or do not spend time working on technique or fitness to improve performance. Young athletes whose parents want them to see a sports psychologist are not good candidate either. It is very important that the athlete desires to improve his or her mental game without having the motive to satisfy a parent. Similarly, an athlete who sees a mental game expert only to satisfy a coach is not going to fully benefit from mental training.

Sports Psychology does apply to a wide variety of serious athletes. Most of my students (junior, high school, college, and professional athletes) are highly committed to excellence and seeing how far they can go in sports. They love competition and testing themselves against the best in their sport. They understand the importance of a positive attitude and mental toughness. These athletes want every possible advantage they can get including the mental edge over the competition.

Energy and the Future of Performance Enhancement

In this month's column would like to give you a little bit of background on the Eastern energy arts and their use in sports training and coaching and then, over the next several issues, we will look in turn at how the Eastern energy arts such as Chi Kung and T'ai Chi can have a positive impact on the four main areas of Sports Science - namely biomechanics, strength and conditioning, endurance and the mental game.

For now though, a development which many athletes and coaches may find interesting comes from within the sports world itself, with many top level sports psychologists and mental game coaches hailing the Eastern energy arts as "the missing link" in sports coaching. From Michael Murphy's classic book "Golf in the Kingdom" to Dan Millman's "Warrior Athlete" and the "Inner Game" concept of Timothy Gallwey, the interest in the Eastern energy arts amongst athletes looking to generate effortless power and mental mastery is now unprecedented.

For instance, training in the Eastern energy arts can increase an athlete's ability to release effortless power, improve their efficiency and economy of motion, develop their mental intent (winner's mind-set), create a more stable core region and enhance relaxation of their "bodymind". They will also learn how to generate ground-strength (peng) in order to use gravitational force in the golf swing, tennis serve, 100m sprint, dive, half-pipe routine and so on and learn to move from their body's natural fulcrum or centre of gravity (t'an tien), thus developing unity of motion and increasing their natural force.

So, what exactly are the Eastern energy arts?

Let's take a quick look at two of the most well known and widely practised of the arts: Chi Kung and T'ai Chi.

Chi Kung

Today millions of people in China and around the world regularly practice Chi Kung as a health maintenance exercise. Chi Kung and related disciplines are still associated with the martial arts and meditation routines practiced by Taoist and Buddhist monks, professional martial artists, and their students. Once more closely guarded, in the modern era such practices have become widely available to the general public both in China and around the world. Chi Kung can help practitioners to learn lower abdominal breathing, an important component of the relaxation response, which is important in combatting stress and indeed, in developing athletic potential.

Chi Kung is an aspect of Traditional Chinese medicine involving the coordination of different breathing patterns with various physical postures and motions of the body. It is mostly taught for health maintenance purposes, but there are also some who teach it as a therapeutic intervention for patients recovering from illness and/or surgery. Various forms of Chi Kung are also widely taught in conjunction with Chinese martial arts, and are especially prevalent in the advanced training of what are known as the Neijia, or internal arts where the intention is the full mobilization, proper coordination and direction of the energies of the body as they are applied to some target. As such, Chi Kung relies on the traditional Chinese notion that the body has something that might be described as an "energy field", known as Chi or qi.

Chi (qi) means breath and, by extension, the energy produced by breathing that keeps us alive; Kung (gong) means hard work and the resultant level of expertise or mastery of an art or craft. Chi Kung translates then as "energy or breath training" or the art of managing one's breathing in order to achieve and maintain good health, and to enhance the energy mobilization and stamina of the body.

In terms of developing athletic potential, the following is a list of various ways sportsmen and women can benefit from Chi Kung exercises:

— Energy cultivation
— Athlete rehabilitation - from injury, stress, poor performance, overtraining
— Athlete wellbeing - balancing work, life and sport
— Resistance to illness
— Quicker recovery rates after strenuous training
— Developing the 'Relaxation Response'
— Strength and physical conditioning
— Endurance

T'ai Chi

T'ai Chi - a martial art based on the principles of Chi Kung, literally translates as "supreme ultimate boxing" or "boundless fist". The concept of the "supreme ultimate" is based on the principles of the Yin and Yang duality of Taoist philosophy. Thus, T'ai Chi theory and practice evolved in agreement with many of the principles of Chinese philosophy and Taoism in particular.

Tai chi training involves learning solo routines, known as forms, two person routines known as pushing hands, as well as the martial applications of the postures of the form. It was created many hundreds of years ago as the lynch-pin of the Chinese martial arts Neijia branch, where the body's intrinsic energy (chi) is directed with the mind (yi); as opposed to the hard, external forms of fighting like Shaolin kung-fu, where more reliance is put on muscular force.

The physical techniques of T'ai Chi as a martial art are characterized by the use of leverage through the joints based on coordination in relaxation, rather than muscular tension, in order to neutralize or initiate attacks. The slow, repetitive work involved in the process of learning how that leverage is generated gently and measurably increases and opens the internal circulation: (breath, blood, lymph, etc.).

Bruce Lee (who's Father was a T'ai Chi practitioner) gave a great anaology for the difference in power between a Karate punch and a T'ai Chi punch. Lee said that to be hit by a karate punch was like being hit with an iron bar, whereas being hit by a T'ai Chi punch was like being hit with an iron ball attached to the end of a chain. Ouch.

T'ai Chi has since developed a worldwide following among many thousands of people with little or no interest in martial training, who practise T'ai Chi for its many benefits to health and health maintenance. Some call it a form of moving meditation, as focusing the mind solely on the movements of the form helps to bring about a state of mental calm and clarity.

For athletes intent on developing their fullest potential, both mentally and physically, T'ai Chi training as an addition to training technique and improving fitness, can have the following benefits:

- Injury prevention, thus extending the sporting life of the athlete
- Developing mental intent (training the mind to lead the body)
- Attention control
- Core stability
- Unity of motion/whole body power
- Athletic alignment
- Immersion, a key component of the 'Inner Game'
- Increased range of motion
- Improved joint flexibility

How to be a champion in sport and life

Do you ever get that feeling deep down that you should be able to accomplish much more than you are at present? Are you looking for a bigger challenge to overcome because your daily workouts are just too easy? Or are you training for a specific goal but feel like something is still missing in your workout program?

There is a good chance that there are a few Olympic hopefuls close to where you live. These are young men and women loaded with talent that is laced by hard work. In fact, you too are loaded with talent and that I am sure has been laced with a lot of hard work. And while these future Olympians are presented with the opportunity of a lifetime, this does not mean that their journey is for the elite only.

The true meaning of the Olympics is about the process or journey of an amateur athlete, an individual who is devoted to continual improvement of oneself. Ultimately, through daily struggle, frustration, and hardship, this athlete experiences personal success and public victories. How about your journey? What do you dream of in your effort to win your gold medal? The exciting truth is that with a little hard work, smart training, and the right supportive environment, you can win your gold. It is like John Maxwell said, "Dreams do not work unless you do."

It would have been too easy to just write an article on physical training with a few sample exercises, but for Olympic athletes training is much more than this. It is about pushing life's limits and having the courage to reach your potential. While it is unlikely that most of us will never compete in the actual Olympic Games, everyone has the ability to be an Everyday Champion™. Apply the following principles of championship athletes and elevate your workouts to Olympic training status.

Turn your ability into achievement

Discipline is what turns your ability into achievement. Without it, your goals will always be daydreams at best. Working out two days last week, five days this week, and three days next week will prevent you from ever reaching your podium. What is missing or what are you tolerating in your life that is preventing you from establishing discipline?

Don't let your competition define who you are

Does this scenario sound familiar? You are right in the middle of your workout at the gym and feeling great, only to look over across the room and see your nemesis, the individual who has everything you are trying to attain. Maybe you want that perfect looking body, blazing speed, or the lungs of Lance Armstrong. Too often we are guilty of comparing ourselves to our team mates, a training partner, or another individual that we do not even know. If you want to win your game, you first have to win your inner game. The competition is not you versus them. It is about you versus you. How much better can you make yourself in your pursuit of athletic excellence?

Monitor Your Training

Just because you are active does not mean that you are actually accomplishing anything. In fact, this approach actually could be detrimental to your body. How many people do you know workout four or five days a week but do not actually have a goal in mind? Better yet, if you were to ask them what they did two weeks ago they probably could not tell you. Many athletes keep a journal, but most of the time they only log physical qualities of training. Unfortunately this does not give a complete picture of what is going on in your body. Olympic athletes know their bodies inside and out as well as every facet of their training program. They can tell you their daily training volume, how much weight was lifted today versus last week, and even if they feel signs of overtraining from the previous day.

Sports psychology guidelines for sports parents

Dr. Patrick Cohn explains how parents can help make sport a successful and fun experience for young athletes Sports parents have a big impact on their young superstars. A healthy and successful sports experience will depend on the sports parents' ability to instil confidence and self-esteem in athletes. Parents have a tremendous impact on how children will engage in sports. Below are some simple guidelines for sports parents to adopt with youth athletes.

Guidelines for Sports Parents

Sports should be fun for kids. Treat sport as a game, it is not a business for kids. With all the money in professional sports today, it is hard for parents to understand that it is just good fun to young athletes. The primary goal should be to have fun and enjoy the healthy competition.

Your own agenda is not your young athlete's. They compete in sports for many reasons. They enjoy the competition, like the social aspect, engage with being part of a team, and enjoy the challenge of setting goals. You might have a different agenda than your young athlete and you need to recognize that it is their sport, not yours.

Emphasize a mental focus on the process of execution instead of results or trophies. We live in a society that focuses on results and winning, but winning come from working the process and enjoying the ride. Teach your young athlete to focus on the process of the challenge of playing one shot, stroke, or race at a time instead of the number of wins or trophies.

You are a role model for your young athlete. As such, you should model composure and poise on the sidelines. When you are at competition, your young athlete will mimic your behaviour as well as other role models. You become a role model in how you react to a close race or the questionable behaviour of a competitor. Stay calm, composed, and in control during games so your young athlete superstar can mimic those positive behaviours.

Refrain from game-time coaching. During competition, it is time to just let them play. All the practice should be set aside because this is the time that athletes need trust in the training and react on the court or field. "Just do it" as the saying goes. Too much coaching (or over-coaching) can lead to mistakes and cautious performance (called paralysis by over analysis). Save the coaching for practice and use encouragement at game time instead.

Help your athlete to detach self-esteem from achievement. Too many athletes attach self-worth to the level of performance or outcomes. Help your young athlete understand that they are a person FIRST who happens to be an athlete instead of an athlete who happens to be a person. Success or number of wins should not determine a person's self-esteem.

Ask your young athlete the right questions. Asking the right questions after competition and games will tell your young athlete what you think is important in sports. If you ask, "Did you win?" they will think winning is important. If you ask, "Did you have fun?" he or she will assume having fun is important.

10

Power of Thoughts

There is scientific proof that negative thinking does play a role in producing negative outcomes. If you do not believe it then try this experiment: You will need another person to serve as a volunteer. Tell the volunteer that you are going to be conducting a test in muscular strength and how positive and/or negative thoughts and words affect muscular strength. Make sure that your volunteer has no arm, shoulder, or elbow injuries before undertaking this test.

Instructions

Extend your arms straight out to the side, shoulder height, parallel to the floor. Now close your eyes and lower your arms. See yourself doing something negative. It could be failing a test, not playing well, blowing a sale, or even tripping and falling. Say out loud your favourite putdown words. Repeat them out loud several times. After they repeat their favourite putdown words out loud 6-8 times, have them raise their arms again. They are to continue saying their favourite putdown words. Once again place the two fingers on their wrist. Ready? Go.

What Happens?

Normally, they are unable to apply much resistance and

their arms go down much easier. Now, close your eyes again and lower your arms.

What were the results this time?

In most cases, your volunteer will be at least as strong, if not stronger, then in the first test. Ask the volunteer what their impression was. Most will tell you that they felt much stronger and felt better about themselves.

So what does this little experiment prove?

It shows us the power of our thoughts over our bodies. When we say negative things, we tend to zap our strength and easily lose mental focus. When we fill our subconscious with positive thoughts, we become stronger and mentally more alert. Still not sold on the concept? Think about a class you took or are taking in school that you did not like. As an athlete, there might be a part of your training regiment that you strongly dislike negatively affecting your overall performance. And in sales, if you hate to make cold calls, you are probably not going to be a very good salesperson.

Conversely, if you can change the words from ones of dislike or hate, to words of like or love, you strengthen your body which in turn strengthens your mind. When your body is feeling stronger, and your mind is sharp and focused, you will be more effective in whatever you do. As a result you will feel better about yourself and will be more enjoyable to be around.

Which sports seem to produce low self-esteem?

A strange paradox of sporting activity is that participation often leads to higher self-esteem. In certain sports it can also lead to an increased risk of developing eating disorders such as anorexia nervosa and bulimia, both of which are usually associated with low self-esteem. Certain sports seem to carry an increased risk of eating problems.

For example, in the United States, about 93% of collegiate athletes who develop eating disorders are female, and these athletes are usually found in a fairly small number of sports, including gymnastics, cross-country, swimming, and track and field. The few cases reported in men are clustered in the sports of cross-country, track and field, gymnastics, and wrestling.

What actually causes the eating disorders?

A combination of individual and family factors is often involved in producing an eating problem, and cultural factors apparently put females at especially high risk. Over the past three decades, the socially acceptable weight for women in Western societies has progressively decreased, while the incidence of eating disorders has steadily risen.

Why are eating disorders linked with certain sports?

Individuals dissatisfied with their bodies may be drawn to "calorie-burning" sports like running and swimming. In addition, scientific research suggesting that "lean is better" for performance may contribute to the problem, and aesthetic sports such as gymnastics probably place far too high a premium on being super-thin. Recovering from an eating disorder is a complex process involving counseling and the raising of self-esteem and self-acceptance. Athletes can do a number of things to reduce their risk of developing an eating disorder, and coaches should realise that they can take steps to help prevent eating disorders in their athletes.

Alice Lindeman, an eating disorder researcher at the University of Indiana, recommends that athletes be aware of the following facts:

— There is a range of weight, which is appropriate for any particular sport. No one weight is ideal and the lowest possible weight is usually not an option. Eating too little can actually depress metabolism and make one fatter, not slimmer.

— Eating more food can be a great way to improve body composition, because the increased caloric intake replenishes muscles and allows higher-quality training, which burns away fat naturally

— Fear of fat in the bódy should not translate into fear of fat on the plate. Fat is an essential nutrient required for the absorption of vitamins D, E, A, and K, so some fat must be included in the diet

— Taking in more calories can improve menstrual function, which heightens bone health and reduces the risk of osteoporosis.

Coaches should de-emphasise weight and refrain from commenting on body weight as they speak with their athletes. Coaches should also avoid group "weigh-ins", which can heighten humiliation and embarrassment for the athlete who feels too fat and may push an athlete onto the road leading to a full blown eating problem. These 24 questions could help you find out why you had a poor performance in your last race

1. Were you rested enough 48 hours before the race?
2. Were you travel-weary on the day?
3. Did your last meal before the race have enough time to be digested?
4. Did your last meal before the race contain gaseous food - egg, for instance?
5. Did you have your usual warm-up?
6. Did you have a race plan? Was this carried out as planned? If not, why not?

7. Did you taper for this race?
8. If the race was in excess of 10K, did you take in extra carbohydrate for the past 72 hours?
9. If the race was in excess of 10 miles and the temperature above 70 degrees F, did you take on board adequate fluid replacement?
10. Did you feel tired as you lined up for this race in spite of 48 hours rest? To what did you attribute this tiredness?
11. Have you suffered recently from pins-and-needles in the feet and hands, or numbness in the feet? If so, you should have a comprehensive blood test for iron and magnesium deficiency.
12. Have you suffered from frequent infections during the past six weeks? If so, you may have a zinc deficiency in your diet.
13. Did you practice visualisation for the race? This involves being alone in a state of quietness, and first, watching yourself running in the race, then second, being in the race and actually taking in everything involved, such as crowd noise, sound of running feet, and carrying out your plan.
14. What was your mental state before this race? Being nervous is a natural reaction to being tested, both physically and mentally.
15. Was your nervousness excessive? If so, did you try to think positively by telling yourself what your race plan was and firmly establishing in your mind how you were going to carry it out?
16. Did you feel before this race that your training was adequate both in quantity and quality? If not, what element of it do you think was lacking? If you had some misgivings, and if coached, did you express your doubts to your coach? If not, why not?

17. Do you think your coach understands the needs of your event?
18. Do you think your coach understands your capabilities and goals?
19. Are you over trained or under trained?
20. Have you in your own mind a clear idea of what is required in training for your event?
21. Do you know the physiological breakdown of your event - in other words, what is aerobic and what is anaerobic, what aerobic training involves and what anaerobic training involves?
22. Are you over stressed in your non-athletics life? You may work full time, do you consider this a hindrance to your athletics progress? If so, is it possible for you to become a full time athlete or a part time worker?
23. If you feel over stressed other than by a full time job, can you pinpoint stresses and take active steps to reduce them?
24. Most athletes have a bee in their bonnet about some aspect of their preparation - it may be more speed, more mileage, or even less of both. Have you such a bee in your own bonnet? If so, have you discussed it with your coach?

Is it sensible to exercise when you are ill?

You wake up in the morning with a bad cold, but you have been planning the day's workout for a long time, and you really do not want to miss it, or you have been overeating during the holidays and you really need to lose some weight. Should you go ahead and complete your training session, or take the day off?

To answer that question, a little common sense is in order. The reality is that if you are ill, you are probably tired, and your muscle strength is below par. That being true, you might as well face the fact that your workout is going to be sub optimal, so why do it? Some additional rest will actually leave you in better shape to train intensely in a day or two.

From a health perspective, insisting on working out when you are sick can be downright dangerous. Instead of having a rhinovirus infection, you might actually be infected with something more lethal, like a virus that can cause pneumonia, or a "Coxsackie" virus, which can infect your heart and even cause sudden death as you train.

If you do not buy these first two arguments for rest, then use what exercise and health experts call the "neck check" to determine whether you can train. If all of your symptoms are above the neck, it is okay to start your usual workout at about half speed. If you feel better after 10 minutes or so, you can increase your intensity and finish your workout.

Otherwise, take some chicken soup, vitamin C, and fluids to bed with you, and try again in a day or two. However, by all means do not work out if you have a fever or symptoms below the neck (aching muscles, a hacking cough, nausea, vomiting and/or diarrhoea). Working out under those conditions is risky, and you will recover much faster from your illness if you rest.

Self-esteem in the athlete

Many athletes and performers work with often wrongly determine their self-worth by how successful they feel about their sport. When an athlete performs well or feels successful, he or she can feel good about him or herself. However, the opposite is also true: despair and low self-esteem results when this person does not perform well or view him or herself as a failure.

Athletes are especially vulnerable to this problem of attaching self-esteem to one's performances because you are judged by how well you perform. However, society sends subtle signals that you must achieve in your sport to feel worthy as a person and that is the trap that many athletes fall into. In addition, if you are perfectionist, it does not help your self-esteem because you have such high expectations and are always so critical and hard on yourself.

If you fall into this trap, your emotions, and how you feel about yourself, are heavily influenced by the perceptions of your performance, which can naturally vary from day to day. Thus, one day you have self-esteem and the next day it erodes due to what you think is a poor performance or practice.

What is self-esteem?

Self-esteem is the regard you hold for yourself. All of you have a concept of your person (self-concept). If you like your self-concept (who you think you are), then you have self-esteem. Self-confidence is different. Self-confidence is the belief in your ability to perform a task - it is not a judgment. You can have self-confidence, but not self-esteem, and vice versa. Optimally, you want both high self-confidence in your abilities and self-esteem.

Self-esteem should be based on who you are as a person instead of how well you can perform in your sport or how high you go in a sporting career. Think about this: if you take away the part of you who is an athlete, how would you describe yourself? What are your personal characteristics that describe you? This is what self-esteem should be based on. If you feel like you struggle with self-esteem, have hope. Here are some other ideas about gaining self-esteem.

Assume the Role

When you are performing, you are in the role of an athlete. You want to be into that role fully when practicing and performing, but when you leave the sporting arena, it is time to switch roles into other parts of your life and let go of judgments. Do not superimpose the role of an athlete (or how well you can perform) into other areas of your life.

True Friends

People, who are your true friends and family members, love you for who you are as a person first. They do not judge you based on your performance or change their view of you because of how good you are as an athlete. If they do, they are not your true friends. They like you for what you bring to a relationship as a person, not as an athlete.

Stop the Comparisons

You do yourself harm by making comparisons to other athletes who you think are better or more talented than you are. This only serves to hurt your self-esteem and confidence because you put others on a pedestal and criticise your faults. Everyone is unique. Think about how well you did compared to your last performance instead of making comparisons to others.

Accept Your Body Image

No one can be perfect or has the perfect body for their sport. Some people are born with more hand-eye coordination, stamina, or balance, but that is what makes us unique. Accepting your body image is the first step to gaining self-esteem. Make the best of what you have by focusing on your strengths and capabilities as an athlete!

Balance in Life

If your life is sport, you are at greater risk for self-esteem problems because you have "all your eggs in one basket" and cannot separate the different roles in you life. Strive to find a balance in your life with your family, school, friends, and other career aspirations. This will help take the pressure off your sport and allow your self-esteem to grow.

Be Your Own Best Coach

You are your own worst critic and your best friend wrapped into one. We are often harder on ourselves than we are on our best friends. What would you say to a best friend who is feeling depressed? Be at least that supportive of yourself. Always give yourself words of encouragement and reward after a performance or practice. Pretend you have the most positive coach on your shoulder giving words of encouragement.

Define Your Self-Concept Outside of your sport

A good exercise is to define who you are outside your sport. Use only descriptions that apply to your personal characteristics that you bring to every aspect of your life. Make a list of these positive characteristics and review them every day. Do you like what you see? If so, you have self-esteem. Is there something you do not like? If so, work to change that part of you .

Running Buddhas

We will be looking at the Japanese Marathon Monks of Mount Hiei, who perform an incredible 1000 days of marathons, as part of their training in Tendai Buddhism - exploring the training they undertake to perform such a feat of ultra-endurance and how you can apply some of their training to your own extreme and/or endurance sports.

The Marathon Monks

The marathon monks of Japan are a group of Buddhists who push the limits of human endurance in search of a higher plane of spirituality. The ritual followed by these monks is almost beyond belief:

— 1st year: 100 consecutive days of 26.2-mile marathons, beginning at 1:30 a.m., each day after an hour of prayer

— 2nd year: 100 consecutive days of 26.2 mile marathons

— 3rd year: 100 consecutive days of 26.2 mile marathons

— 4th year: 100 consecutive days of 26.2 mile marathons - performed twice

— 5th year: 100 consecutive days of 26.2 mile marathons - performed twice

— On the 700th day, the monks undergo a 9 day fast without food, water, rest or sleep - a mind-boggling feat which would result in certain death for most human beings, before having a short rest of a few weeks and increasing their gruelling schedule

— 6th year: 100 consecutive days of 37.5 mile marathons

— 7th year: 100 days of 52.2 mile marathons and 100 days of 26.2 mile marathons.

Throughout the night they run and pray, stopping at different stations along the way to recite prayers and perform ritual chants. Upon completion of each day's marathon, the monks perform chores such as cleaning the temple and they continue to pray throughout the day, until retiring at 8:00 or 9:00 p.m. The ritual begins again a few hours later. If at any time the monk finds himself physically or mentally unable to complete the 100-day ritual, he is duty-bound to commit suicide by hanging himself with the belt from his robe or through ritual disembowelment. And you thought the London Marathon was difficult!

Is it physically or mentally healthy to push the limits of your endurance?

Like any sporting endeavour, running ultra long distances is an individual thing; it comes more easily to some than others. Women in particular, seem to possess the ability to trot along for hours on end. In addition, advances in nutrition and supplementation, along with high-tech gear and shoes have made ultra runs easier than they used to be. For all of us however, running like this will take its toll on joints, tendons, and connective tissue. Furthermore, the training can be time-consuming and tiring. It is tough to squeeze a 20 mile training run into a busy schedule, as unlike the marathon monks, most of us have full-time jobs, families and children to raise, on top of our athletic goals.

So, should you try to stretch the limits of your own endurance?

Well, there are some pretty good reasons why you might want to. As with anything in life, the maxim "nothing ventured, noting gained" applies. Psychologists believe the only way for each of us to be truly happy and content in life is to know that we are striving towards and accomplishing something each and every day. The human mind needs goals, something to focus on. Our bodies too need to reach, stretch, achieve and excel. We gain energy by using energy. We conquer our limitations by literally conquering or surpassing them. Yet the investment of time you need to make in endurance sports is substantially larger than in say tennis, football or golf - but otherwise there are no other requirements needed to try to double or triple your mileage or run more marathons more frequently than you have before. Sure, someone else has probably already done it, but by reaching beyond what you think you are capable of, you stand to learn a lot about yourself.

How do the Marathon Monks Train?

Interestingly, in order to qualify as a mountain marathon runner, a trainee monk has first to master seated meditation, with major emphasis placed on deep abdominal breathing. Other essential factors are chanting, proper rhythm and intense concentration which enable the monk to cover meters and meters on each breath, keeping pace with the beat of their mantra. An experienced monk flows along naturally, maintaining the same speed for climbing up or down the mountain paths and does not allow himself to become distracted by any obstacle, whether external or internal. In his book about the monks, John Stevens details the end result of their practise: "In the last 300 days of the marathon, the focus shifts..a balance is struck between practise for one's own sake and practise for the benefit of all. At the end, the marathon monk has become one with the mountain..The joy of practise has been discovered..The stars and sky, the stones, the plants, and the trees, have become the monks trusted companions; he can predict the week's weather by the shape of the clouds, the direction of the wind, and the smell of the air..and he takes special delight in that magic moment of the day when the moon sets and the sun rises, poised in the centre of creation".

What can you learn from the Marathon Monks?

Sports Psychologists are fast coming to the conclusions long known by those following Eastern traditions - that is, that the mind rules the body. In any aspect of training, it is always the mind that quits first and the body that follows - hence, the marathon monks' training for their 7 year long ultra-endurance feats are almost entirely about training the mind to ignore distractions of any shape or form, from physical pain, mental anguish, loneliness, boredom etc

Here are some things you can do to train your mind to maintain a calm, even and neutral state, which will allow your body to move uninhibited and keep you free from doubt, anxiety and all other mental symptoms.

Meditation Training

Very simply, meditation is the art of sitting quietly, doing nothing but focusing on your breathing. Breathing is obviously the most important of all your bodily functions - your very life depends on it - but it is probably the most widely neglected of all our daily activities. Breath is the first thing given to us and the last thing taken away, the most precious thing of all, yet we generally ignore it or pay it minimal attention. The brain undergoes subtle changes during meditation.

Research shows that meditation can actually train the mind and reshape the brain. Tests using the most sophisticated imaging techniques suggest that meditation can actually reset the brain, changing the point at which a traffic jam, for instance, sets the blood boiling. What the scientists discovered through these studies is that with enough practise, the neurons in the brain will re-shape themselves, and many parts of the brain responsible for taking in information, actually slow down or go off-line altogether during meditation, enabling the practitioner to have a more positive experience of themselves and detach from negative feelings and situations.

Meditation also results in a pronounced change in brain-wave patterns, shifting from the alpha waves of aroused, conscious thought to the theta waves that dominate the brain during periods of deep relaxation.

Contentment and a real sense of inner peace are the natural result.

How to Practise

Hide your car, switch off your mobile phone and tell everyone you have gone to Alaska! In other words, find a quiet time and space where you will not be disturbed by everyday activities. Sit on a chair, with your feet firmly on the floor or sit cross-legged on a cushion on the floor. Make sure your back is straight, your shoulders are relaxed, your chin is tucked under and the crown of your head is lifted up towards the ceiling. Place your left palm inside your right palm (palms facing upwards) and gently press the tips of your thumbs together. Rest your hands in your lap. Once you are comfortable, concentrate on your breathing, specifically, on counting each breath e.g. breathe in and breathe out and count one. Breathe in and breathe out and count two. Breathe in and breathe out and count three.

The idea is to count each breath from one to ten. If you lose your place by getting distracted with other thoughts, gently bring your mind back to what you are doing and start again from one. When you get to ten, start from one again.

If thoughts come up, which they invariably will, just let them pass through your mind like clouds moving across the sky on a windy day. Relax fully. Do not try to take deep breaths, just be mindful of keeping your body posture strong but relaxed, and quietly focus on counting your breath.

What to Expect

Over time, you will gradually find your breathing becomes deeper and slower. You may also feel heat in the lower abdomen because as you learn to relax, your breathing will naturally deepen and you will find your lower abdomen moving up and down as you breathe in and out, rather than your chest and shoulders. If at any time during your practise, you feel dizzy or light-headed, simply stop training and rest quietly for a while. Continue the next day. Start your meditation practise by concentrating for just a few minutes each day and build up your training gradually. Over time you will find yourself getting physically and mentally stronger and feeling more relaxed.

Introducing Distractions

Once you can meditate peacefully without distractions, try to introduce some background irritations. For instance, you can try meditating while the kids are getting ready for bed or while the radio is on or with a clock ticking in the room or with your partner tapping away at the computer in the background. Also, try meditating while you are physically uncomfortable, for instance sitting on the edge of a chair or kneeling on the floor. This way you are introducing mild annoyances, which you must learn to ignore, while you continue to concentrate on your breathing. You can then progress to moving while you mediate.

Practise your deep breathing while getting ready for your run or event, while putting on your training kit and shoes. Revisit this state in the locker room at the gym, with other people buzzing around. Practise your meditation for a few minutes while on the starting line of your next marathon and of course, focus on breathing long, deep and slowly while on your next run. Each time your mind gets distracted by your watch, tight calf muscles, stitch in your side and so on, calmly and quietly bring your mind back to your breathing.

Chanting and Mantra's

You do not have to be religiously or spiritually inclined to practise mantra meditation - the constant repetition of a phrase, either quietly to yourself or spoken aloud in a constant refrain. Any phrase that taps into your potential and focuses on what you want to achieve will suffice.

Try keeping part of your focus on your breathing, while calmly reciting over and over again (either aloud or in your mind) any of the following phrases - or make up some of your own:

— I am Lean, Strong and Relaxed

— My Running is Fluid, Smooth and Relaxed

— Powerful and Graceful, I Can Run This Way For Hours

— Easy Does It. Stay Relaxed.

Zen Mind, Sports Mind

Hi. I am Jayne Storey, welcome to my new monthly column, which will help you to prepare your mind to access "the sporting zone" - a state of peak performance where actions are automatic, intuitive and unconscious and where bursts of 'spontaneous excellence' occur naturally and effortlessly. As a performance enhancement specialist, coach athletes and sports-teams in T'ai Chi (one of the world's oldest forms of kung-fu) and its component parts like abdominal breathing, balance, postural exercises and meditation - to help maximise training, performance and recovery.

T'ai Chi

Combined with traditional training in sports psychology (Effective Thinking-Skills, Attention Control, Goal Setting, Visualisation and Stress Management) - T'ai Chi can help athletes and teams develop better results in training and performance by helping to unite the mind, the body and the breathing to achieve 100% relaxed concentration. Phrases like peak performance, transcendence, flow and the zone, all refer to the bursts of spontaneous excellence experienced by top athletes, and describe a state where actions are easy, focus is 100% and the player knows instinctively what to do to succeed.

Research shows that skill, passion and immersion equal peak performance - the ultimate experience of which is the flow state or sporting zone. Action and awareness merge when the athlete becomes totally absorbed in what they are doing - when they have the skills to meet the challenge and focus all of their attention on the task at hand.

Perhaps the most systematic approach that research shows is consistent with achieving the zone, is that used in the martial arts. In Kung-fu, T'ai Chi and Karate the competitor seeks to lose all distractions of ego, analysis and self-referring thoughts, immersing him or herself completely within the activity. Zazen, the formal practice of seated meditation, is the cornerstone of Zen training. In its beginning stages, Zazen is a practice of concentration, with a focus on following or counting the breath.

In sports, we tend to view the body, breath, and mind separately, but in Zen they come together naturally as one reality. By concentrating on the breath you are empowering yourself with the ability to put your mind where you want it, when you want it there, for as long as you want it there. By disciplined training, the mind can be re-programmed to acknowledge distractions, whether internal (anxiety, fear of failure, pressure of expectations) or from the environment (crowd noise, other competitors, weather conditions) - without holding on to them or paying them any attention.

The emphasis in Zazen is to breathe naturally, deeply and quietly and simply to be aware of our breathing, while letting all other thoughts, feelings and distractions pass through the mind like clouds moving over-head on a windy day.

How to Practise

— Sit upright on a stool or hard-backed chair with you feet firmly on the ground, palms resting on your thighs. Hold the crown of your head up, as if it were held by a hook or thread. Tuck your chin under slightly and relax your shoulders. Look down at the floor or a blank wall about a metre or so in front of you.

— Once you are comfortable, concentrate your mind at the hara or t'an tien - a point inside the lower abdomen, about 2 inches below the navel. It is important to centre your attention in the hara. The hara is the well-spring of your physical power and your body's natural centre of gravity. Put your attention there; put your mind there. As you develop your Zazen, you will become more aware of the hara as the centre of your attentiveness.

— Relax your stomach. Touch your tongue to the roof of your mouth and breathe in and out through your nose. When you breathe in, allow your lower abdomen to come out (expand) gently. Do not force your breath. Just try to relax and let it happen naturally.

— To aid your practise, you can visualise a small balloon inside the stomach, below the navel. As you breathe in, this balloon gently expands, and when you breathe out, the balloon gently releases the breath.

— Relax fully. Do not try to take deep breaths, but just keep your mind on the hara centre for the duration of the exercise and quietly observe your breathing.

What to Expect

Over time, you will gradually find your breathing becomes deeper and slower. You will also feel heat in the lower abdomen. Start your Zazen practise by concentrating for just a few minutes each day and build up your training gradually. Over time you will find yourself getting physically and mentally stronger and feeling more relaxed.

Daily training

The ability to achieve a relaxed and focused state of mind needs to be trained and experienced on a daily basis, and is not a technique that can be pulled from the bag on the day of competition. You need to start preparing your mind by learning to detach from all the trivial problems which beset every-day life. Start gradually by meditating for 5 or so minutes and work up another minute a day until you can sit comfortably in silence for at least 20 minutes.

In skills training/practise

Here you will be learning how to meditate while in action, and can quietly start training yourself to focus on your breathing while putting on your sports gear, warming-up and during your practise routines.

Competition

The night before a competition, it is helpful to meditate for a few minutes before going to bed. Sit quietly for a while, without reading or watching the television and then quieten your mind completely by practising Zazen for a few moments. If you feel restless in the night, get up and do some gentle stretching, then sit and meditate for a little while. This will help you relax your nerves again before going back to bed.

In the morning, start with ten minutes of meditation and then do short bursts throughout the day while you get ready and prepare yourself for the event. In the locker-room, you can continue to stay focused on your breathing and perform your Zazen training without anyone knowing what you are doing or being able to distract you.

During the game itself, use your meditation training as a trigger to increase your focus and relaxation during moments of intense pressure. Gently pushing down the diaphragm and sinking your awareness to the hara while exhaling, is a great way to stay strongly present in your body.

The benefits of Standing Practise (Zhan Zhuang) in martial arts circles are legendary, as each of the Shaolin and Wu Dang temple arts (T'ai Chi, Hsing Yi, Wing Chun etc.) used standing or rooting exercises as part of the mental and physical discipline required to perform kung fu at an advanced level. Founded as an individual art by Wang Xiang Zhai (1885 - 1963), Standing Practise has an even older history in Taoist and Buddhist cultures, even as far back as 500 B.C.

The 6 Benefits of Standing Practise

1. Physical strength and stamina
2. Relaxation
3. Grounding
4. Breathing
5. Opening the energy gates of the body

6. Cultivation of intrinsic energy Other benefits include correcting misalignments of the skeleton and cultivating a calm mental state.

The First Posture

Wu Chi, also known as the posture of 'Emptiness' is the mother of all standing postures, the easiest posture to hold with the body, yet Wu Chi challenges the mind and mental state if you are not used to being still for extended periods of time.

Wu Chi - Structural Points

— Stand with your feet shoulder-width wide or slightly wider

— Unlock your knees and sink your weight into the balls of your feet

— Gently tuck under your lower back to take out the lumbar curve

— Relax your shoulders

— Let your arms hang down naturally at your sides, with your palms gently touching your legs

— Keep your chin tucked under, to take the curve from the neck and hold your head upright, imagining the crown of your head is suspended by a balloon on a thread

— Gently touch your tongue to the roof of your mouth. Breathe in and out through your nose.

— Relax all the muscles of your body and try to be aware of your breathing.

Try 3 minutes at first and gradually work up to 10, 15 or 20 minutes.

The 6 Benefits Explained

The benefits of Wu Chi have been verified by

Physiotherapists and Chiropractors, as essentially, this posture helps to correct muscular-skeletal misalignments and greatly relieves pressure on the lower spine and the neck areas. Cultivating calm, aware "here and now" thought - which you will gain through extended practise of Wu Chi - is fundamental to any and all 'mental game' training.

1. Physical strength and stamina

Standing aims to increase muscular strength and endurance in two main ways. Firstly, most people use more muscular effort to perform any given task than is actually required. By learning to use the minimum amount of effort necessary, we are in effect increasing the efficiency with which we use our muscles. Additionally, we are learning, though standing, not to use muscle groups that are antagonistic to the task we are trying to perform - i.e. we stop fighting ourselves.

Secondly, standing excels at developing the postural muscles. These are deep fascia muscles which, as the name suggests, hold the skeleton in position. These muscles naturally have greater strength and endurance than the phasic, or movement muscles. Through training to rely more on these muscles (using body structure rather than brute force), we can begin to use the whole body in our movements, rather than one isolated part. Also, holding the posture(s) is physically tiring - it is real exercise!

2. Relaxation

We are aiming to achieve a state that the Chinese call "sung". This describes a state that is relaxed, but not to the point of floppiness that we in the West sometimes associate with complete relaxation. It is more like the softness of a bale of cotton, which is so dense that it can stop a bullet. As previously mentioned, we are aiming to use only the correct amount of muscle tension needed to perform the task, and no more.

3. Grounding

Grounding is the result of relaxation coupled with correct alignment of the skeleton - i.e. proper body posture. This allows the weight of the body to fall naturally to its lowest point. In fact, without correct alignment and posture, true relaxation is not possible, as effort is required just to hold the body up!

4. Breathing

If we drop the diaphragm and expand the belly, rather than expand the rib cage and puff out the chest, this has a number of advantages:

1. Relaxation - "Abdominal breathing" encourages the awareness to fall to the centre of the body, helping to create a feeling of sinking and relaxation.
2. Efficiency - Most people use only a small portion at the top of their lungs during normal breathing. Abdominal breathing inflates the lungs from the bottom up, allowing a much fuller breath.
3. Massage - The contraction and expansion of the abdominal cavity during abdominal breathing has a massaging effect on the digestive organs, which is beneficial for general health and well-being.

5. Opening the Energy Gates of the body

As we learn to relax and let go of stiffness, the body will begin to "open up", allowing greater circulation of blood and energy ("chi"). Certain points on the body are vital, according to traditional Chinese medicine (TCM), with regard to the exchange of energy with the environment and circulation of energy within the body. The three energy gates of the spine are of particular importance, as opening these is the first step in encouraging the circulation of energy up the spine (governing vessel) and down the middle of the front of the body (conception vessel).

This circulation is known as the small circulation or "microcosmic orbit", and connecting the two vessels is the reason for placing the tongue at the roof of the mouth. The energy gates of the spine are located at the base of the spine (tailbone gate), between the shoulder blades (dorsal gate), and where the top of the spine meets the skull (jade pillow).

Other gates include: centre of palms (lao gung), centre of soles of feet (yong quan), crown of head (ba hui), perineum (hui yin), and of course the "reservoir of energy" (t'an tien), located approximately 2" below the navel.

This is not intended to be an exhaustive list, as there are many energy gates all over the body. Rather, it is a basic introduction to the area where kung fu and TCM theory meet. Many people have trouble accepting the existence of energy gates, meridians and chi and blind faith in their existence is not necessary to progress in Standing Practise. However, as your training develops, you may find that your opinions change.

6. Cultivation of intrinsic energy

Most Eastern cultures accept the existence of energy which can be absorbed through air and food, and developed within the body through certain postural/ movement practices. In the West we have no such concept; so many people find thinking of chi simply as vitality is a helpful solution. One thing chi is definitely not, however, is some mystical force that can be harnessed to give the practitioner superhuman powers. Martial artists (such as the Shaolin monks) who can display feats which seem to defy the laws of reality are normally showing the results of extreme mental and physical conditioning and correct physical connections/ alignment.

Taoist Standing Practice - Core Stability

A traditional exercise practiced by martial artists over the centuries, Standing Practice (Zhan Zhuang) is known for its surprising toughness (postures are traditionally held for at least 60 to 80 minutes) and for its ability to develop health, strengthen the bones and tendons, increase core stability, correct any muscular-skeletal misalignments (crucial for lop-sided sports like golf, javelin, tennis etc), increase sensitivity to balance, and develop a powerful competitive spirit The six benefits of Standing Practice are as follows:

1. Physical strength and stamina
2. Relaxation
3. Grounding
4. Lower Abdominal Breathing
5. Opening the energy gates of the body
6. Cultivation of intrinsic energy

Other benefits include correcting misalignments of the skeleton and cultivating a calm, aware mental state. The more advanced posture you are going to learn here, will continue to help train all the above, and due to its intensity and demanding nature, it will help to prepare your mind for increased focus, intent and competitiveness.

San Ti Shi - Three Body Posture

The foundation of Xingyiquan (Hsing Yi Ch'uan) is its stance keeping practice of San Ti Shi, which means "Three Body Posture" or "Trinity Posture". Hsing Yi

Ch'uan is one of the three Chinese internal martial arts, alongside the more well-known T'ai Chi and the more esoteric style of Ba Gua Ch'uan. To get a rare glimpse of these ancient arts in action, watch a film called "The One", staring Jet Li, in which he plays two roles - a good guy and a bad guy - the first using the fighting skills of Ba Gua Ch'uan and the other using Hsing Yi Ch'uan . These arts are known for their physical toughness and for their ability to develop the practitioner's mind to a level where the mind sets the intent for the physical movement - Hsing Yi Ch'uan actually means "the mind that forms the fist". The exercise you are going to learn here will help you set your mental intent for the movement skills of any sport and is particularly good if you are a competitive athlete, as it will help to increase your level of intent or desire by training your mind, breathing and nervous-system to stay focused yet relaxed under pressure.

San Ti Shi - How to Stand

— Stand with your feet about half shoulder width wide, the toes of both feet parallel and pointing straight forward

— Gently tuck under your lower back to take out the lumbar curve

— Unlock your knees and sink your weight into the balls of your feet

— Turn your right toes out about 45 degrees and shift your weight onto your right leg - then step forward with your left leg, keeping your left toes facing straight ahead

— Keep your weight 70% on your right leg and 30% on your left leg

— Keep your centre of gravity mid-way between your feet, rather than predominantly on either the right or left leg

— Turn your hips and shoulders 45 degrees to the right, matching the direction of your right toes - your eyes and head point straight forwards, in the direction of your left toes

— Relax your shoulders - bring your left arm in line with your left leg, arm and fingers pointing straight forward and your elbow relaxed and in line with your left knee

— Bring your right arm in front of you - waist height - and touch the outside edge of your right thumb against your lower abdomen, about 2" below your navel (this is your T'an Tien - the body's natural centre of gravity) - your right fingers point forward and your elbow is relaxed and holding your ribs

— Keep your chin tucked under, to take the curve from the neck and hold your head upright, imagining the crown of your head is suspended by a balloon on a thread

— Gently touch your tongue to the roof of your mouth

— Breathe in and out through your nose

— Relax all the muscles of your body and try to be aware of your breathing

— Look straight ahead

For a left back-stance, simply mirror the posture on the other side of your body. Try 3 minutes each side at first and gradually work up to 10, 15 or 20 minutes each side.

What to expect

With your waist and shoulders facing right, while your eyes, fingers and intent are directed forward, you are learning to train your ability to release energy from the T'an Tien - your body's natural centre of gravity - which is used all the time in sports yet rarely trained in isolation. In the martial arts, this stance is used to develop Fa Jing or explosive power in your punches, and if you want to experience this, try this exercise once you can hold the San Ti Shi posture each side for at least 5 minutes:

— Starting in San Ti Shi, sink your weight deeper into your feet

— Make a loose fist with your right hand

— Throw your hips forward and release the punch at waist height, keeping your shoulder, elbow and wrist relaxed - your punch should end up in line with your T'an Tien (2" below your navel) - your hips and shoulders will now be facing forwards

— As you punch, simultaneously grip and pull your left hand back to your waist, turning your left closed fist upwards as you do so - feel as if you are grabbing and twisting someone's belt-buckle and are pulling them towards you with your left hand, while punching with your right

— Focus on the T'an Tien - the pivot point around which the hips turn - this is an energy centre about the size of a golf ball, located 2" below your navel. Imagine the ball rotating and that in turn, your hips, shoulders, arms and fists are all thrown into place as a result

If you really want to give yourself a challenge, try this exercise standing in front of a lighted candle and use the intent, relaxation and speed combined in your punch to generate enough force to put out the flame. Once you can do this up close to the candle, step back a little and try again.

Learning to hold the San Ti Shi stance for 10 or more minutes each side will really train your core stability muscles to keep you relaxed and poised while keeping only a narrow base. Usually we are comfortable with a wider base and generally stand and play sports with our feet under our shoulders. Narrowing your stance like this while lengthening your stride will help to lower your centre of gravity and increase your relaxation response, which in turn makes your body denser and stronger. This type of training also strengthens the bone marrow and tendons and is used a great deal in Traditional Chinese Medicine where it is considered a form of Chi Kung or energy training.

Having a strong intent and competitive nature is vital to achievement in sports, whether you are competing against others, against your own self, or against the time-marker on the treadmill. Masters' level swimmers who have trained in San Ti Shi, agree that their intent pool-side while warming up and getting ready to enter the water has increased dramatically, as has their opponents reactions to them on account of their indomitable body-language.

Any time you need to initiate an all-out performance of pure action without heed to reaction, internal chatter or self-observation, then San Ti Shi is the training tool for you. But remember, the exercise really starts to work, just at the point when your mind wants to give up.

Stay with it, relax and breath and in no time you'll be stronger, quicker, ready for competition, and above all, focused. Next time, we will look at elements of T'ai Chi for extreme and endurance sports.

Bibliography

Asimov, Isaac, *The Brain*, Boston, MA: Houghton Mifflin, 1963.

Bandler, Richard, *Using Your Brain for a Change*, Moab, UT: Real People Press, 1985.

Baum, Ken; Trubo, Richard, *The Mental Edge : Maximize Your Sports Potential With the Mind/Body Connection*, Perigee, 1999.

Chernow, Fred B., "The Sharper Mind", *Mental Games for a Keen Mind and Foolproof Memory*, New Jersey: Prentice Hall, Inc., 1997.

Douillard, John; King, Billie Jean; Navratilova, Martina, *Body, Mind and Sport: The Mind-Body Guide to Lifelong Health, Fitness, and Your Personal Best*, Three Rivers Press, 2001.

Gardner, Howard, *Frames of Mind*, New York, NY: Basic Books, 1983.

Hill, Napoleon and Stone, W. Clement, *Success Through A Positive Mental Attitude*, Simon & Schuster, reissue 1992.

Holtz, Lou; MacKay, Harvey, *Winning Everyday*, HarperBusiness, 1998.

Hutchison, Michael, *MegaBrain: New Tools and Techniques for Brain Growth and Mind Expansion*, New York, NY: Ballantine, 1991.

Mackenzie, Marlin, *Golf: The Mind Game*, New York, NY: Dell Paperbacks, 1990.

______________ , *Skiing: The Mind Game*, New York, NY: Dell Paperbacks, 1993.

______________ , *Tennis: The Mind Game*, New York, NY: Dell Paperbacks, 1993.

Taylor, C.B., Sells, J.F., Needle, R. (1985) The relation of physical activity and exercise to mental health. *Public Health Report*, 100:195-202.

Van Raalte, Judy L.; Brewer, Britton W., *Exploring Sport and Exercise Psychology*, American Psychological Association, 1996.

Vernacchia, Ralph; McGuire, Rick T., et. al., *Coaching Mental Excellence: It Does Matter Whether You Win or Lose.* Warde Publishers, 1996.

Waitley, Dennis, *Being The Best,* Pocket Books, 1988.

Warren, William E., *Coaching and Motivation: A Practical Guide to Maximum Athletic Performance,* Prentice Hall, 1991.

Whitten, Phillip. Ph.D., *The Complete Book of Swimming,* New York, NY: Random House, 1994.

Wilson, Susan M., *Sports Her Way: Motivating Girls to Start and Stay With Sports,* Simon & Schuster, 2000.

Winter, Arthur, M.D. and Ruth Winters, M.S, *Brain Workout: Easy Ways to Power Up Your Memory, Sensory Perception, and Intelligence.* New York: St. Martin Press, Inc., 1997.

Wise, Anna, *The High-Performance Mind : Mastering Brainwaves for Insight, Healing, and Creativity,* JP Tarcher, 1997.

Wooden, John R.; Jamison, Steve, *Wooden: A Lifetime of Observations and Reflections on and Off the Court,* NTC Publishing, 1997.

Yates, Brad, *Fuel The Fire, Perform With Passion,* HiLevel Productions, 1998.

Zimmerman, Jean; Reavill, Gil, *Raising Our Athletic Daughters: How Sports Can Build Self-Esteem and Save Girl's Lives,* Main Steet Books, 1999.

Index